WEST CORK
THROUGH TIME

Kieran McCarthy &
Daniel Breen

AMBERLEY PUBLISHING

Acknowledgements

We would like to express our gratitude to the curator of Cork Public Museum, Stella Cherry, for her courtesy and encouragement during this project. The old postcards within the book are archived in the Cork Public Museum. The present-day pictures were taken by the authors. We would like to also thank the staff at Amberley Publishing for their vision with this work.

Dedicated to all those who find peace and solace in West Cork.

First published 2013

Amberley Publishing
The Hill, Stroud, Gloucestershire, GL5 4EP
www.amberley-books.com

ISBN 978 1 4456 2074 9 (print)
ISBN 978 1 4456 2079 4 (ebook)

British Library Cataloguing in Publication Data.
A catalogue record for this book is available from the British Library.

Typesetting by Amberley Publishing.
Printed in Great Britain.

Introduction

One cannot but be drawn in when taken on a journey in West Cork. This book is ambitious in its aims, as it takes the reader on a journey into one of the most dramatic landscapes in Ireland. West Cork is known for many aspects: its scenery, its serenity, its culture and its people. This book explores postcards of the West Cork region from the last 100 years (*c.* 1913), and follows in the footsteps of photographers to retake the same scenes in the present day. The old postcards, sourced from the collections of Cork City Museum, embody many memories and representations of the West Cork region. These postcards were sold to visitors and locals a century ago. In their day, they were never neatly packaged in one publication, nor could one ever buy them all in one go in one particular place.

This book takes the reader from Bandon to Castletownbere, through the changing and the unchanging face of the landscapes and the seascapes, and provides an insight into the uniqueness of the region. The necklace of towns and villages are all linked together through a striking section of Ireland's coastline, over 320 km in length, encompassing a raw coastal wilderness with expansive inlets continuously being eroded away by the Atlantic Ocean. With exquisite coastal scenery, undulating inland landscapes, criss-crossed by mountains, hills, streams and rivers, imposing old-world villages, the visitor finds a discovery at every bend of the road.

Researching West Cork, the visitor discovers that each parish has its own local historian, historical society, village/town council, tidy towns group, community group and business community, which have inspired the creation of heritage trails and information panels, each asserting why its area has a strong sense of place and identity, and why it should be visited. Relics from the past also haunt the landscape, with prominent landmarks ranging from Bronze Age standing stones to ivy-clad ruined houses and castles, churches, big houses and cultivated farmlands. All add to the spectacle that is West Cork.

The winding roads bring the visitor on an experience through landscapes, many of which have been frozen in time for centuries. There are places that charm, catch and challenge the eye, especially in the quest to retake photographs 100 years on. Chapter 1 begins with an exploration of what could be described as a gateway country into West Cork. The towns of Bandon and Clonakilty were both founded 400 years ago, and are central to a ribbon of market towns and villages in their vicinity, such as Dunmanway and Drimoleague. All are set against the backdrop of a raw, glaciated, mountainous landscape, and the Bandon River valley and its tributaries.

Chapter 2 explores the settlements and views along the coast, from Courtmacsherry to Mizen Head, which is Ireland's south-westerly point. Here are multiple beaches, large bays, rocky inlets, islands and many twists in the coastal roads that the visitor endures in the attempt to explore this landscape.

Chapter 3 details the regional pilgrimage site of Gougane Barra. According to legend, Cork City's patron saint, Finbarr, is said to have had a monastery on an island in the middle of the area's lake at the base of the Shehy Mountains. Many pilgrims have visited this peaceful site over past centuries. Some have left their mark more than others, in terms of raising funds and acquiring human resources to enhance the collective memory of Finbarr through the construction of pilgrimage cells and an oratory.

Chapter 4 leads the visitor on a journey from Bantry to Bere Island. The dramatic landscape here is amazing, as coastal roads loom out into the coast and back in through tunnelled-out rock. To experience the western tip of this area, Bere Island, on any morning is breathtaking, as the sun, rain or just a few clouds can change the whole character of the location.

Chapter 5 explores the Cork, Bandon and South Coast Railway, which cut a route into the heart of West Cork 100 years ago, and provided a means of goods transportation and a slower method of enjoying the countryside, especially in an age where the car and even good quality roads were rare.

In all, this book, through pictures of the old and new, comprises a myriad of stories made up of different shapes, patterns and colours, just like a painter's palette of colours. Every picture presented is charged with an emotional sense of nostalgia – the past shaping and inspiring present thoughts, ideas and actions. However, this book only scratches the surface of what this region has to offer. West Cork in itself is a way of life where generations, individuals and communities have etched out their lives. It is a place of discovery, of inspiration, a place of peace and contemplation, and a place to find oneself. There is even more to offer the tourist today than there was 100 years ago. What's the best way to see West Cork? Travel through it, sense it and enjoy it!

Kieran McCarthy & Dan Breen

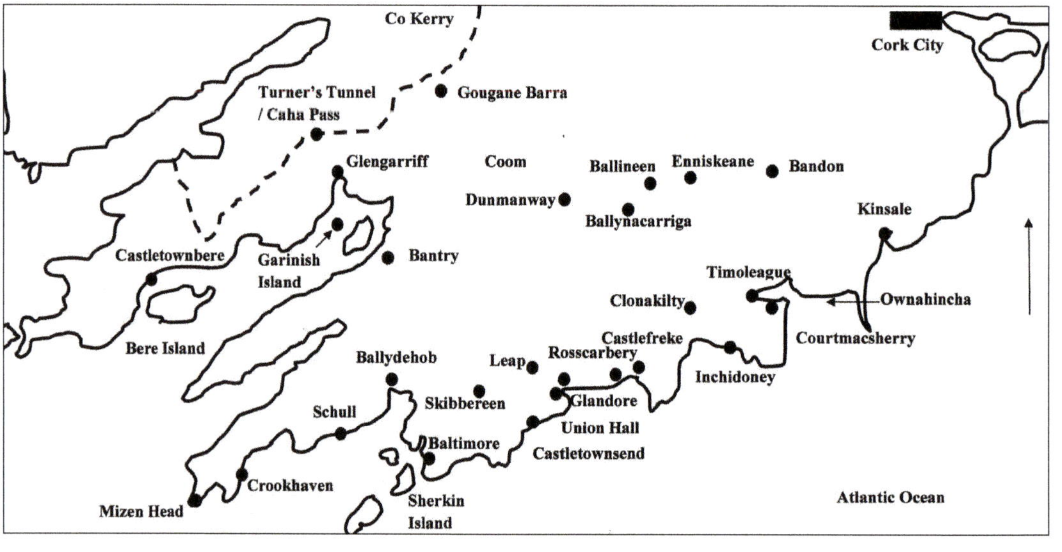

Map of West Cork Locations

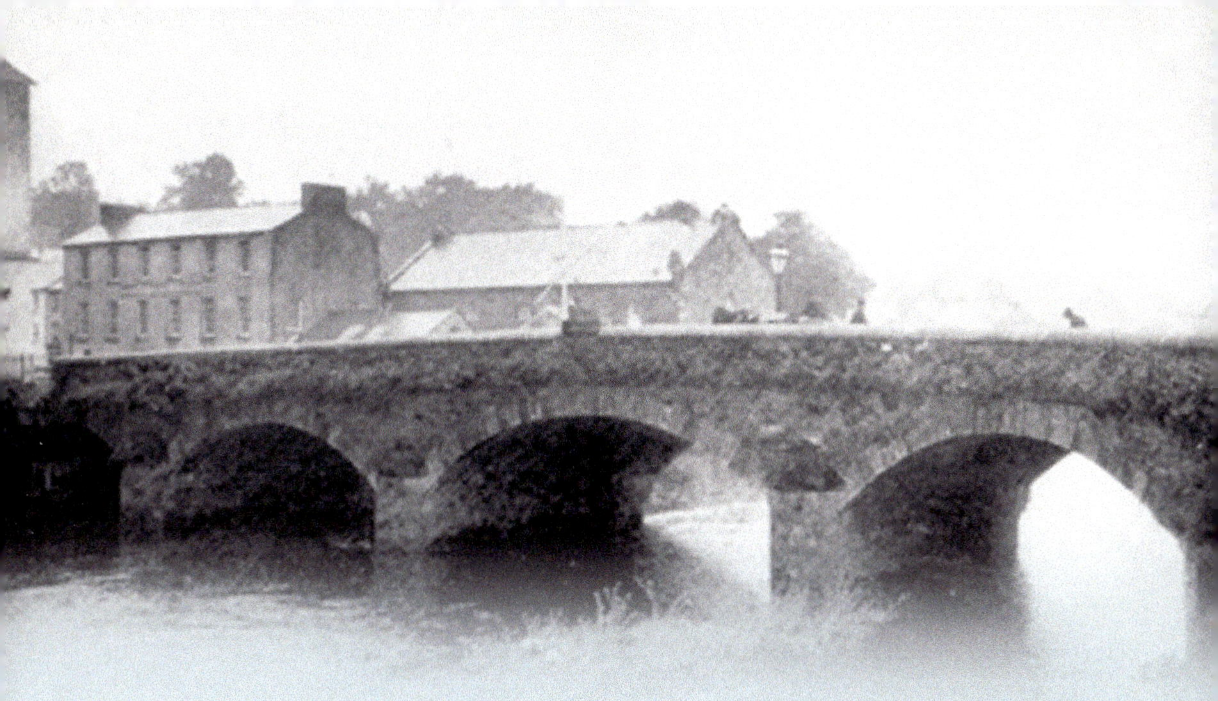

CHAPTER 1

Gateway Country – Making an Entrance

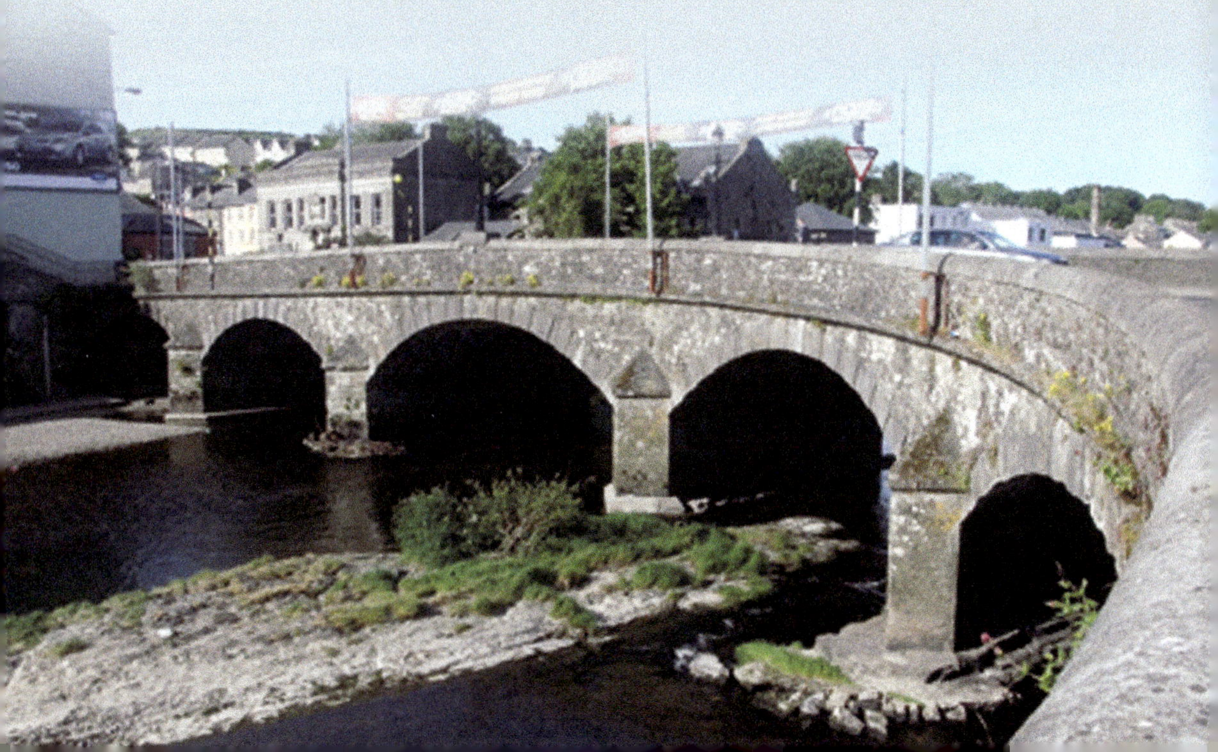

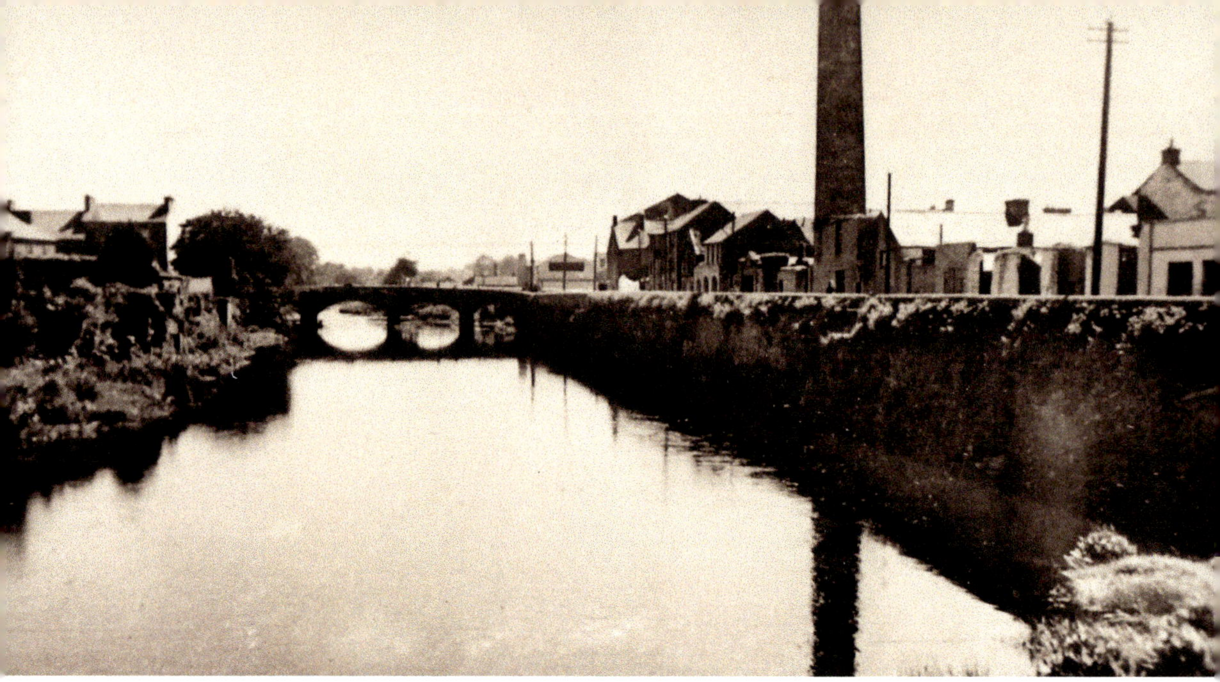

Bandon Bridge

Bandon derives its name from the construction of a bridge over the River Bandon, and owes its origin to English planters in the reign of Elizabeth I. In 1609, James I granted to Henry Beecher the privilege of a Saturday market and two fairs in the town, which were built on the south side of the River Bandon, near the bridge. These grants were purchased shortly afterwards by the first Earl of Cork, Richard Boyle, who promoted its growth and prosperity. He is generally regarded as the founder of the town, which he peopled with a colony of Protestant settlers from Bristol. The town was also enclosed in strong town walls and was protected by three castles. Some of the walls still survive today. The current Bandon Bridge dates to 1838.

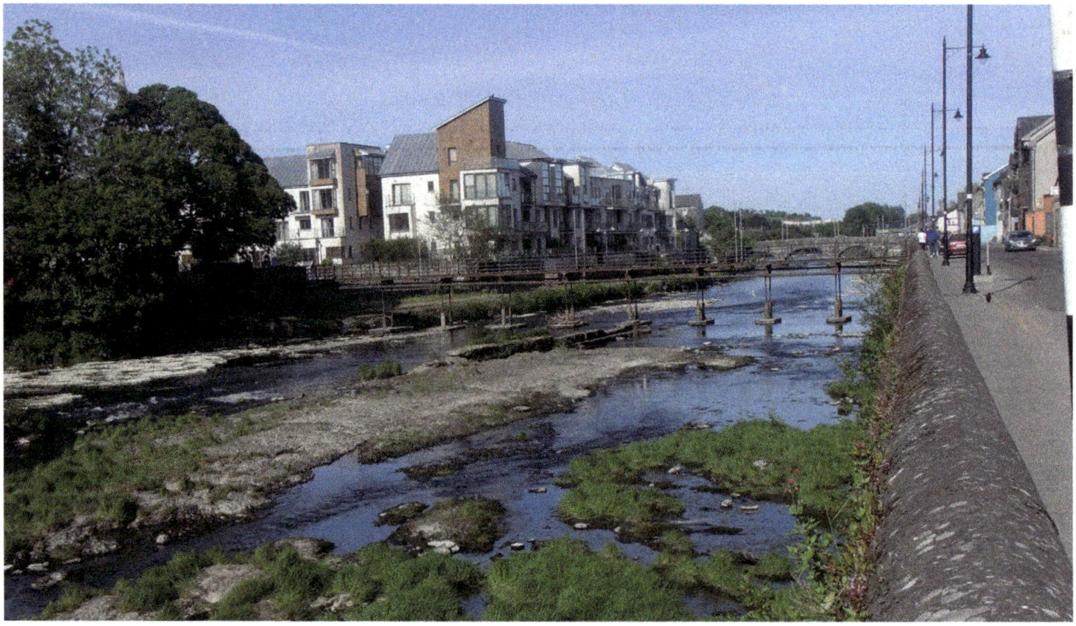

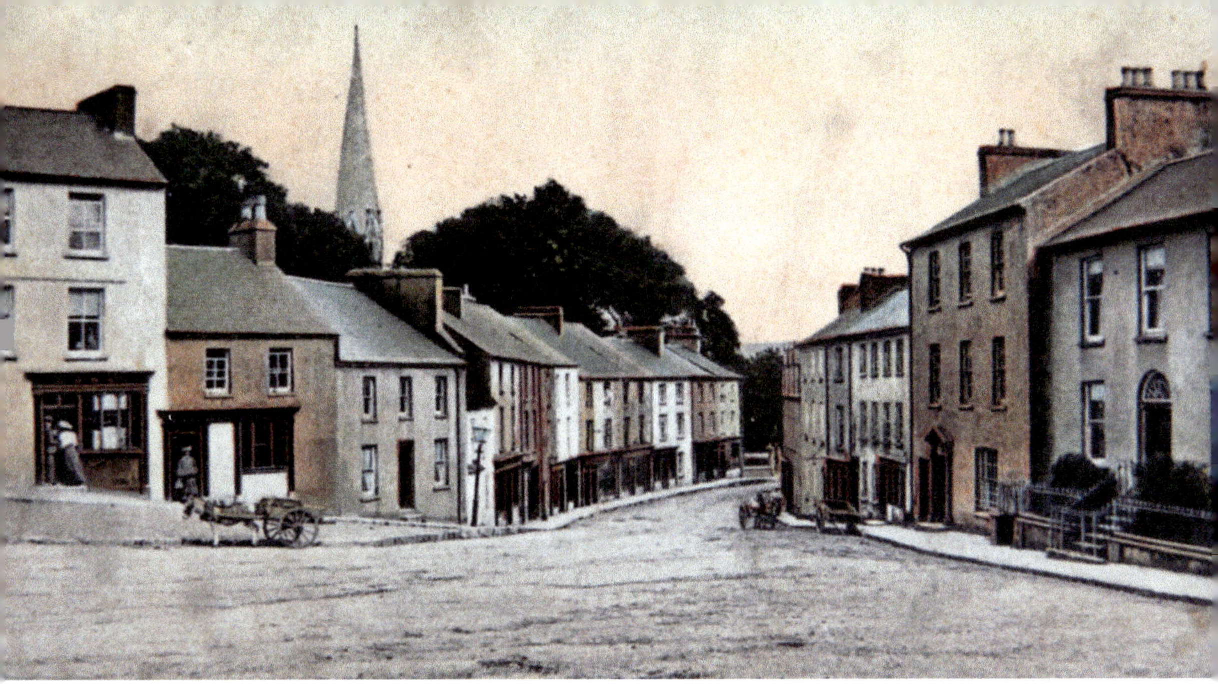

North Main Street, Bandon

The plentiful supply of water from the River Bandon and its tributaries provided a basis for the growth of many industrial pursuits. Among the workers recorded in the early seventeenth century were bakers, blacksmiths, butchers, carpenters, chandlers, cloth workers, coopers, curriers, cutlers, dyers, glaziers, glovers, masons, metal men, shoemakers, tailors, tanners and weavers. Built in 1610, the spire – as shown on the left of both pictures – is that of the former Christ Church, the oldest surviving post-reformation church in Ireland. The present tower and steeple were constructed in 1856. There were many splendid memorials in this church – the oldest being that of Richard Croft, the builder of a portion of the town wall, and Burgess of the Corporation in 1613, who died in 1629. The church was deconsecrated in 1973.

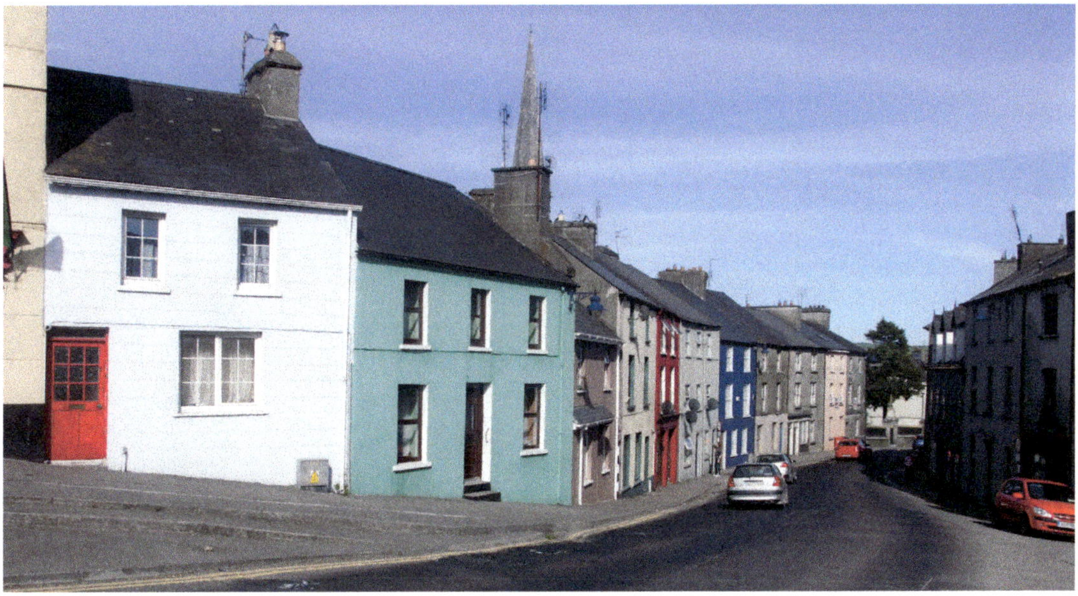

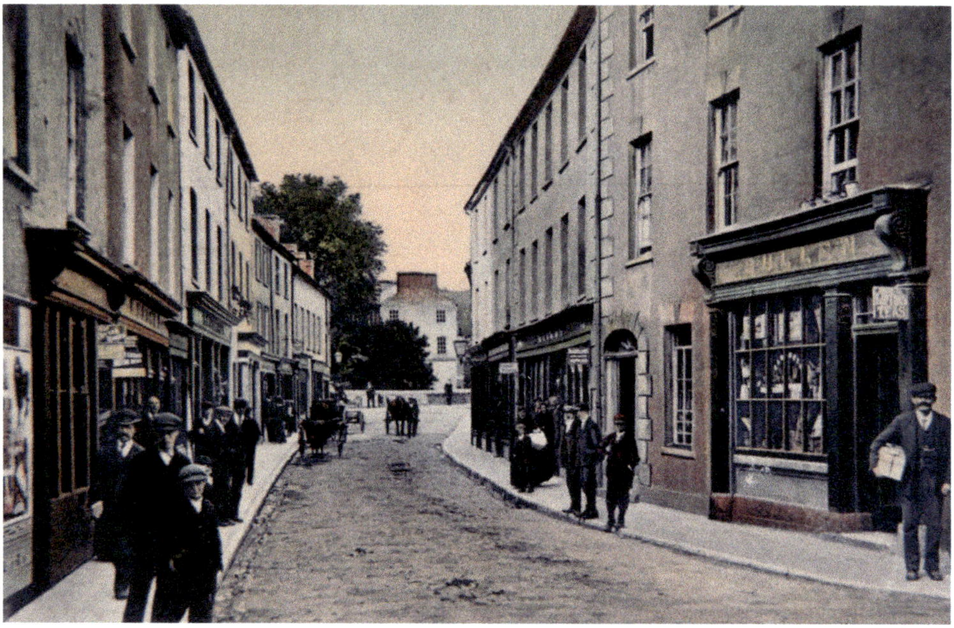

Bridge Street, Bandon

The manufacture of camlets, stuffs and other woollen goods were successful in Bandon to a great extent in the eighteenth and nineteenth centuries. This was taken over by the spinning and weaving of cotton, which continued to flourish until 1825. Spinning mills were erected on a large scale and more than 1,000 people were employed in weaving, but both branches declined. One hundred years ago, the distilling and milling industries were very successful in the town. In 1825, George Allman and his sons began whiskey production at Monarone where the Bandon Mart is today. Their distillery once had an output of over 600,000 gallons of whiskey per year!

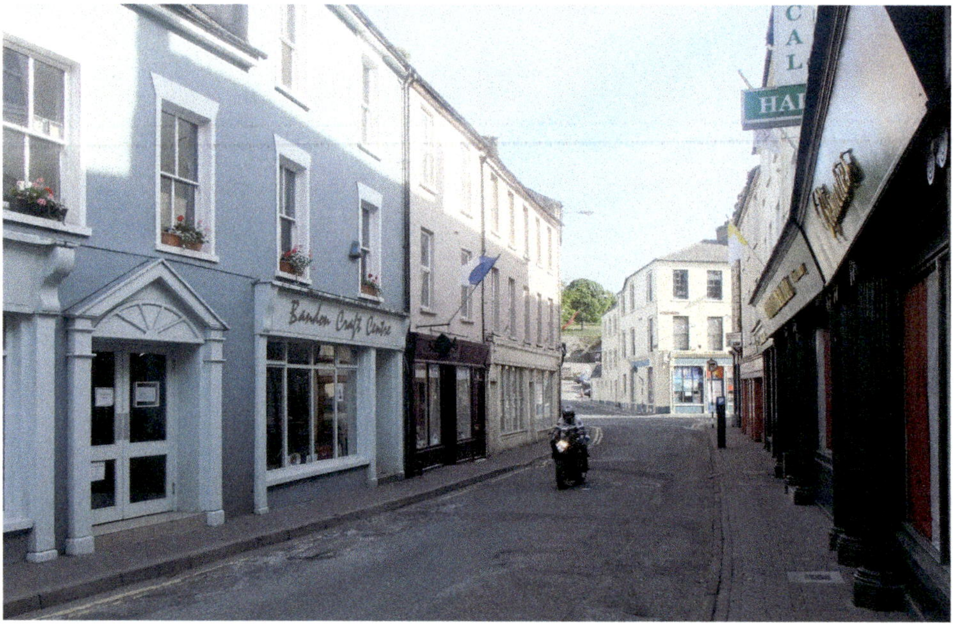

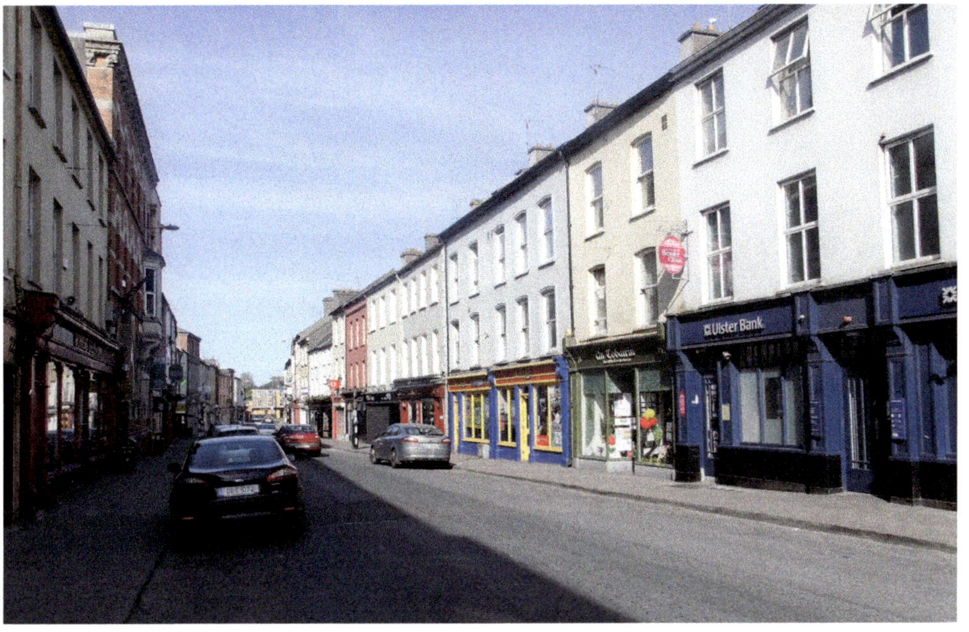

South Main Street, Bandon

Much of the physical structure of shops in South Main Street today date from the nineteenth century. By 1913, Bandon had a population of 3,997 and was – and still is – one of the largest towns in the region. Streets such as this were full of services in 1913: solicitors (six in number), physicians and surgeons (two), a dentist (one), the Bandon Arms Hotel, agricultural implements (four), auctioneers (five), bakers (two), boot and shoemakers (three), a brewer agent (one), butter merchants (two), a cattle dealer (one), china and glass warehouses (five), a coal merchant (one), confectioners (three), corn merchants (three), cycle agents (four), drapers (eight), dressmakers and milliners (six), grocers (ten), and vintners (ten) to name just a few. A further twenty trades are listed on the 1913 street directory for the town.

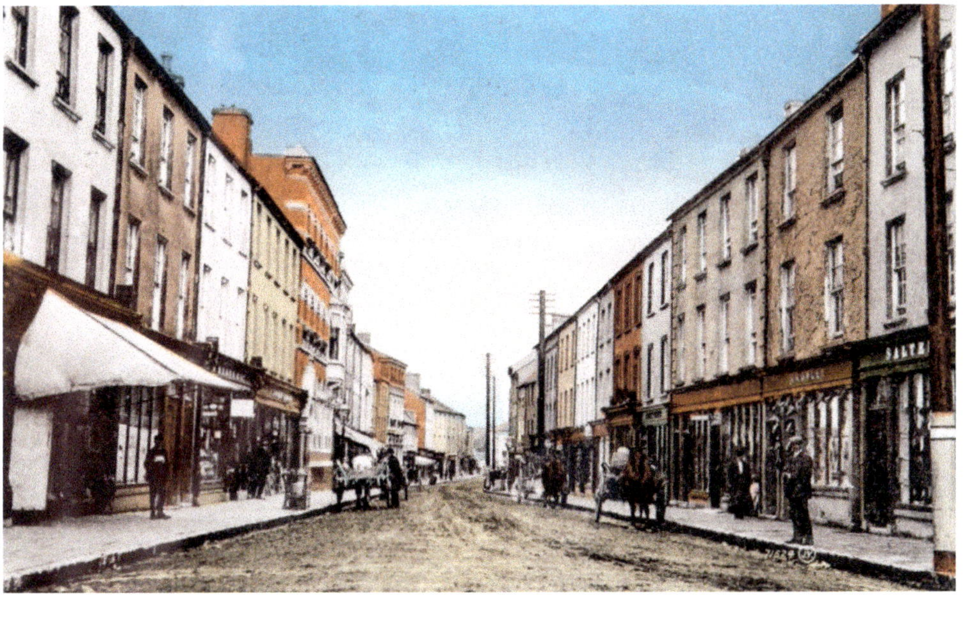

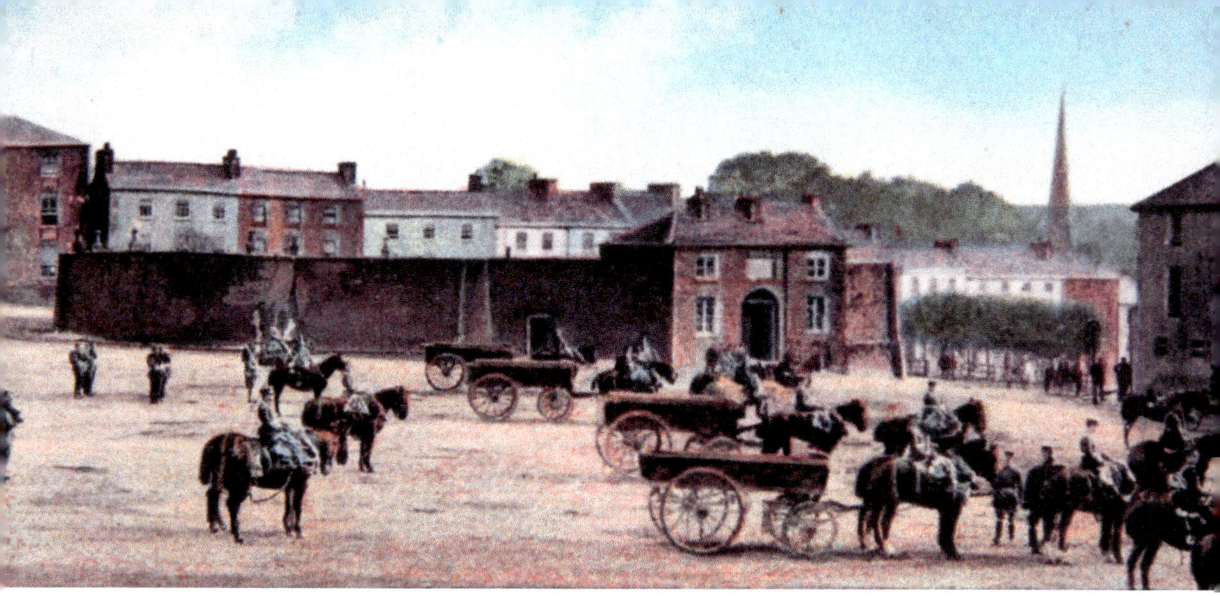

Bandon Shambles or Meat Market

There were three convenient market places in Bandon, built at the expense of the Duke of Devonshire in 1818. One of those, the meat and fish market on the north side of the river, was held in a commodious building in the form of a polygon, surrounded by stalls and forming a piazza for the market people. It had twenty-two stalls rented out to individual traders, a veterinary office and a market jury room. This fifteen-sided building is a rare find in Ireland today and parts of it have survived to the present day.

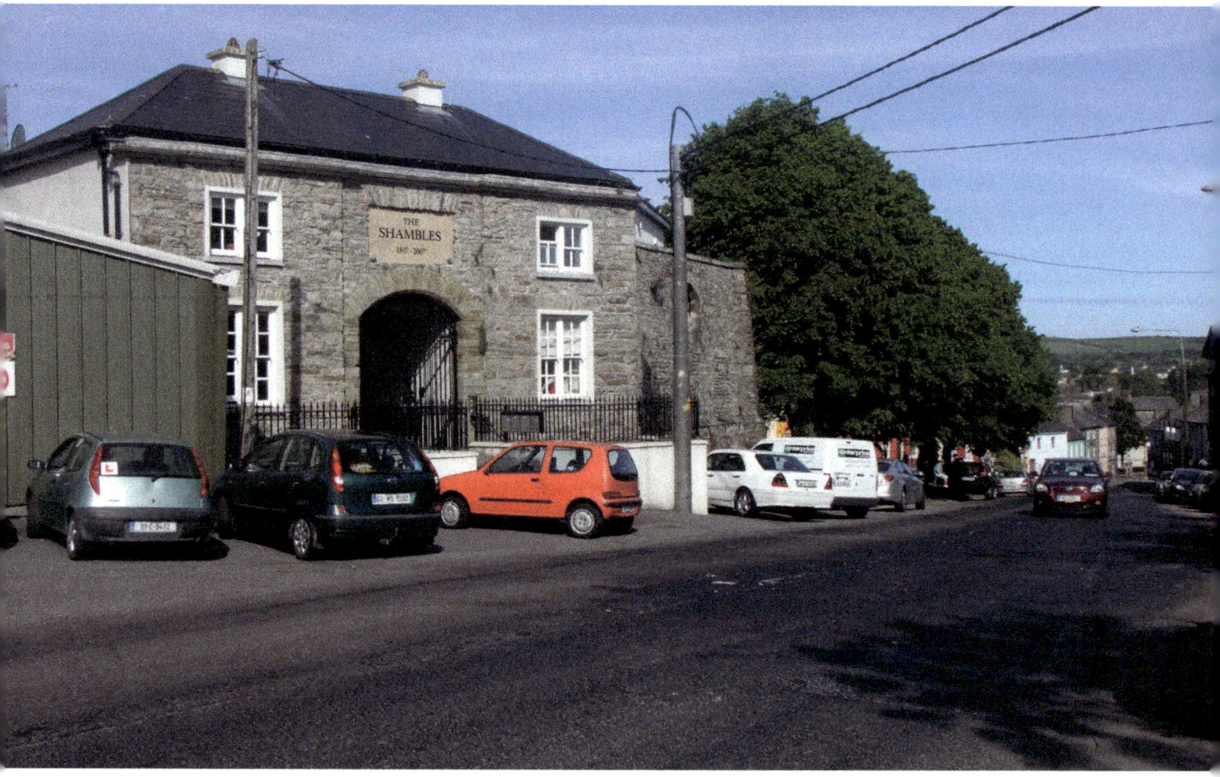

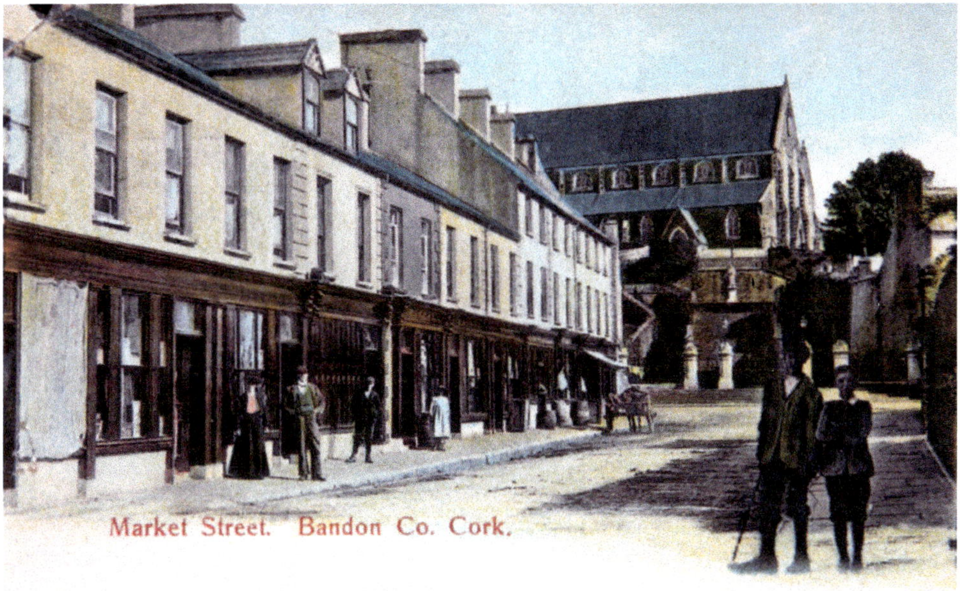

St Patrick's Church, Bandon

The church is one of the finest buildings of its period in the south of Ireland. The architects were Hadfield and Goldie, their design of the building was neo-Gothic and the cost of the building was £11,000. It is built of local sandstone, and white limestone is used in all dressings and ornaments. The foundation stone was laid on 17 March 1856 by Bishop Delaney, Cork, and the church was officially opened on 9 June 1861 at the feast of St Columba. The site of the church was donated by the Presentation Sisters.

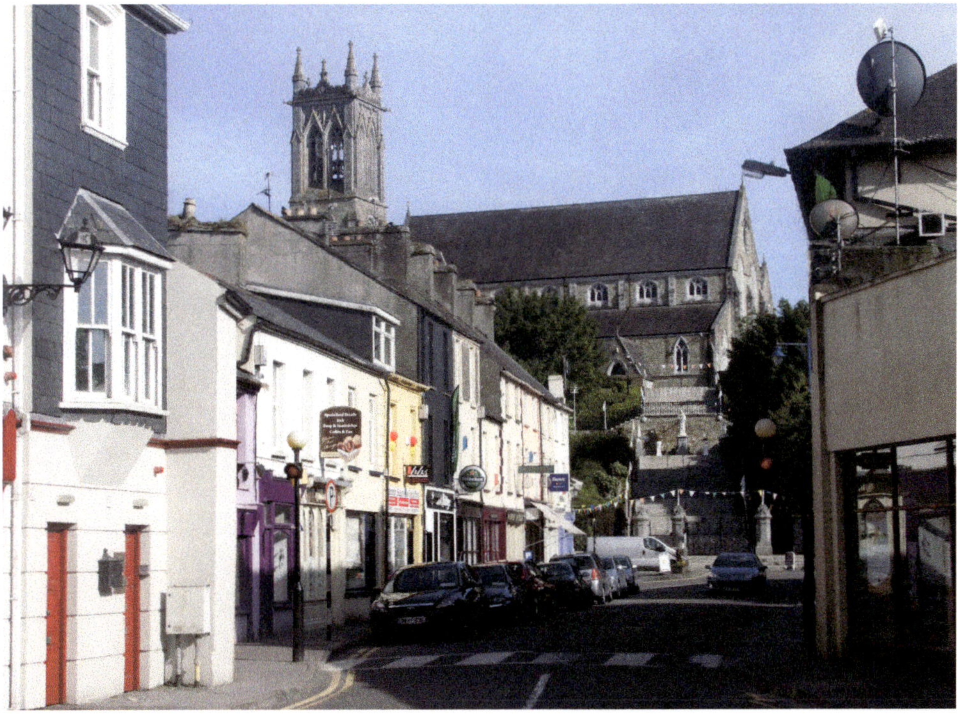

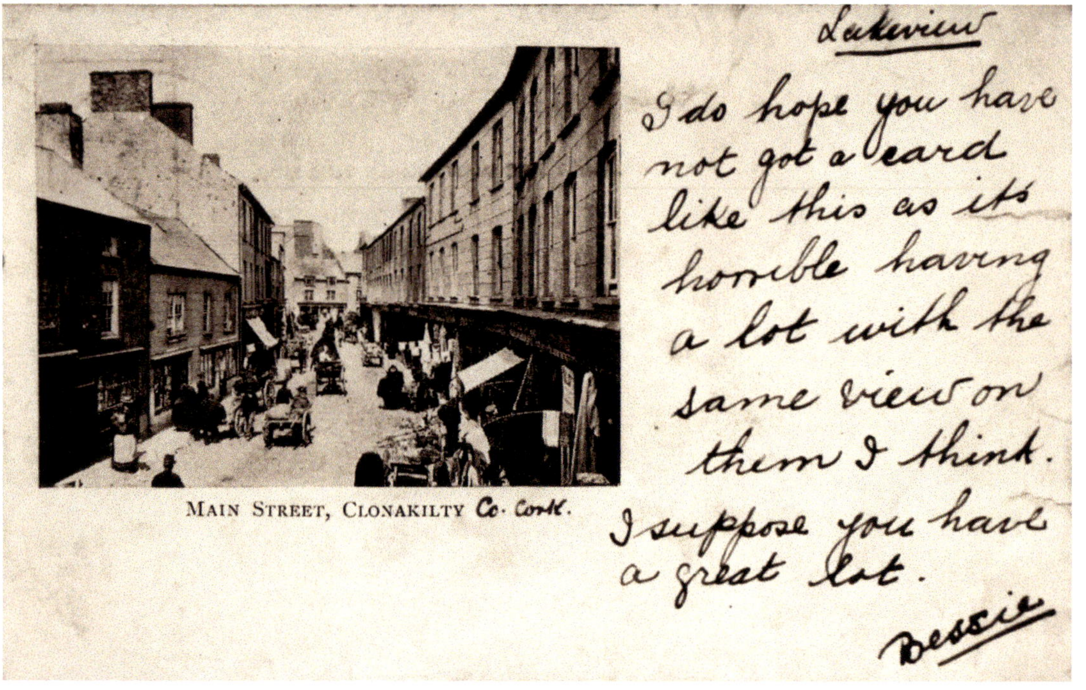

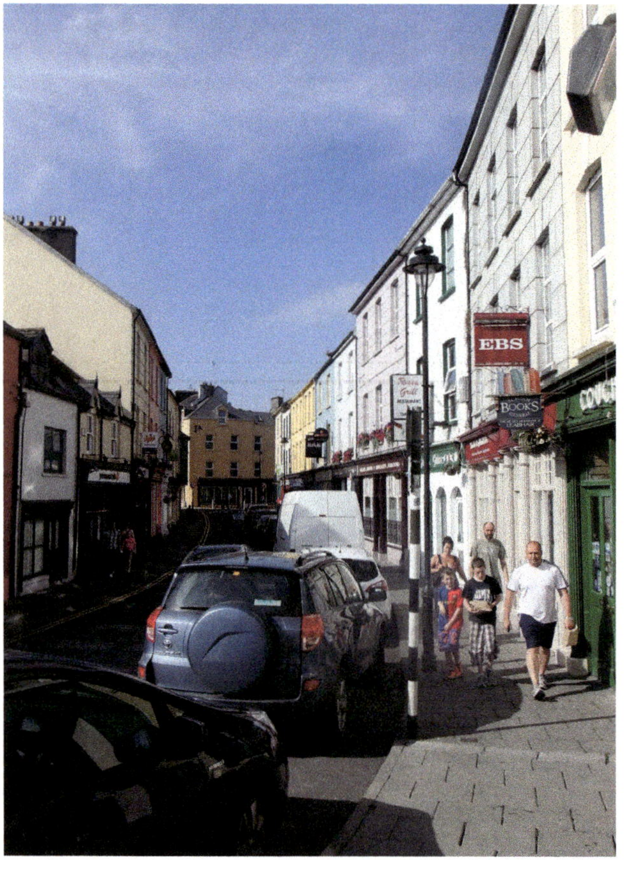

Main Street, Clonakilty

Clonakilty town is rich in ancient monuments and dwelling places. The Anglo-Normans made the area one of their territories, and their castles and surnames survive to the present day. Environed by hills and situated at the head of the spacious but ill-protected bay of Clonakilty, the town derives its name from *Cloch na gCoilte*, meaning the castle of the woods. In 1613, Sir Richard Boyle, first Earl of Cork, obtained for the inhabitants a charter of incorporation from King James I. The town flourished and was celebrated for its linen yarn trade. To mark the 400th anniversary in 2013, the president of Ireland, Michael D. Higgins, visited the town to celebrate four centuries of life, living and a rich cultural heritage.

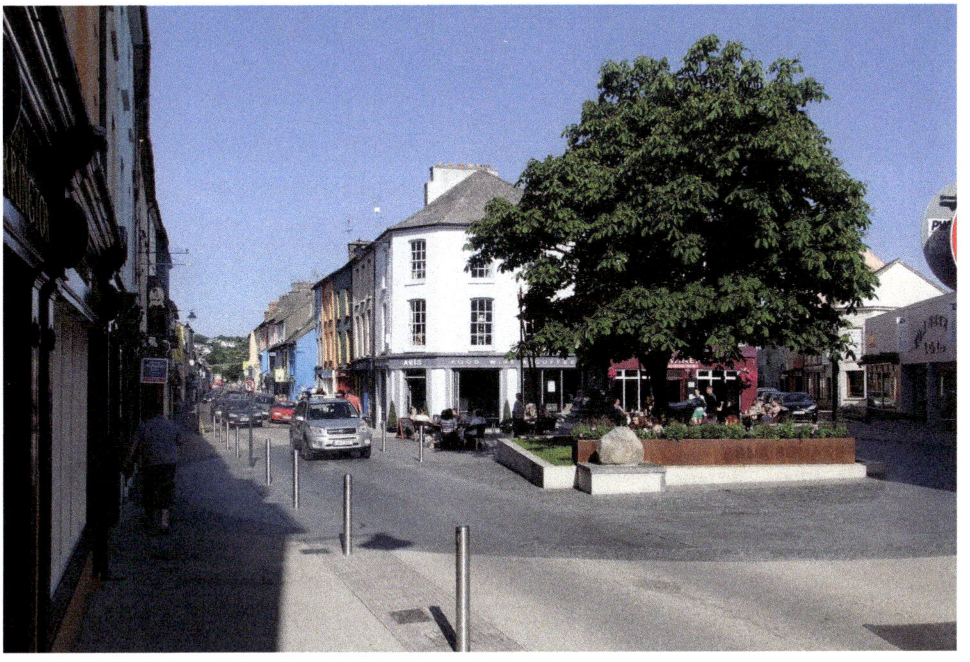

Mill Street, Clonakilty

At one time, the principal staple trade of Clonakilty was linen manufacture – hence the name Mill Street. Its principal factory furnished employment for 1,000 people who worked on 400 looms and who manufactured at the height of its prosperity weekly sales of £1,000. A spacious linen hall was built by the local aristocracy, the Earl of Shannon, as a central focal point for the promotion of linen in the region. The building in the postcard below stood on this site in the centre of the town until its demolition in 1941. Its curved front complemented the curved fronts of the other buildings, which surround what is known as the Cross, or town centre.

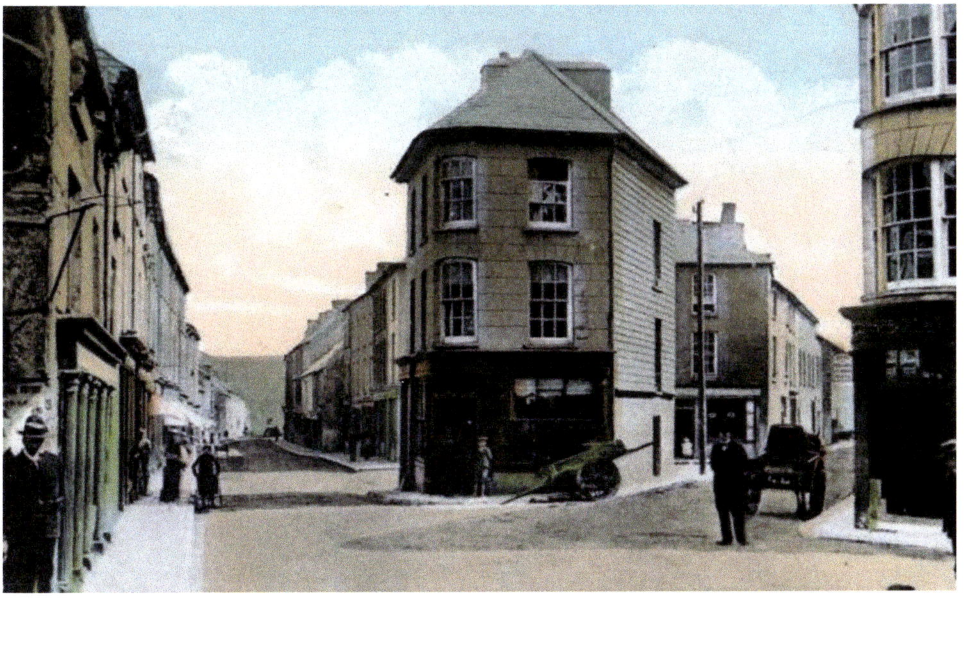

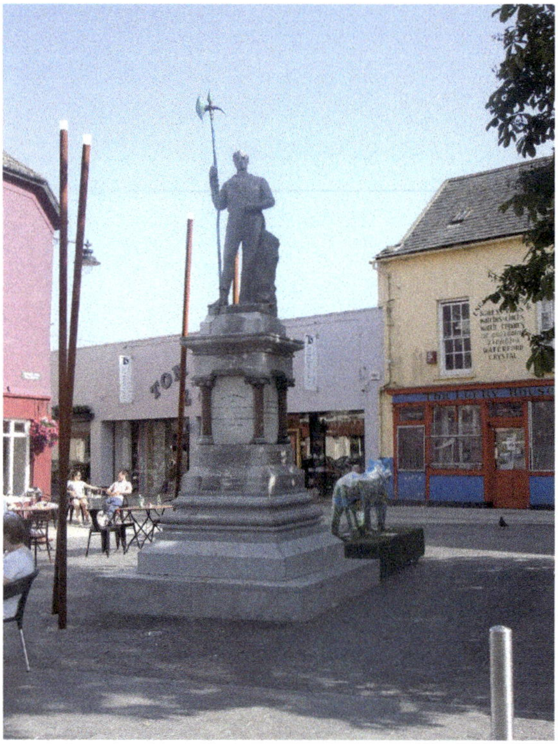

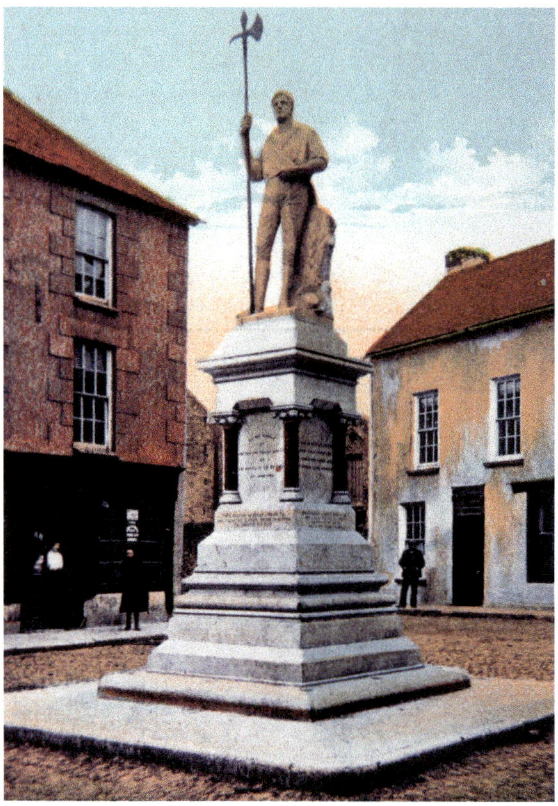

1798 Memorial, Asna Square, Clonakilty

The statue in the centre of Asna Square commemorates the ill-fated rising of Tadhg O'Donovan Asna and his followers, against British forces near Shannonvale, north of the town, in 1798. The battle was the only engagement in Munster during the rising of the United Irishmen in 1798 to overthrow the British rule in Ireland. The lighting (*above*) represents the other soldiers, or 'pikemen', who stood alongside Tadhg. The square also displays the 'Kitty Stone', which is recorded as being from a local Norman castle and was used as a symbol of the town's foundation for centuries.

Roman Catholic, Church of the Immaculate Conception

Up to 1880, members of the Roman Catholic community of Clonakilty were baptised, and prayed in the small church in Western Road where the former boys' National School currently stands. A new church was designed by S. C. Ashlin of Dublin and built in 1880. Designed in the pure Gothic early French style, the church comprises a nave, transepts, ailes, a baptistery and two chapels. In the 1890s, the spire was fitted, and later, in 1898, the bell was installed. The altar of the Sacred Heart was erected at a cost of £350 by James Pearse of Dublin (father of Pádraig Pearse, patriot and leader of the 1916 rising), while the erection of the church itself cost around £36,000 in total. Following renovations in the 1990s, the church interior was restored to its former glory.

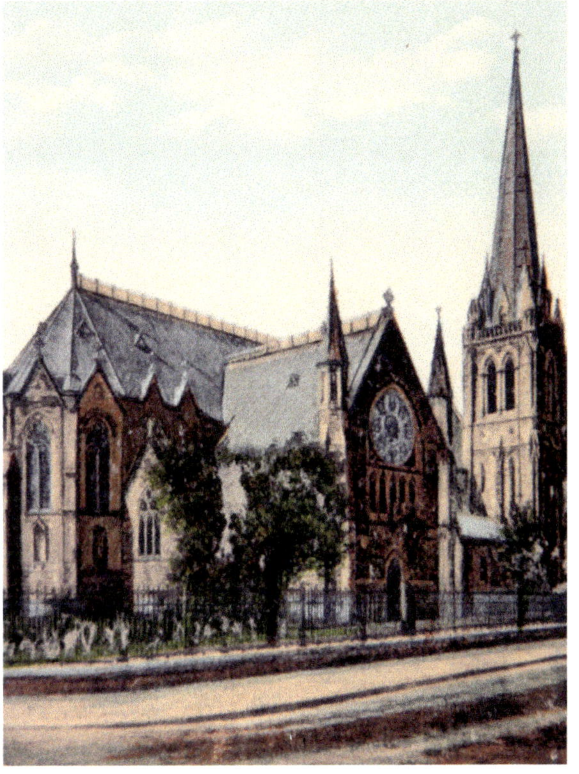

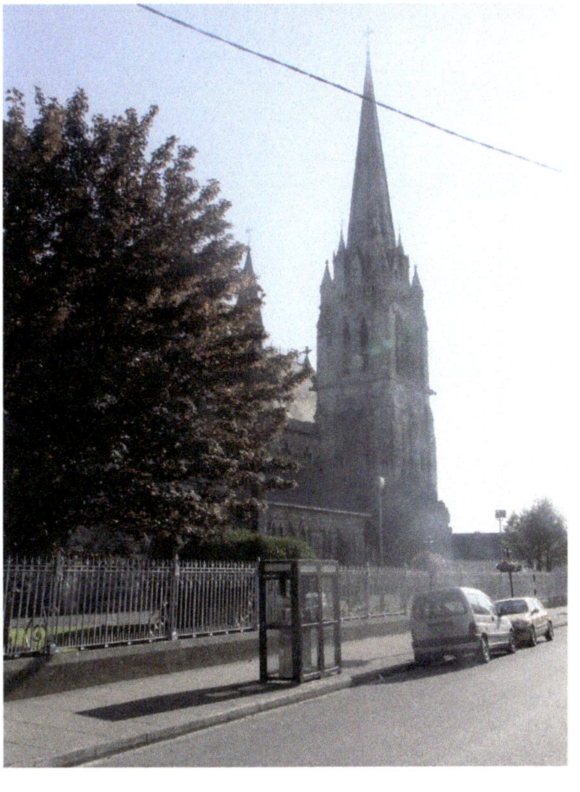

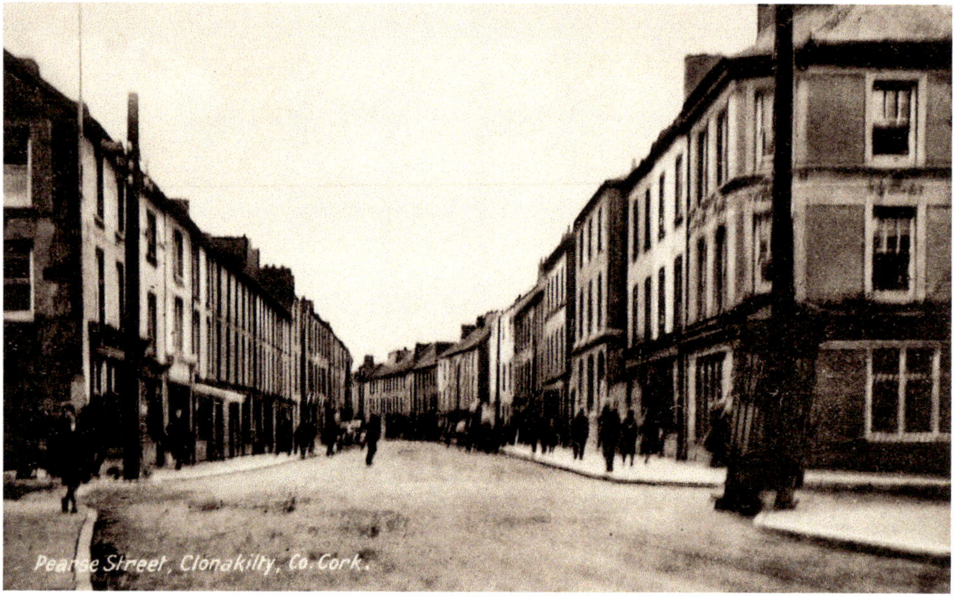

Pearse Street, Clonakilty

Perhaps the biggest alteration in any town's history is a name change, which this street, originally Sovereign Street, underwent. It was renamed Pearse Street following the Irish War of Independence, after Pádraig Pearse, the 1916 Irish leader and signatory of the Irish Proclamation of Independence. His father designed the altar in the local Catholic church. Other signatories are also highlighted in street names: Thomas Kent, Thomas Clarke, and James Connolly. Locally born Fenian leader Jeremiah O'Donovan Rossa is also immortalised, as well as Tomás MacCurtain, Cork's Lord Mayor who was martyred in 1920, and figures from earlier revolutionary history such as Robert Emmett, the United Irishman leader. The nearest settlement to have such street names is Cork City.

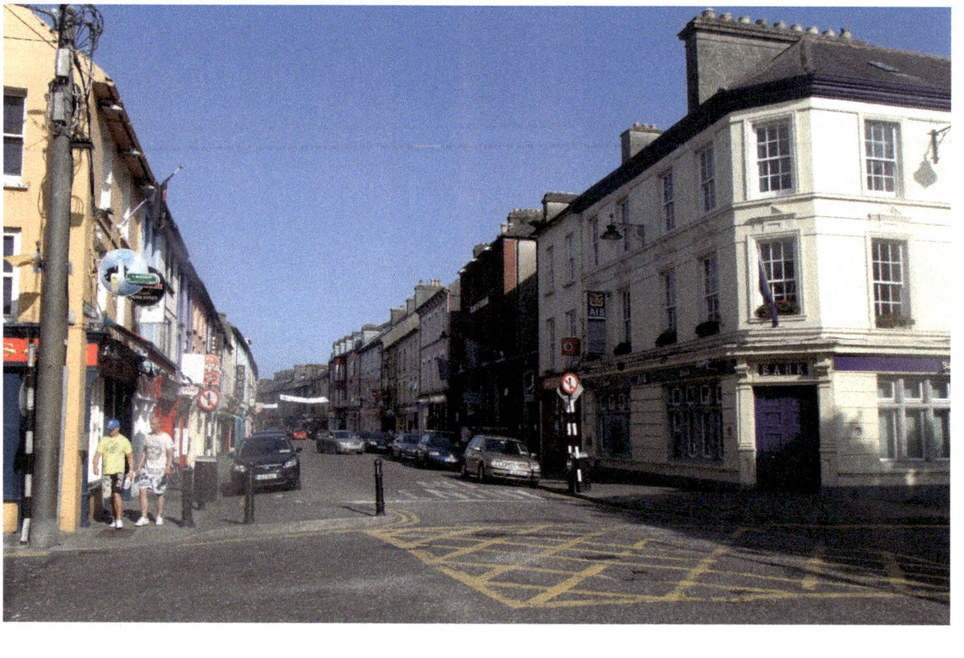

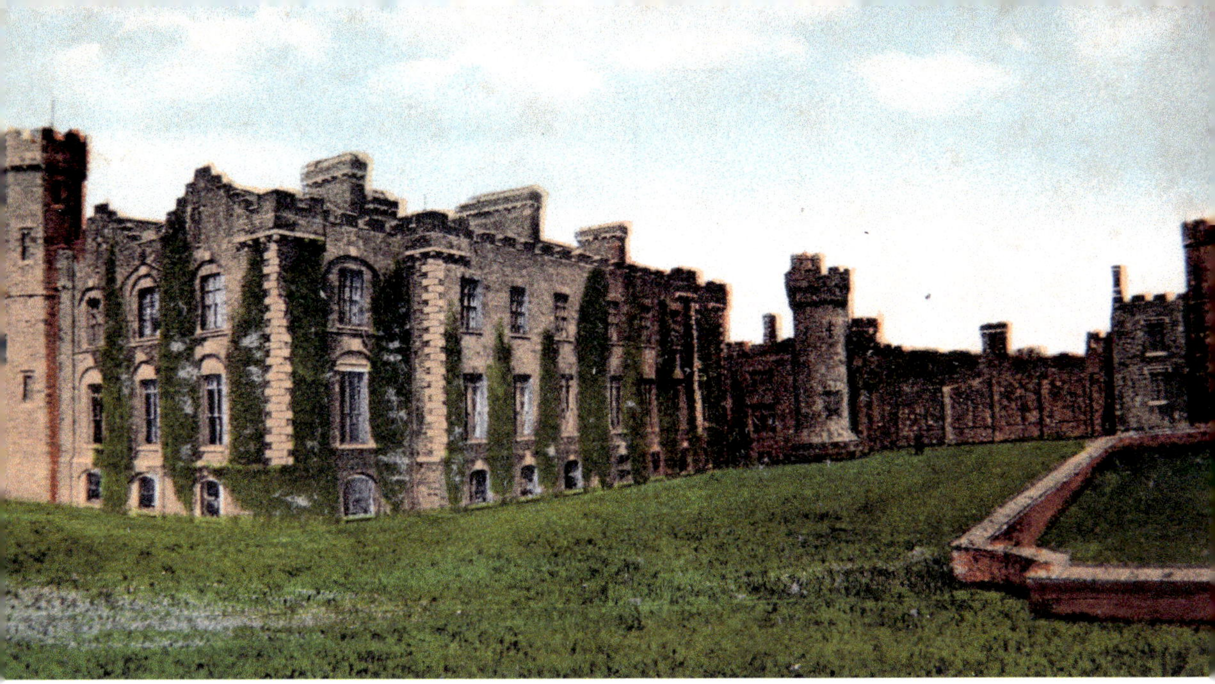

Castlefreke, Clonakilty

The former name of Castle Freke was Rathbarry. As the old castle of Rathbarry was neglected and dilapidated, John Evans-Freke built a new one. Around 1820, a new site was chosen in another part of the estate for a new structure. The renowned architect Sir Richard Morrison altered the castle into its current Gothic-castellated style and the new building contained numerous spacious suites of apartments on the principal storey. In 1910, there was a major fire at the castle. The building was reconstructed to include concrete floors, a lift and electricity. By 1919, the family successor, also called John Evans-Freke, sold the estate and moved to America. A year later he moved to Kenya. Recent renovation work by the Freke family is ongoing.

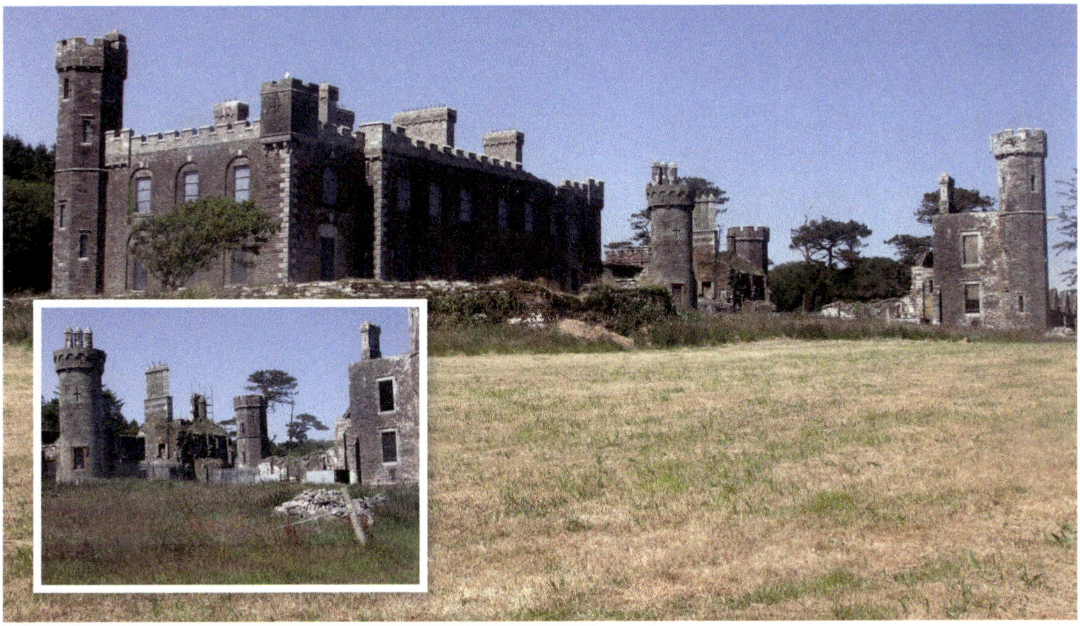

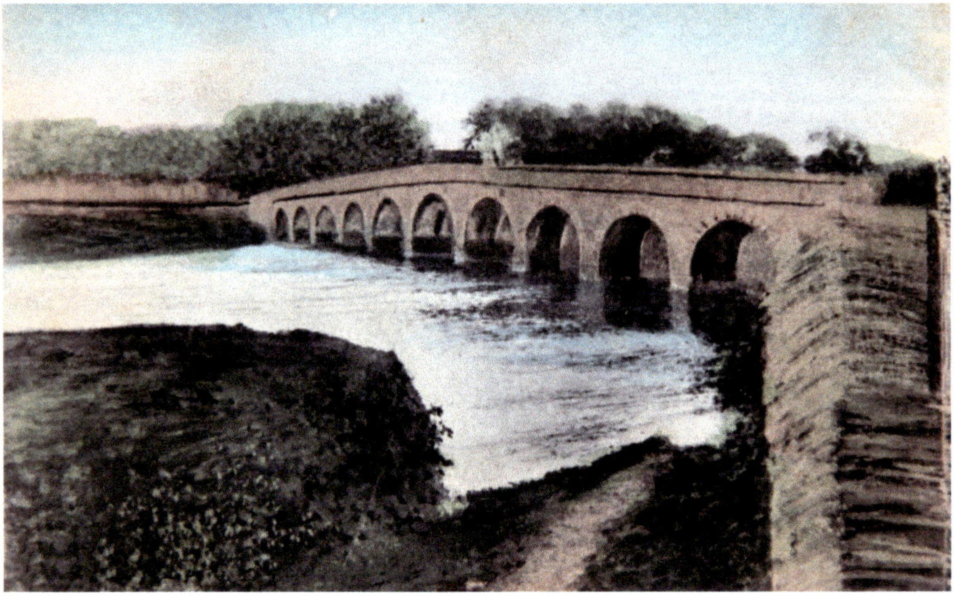

The Bridge, Ballineen

An impressive bridge over the Bandon River, near Ballineen village, has ten semicircular arches gently increasing in height towards the centre. It has tall, pointed, stone breakwaters. Dating to the nineteenth century, the number of arches makes it more unique than the typical three-arched bridge. The decade of the 1820s coincided with enormous investment by local landowners and the Westminster government to improve the road network for the transportation of goods in County Cork. The Bandon River rises in the Shehy Mountains and flows for 72 km in a general eastwards direction, with several tributaries feeding into it. Salmon fishing is licensed from Inishshannon up to 4 km downstream of the bridge. Sea trout and brown trout are also quite common. At the mouth of the river is Kinsale Harbour.

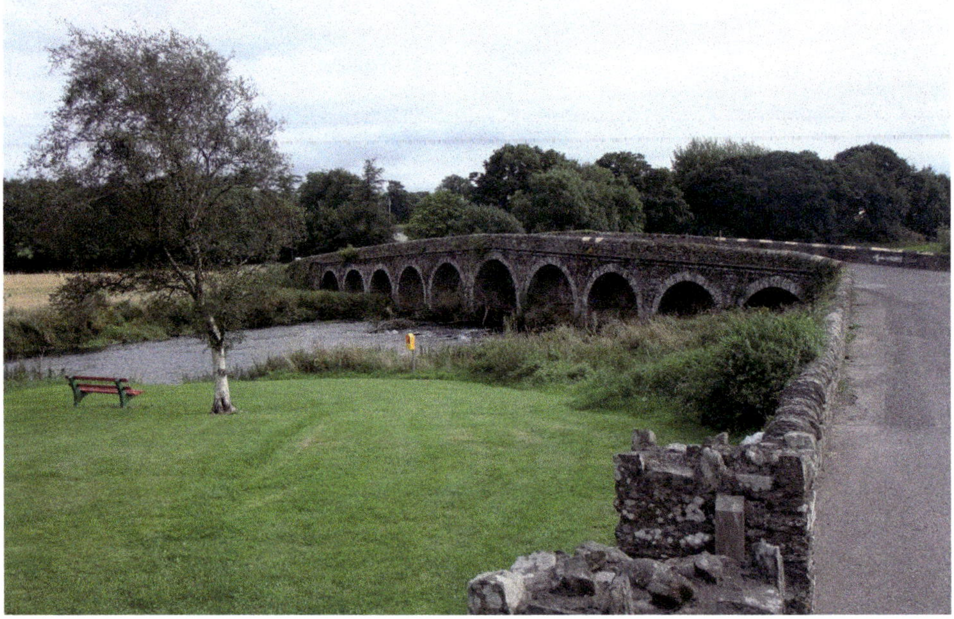

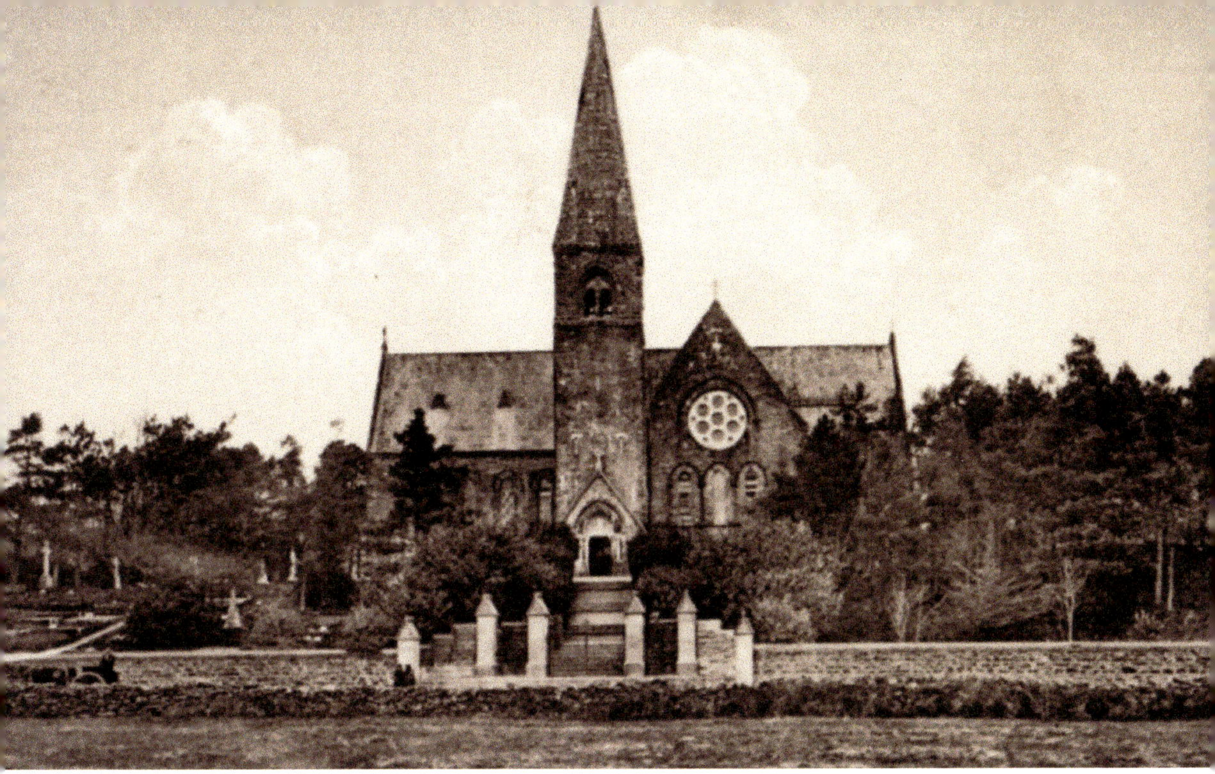

Church of the Immaculate Conception, Enniskeane
The history of the Catholic church in the locality records that, in 1858, a new parish was created with a new parish name: Enniskeane and Desertserges. Shortly afterwards, under the leadership of parish priest Father Daniel Coveney, the people of the parish set about building a new parish church in Enniskeane to replace the local chapel, which had been built around 1750. The foundation stone of the beautiful church of the Immaculate Conception was laid by Bishop William Delaney on 7 May 1871. Richard Evans designed the church in the Gothic style.

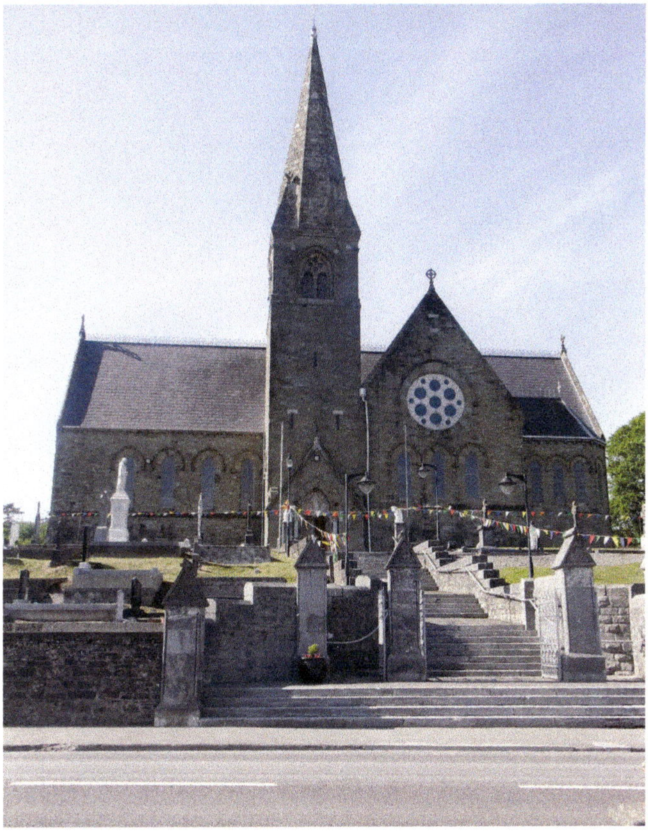

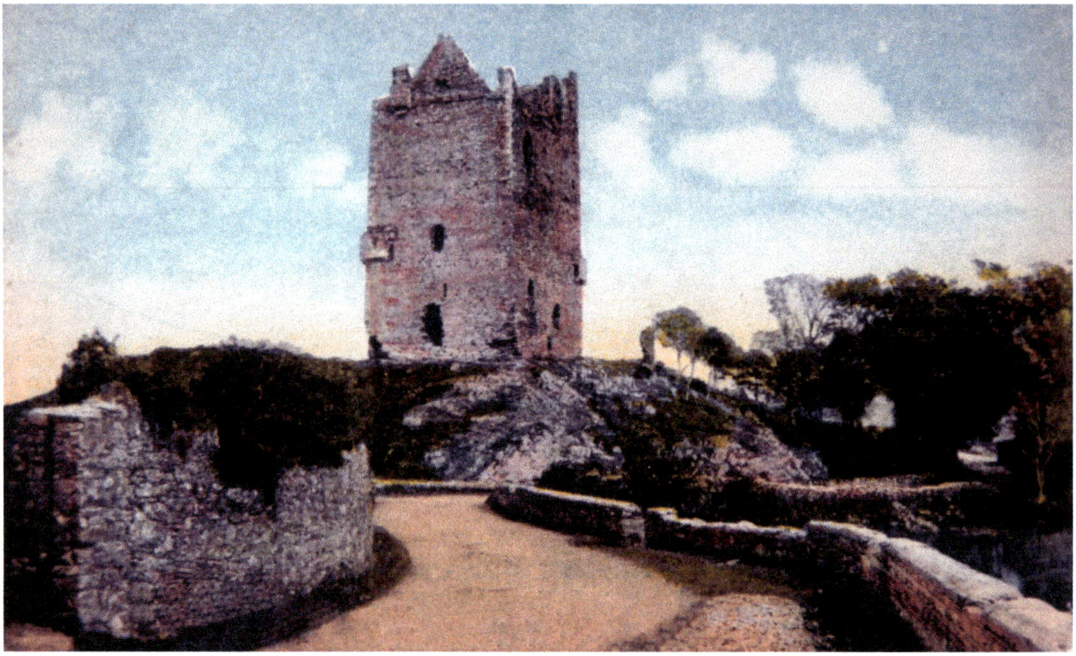

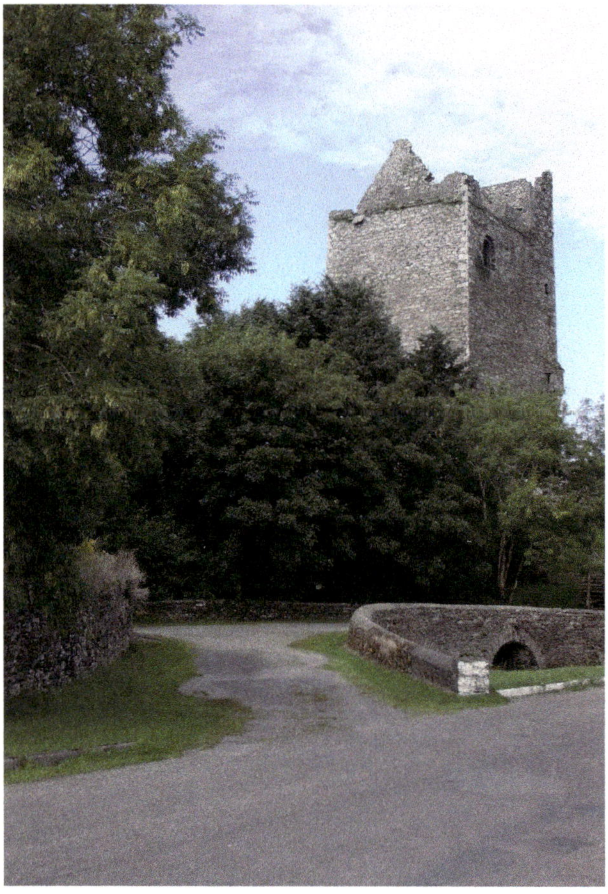

Ballinacarriga Castle, Ballineen

Béal na Carraige means the mouth or passage of the rock. Halfway between the towns of Ballineen and Dunnway, just off the beaten track, lies Ballinacarriga Castle. The castle is atypical of a tower house; it is a four-storey tower built on a rocky outcrop, with good views in all directions. On what was the third floor – which is accessible by a circular stairway built into the thickness of the wall – are the initials R. M. C. C. and the date 1585, carved into the soffit on the north window. These are thought to be the initials of the Irish chieftain Randal Murlihy (Hurley) and his wife Catherine Cullinane, while the date refers to the year of the erection of the building. It is generally accepted that the greater part of the castle is older, and may have been in the possession of the MacCarthy Irish clan before the Hurleys took over.

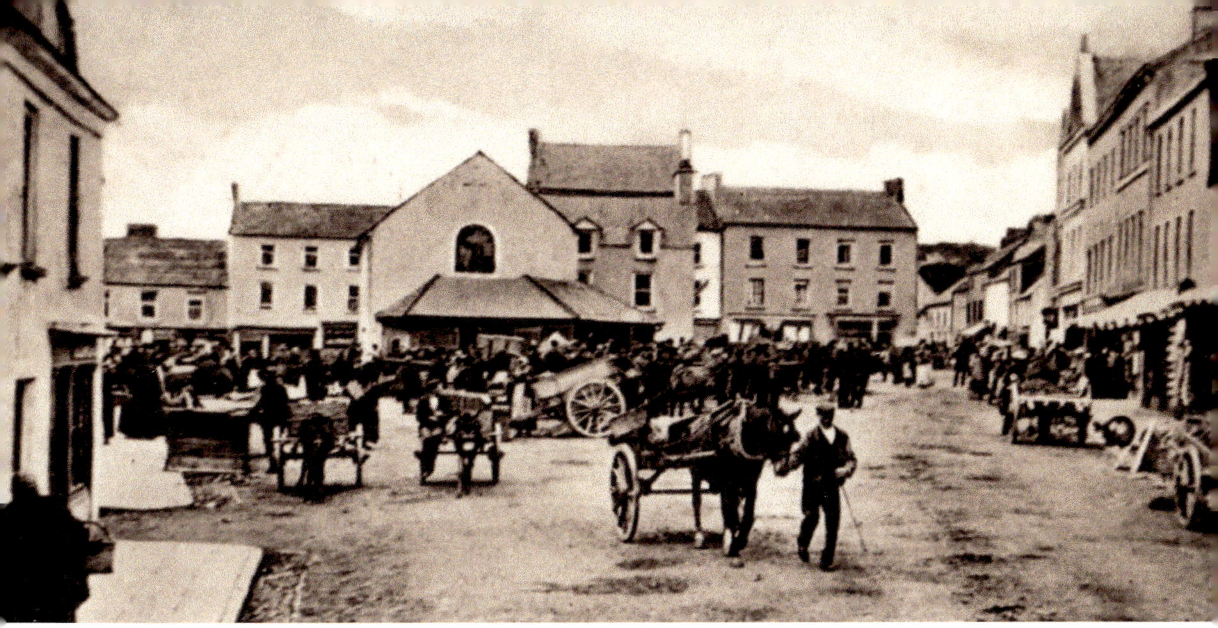

Dunmanway

Dunmanway is a seventeenth-century planned town, and the two original triangular squares still survive. Various sources list its meaning when translated from Irish as 'the castle of the yellow river', 'the castle on the little plain', 'the fort of the gables (or pinnacles)', or 'the fort of the yellow women'. It is best known as the birthplace of Sam Maguire, the man after whom the All-Ireland Senior Football trophy is named, and a statue (*inset*) of him is on the public square (*below*).

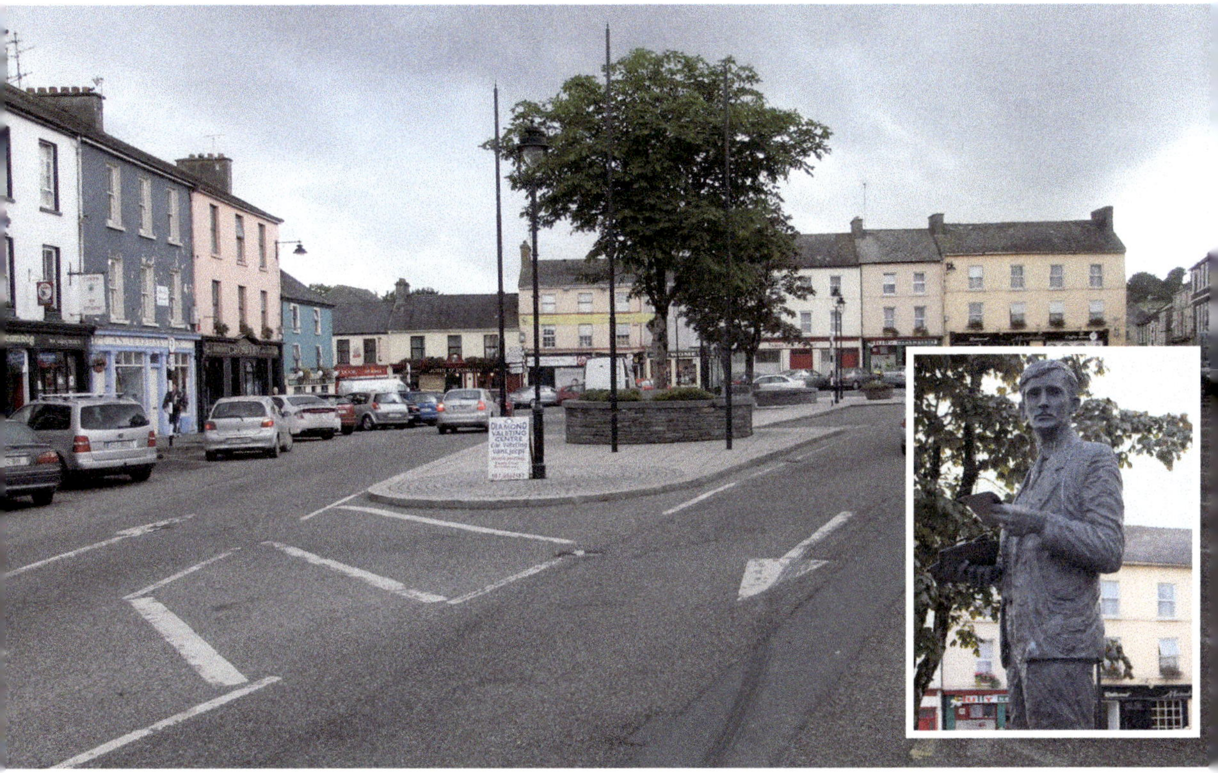

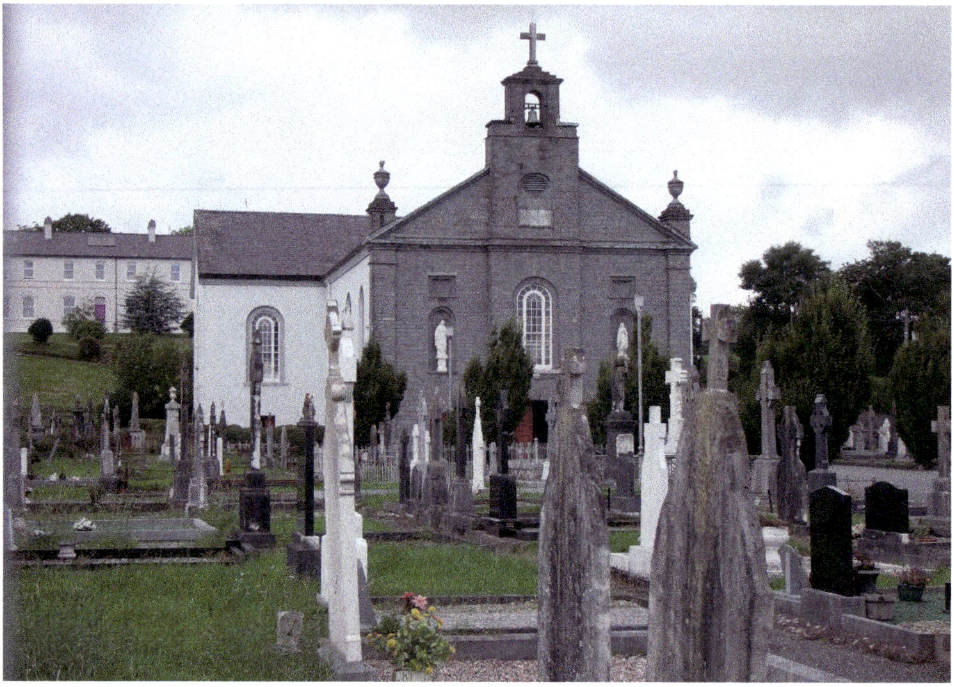

St Patrick's Church, Dunmanway

Built in 1834, the church was designed by Brother Michael Augustine Riordan, a Presentation Brother who had been a draughtsman before joining the order. Built around an older small church, it was constructed in an era following the Roman Catholic Relief Act, which was passed by the British Parliament on 24 March 1829. The act permitted members of the Catholic Church to openly worship and sit in parliament, something previously forbidden, even if they won an election. The Catholic middle classes could now have new careers in the higher civil service and the judiciary. In addition, the new act allowed many Roman Catholic churches, similar in architecture, to be built across Ireland, many replacing old and rundown structures.

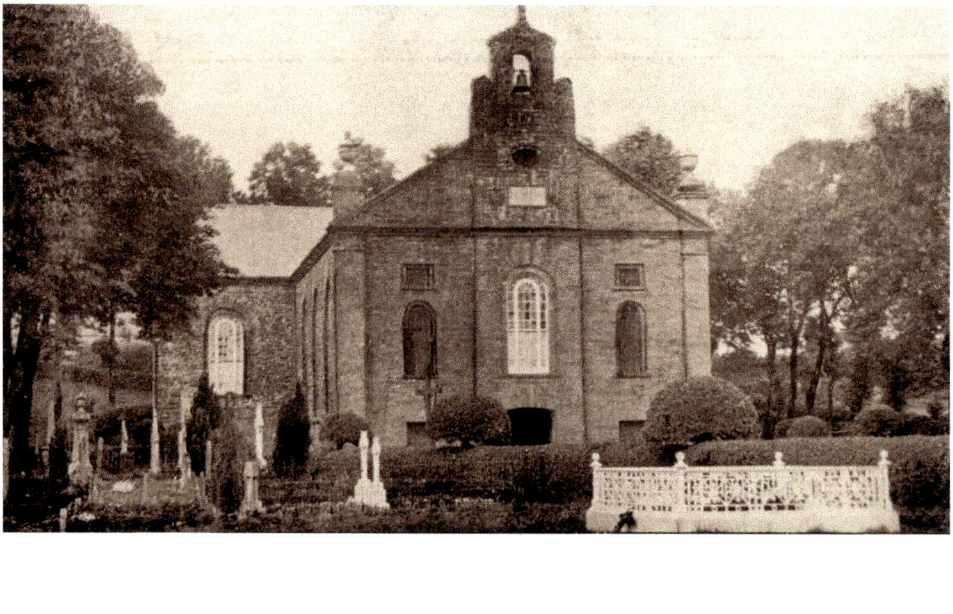

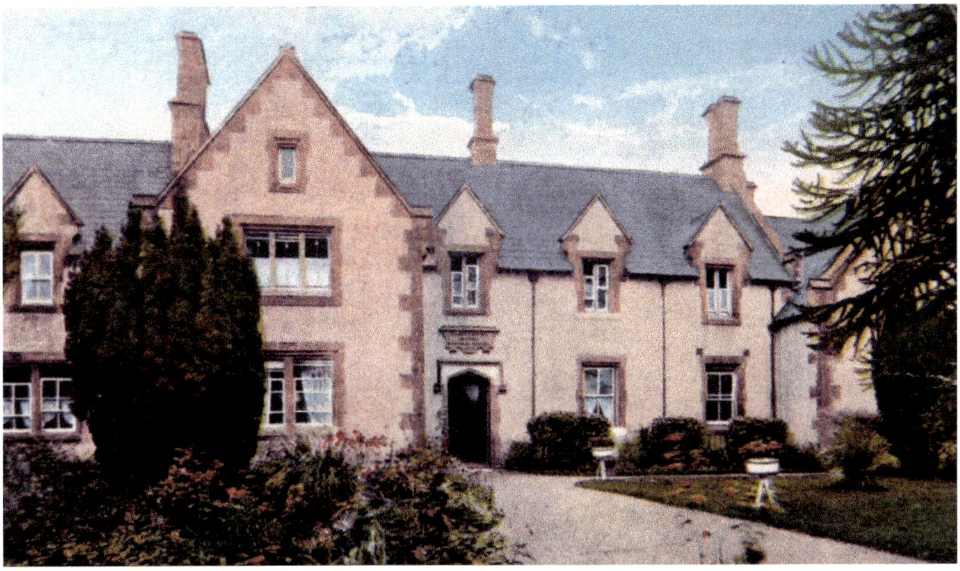

Model School, Dunmanway

The school was founded in 1848, and was established along with twenty-five other 'model schools' around Ireland to represent a high standard of educational practice, and to begin the training process for teachers. Also attached were agricultural departments and farms, complete with trial plots. After some years as monitors in the model school, the trainees would go to Dublin for six months to complete the course and become qualified in Dunmanway. Today, the school's patron is the Irish Minister for Education and Skills, rather than the Bishop of Cork, Cloyne and Ross. Local Church of Ireland schools have been amalgamated into it.

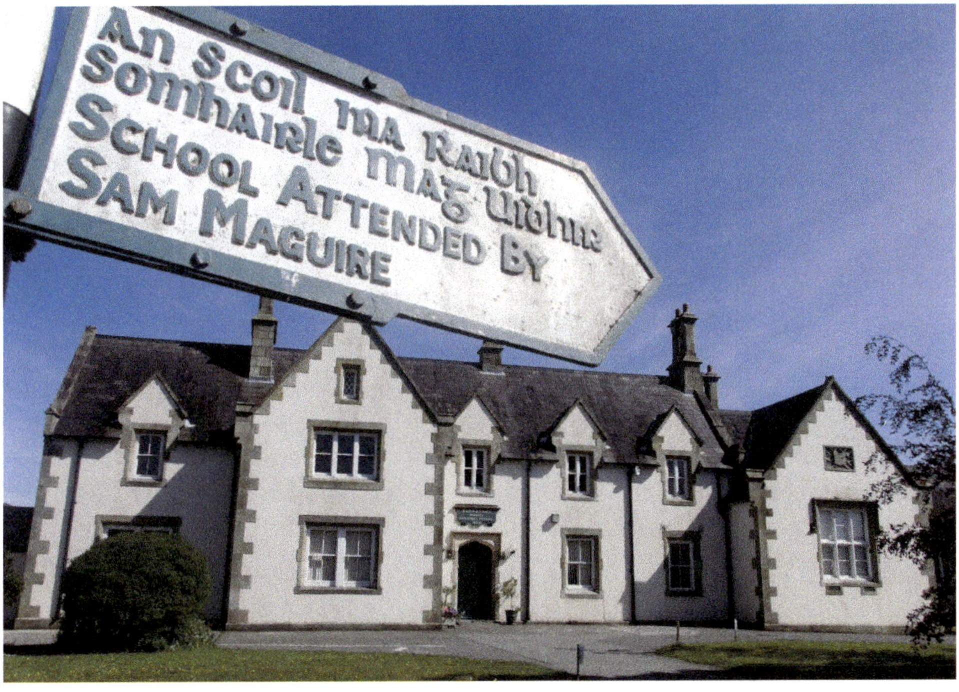

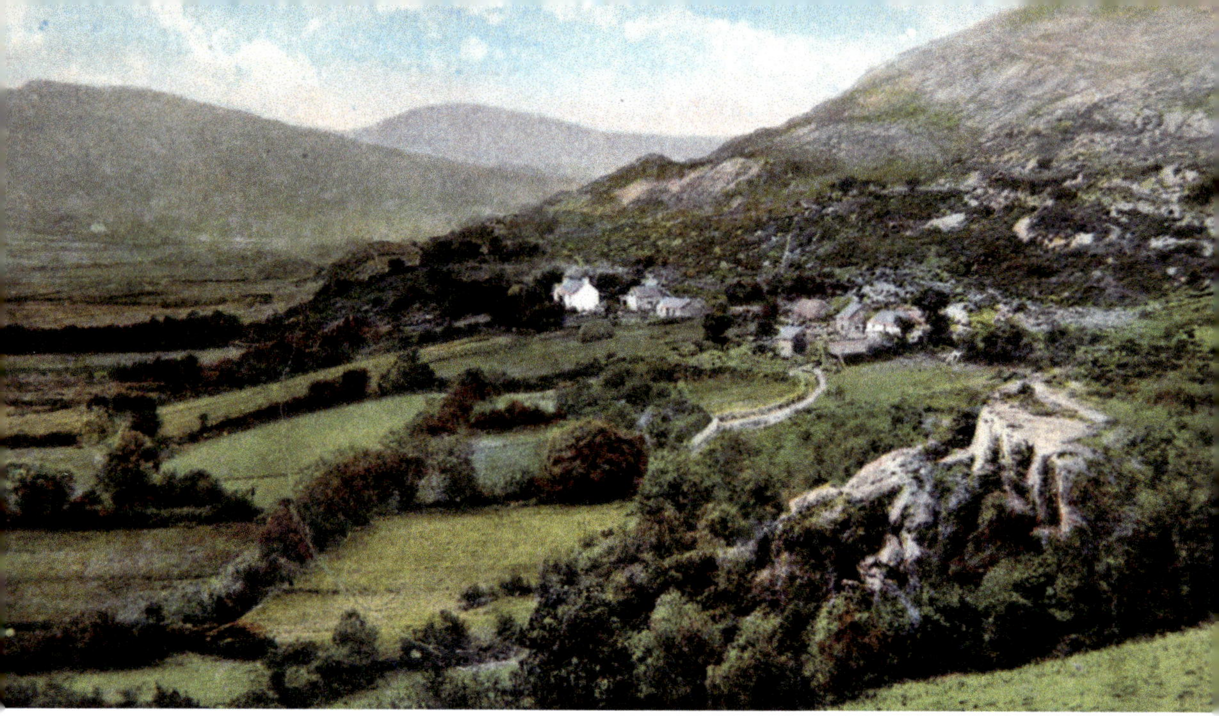

The Coom, Dunmanway

Dunmanway is encompassed by spectacular scenery, with hills and lakes to the north, south and west. The settlement can lay claim to being 'The Gateway to The Mountains', and is ideal for hillwalking, fishing and horse riding. Because of its central location, Dunmanway is the ideal base from which to visit and explore the renowned beauty of West Cork, and to sample its culture, cuisine and hospitality.

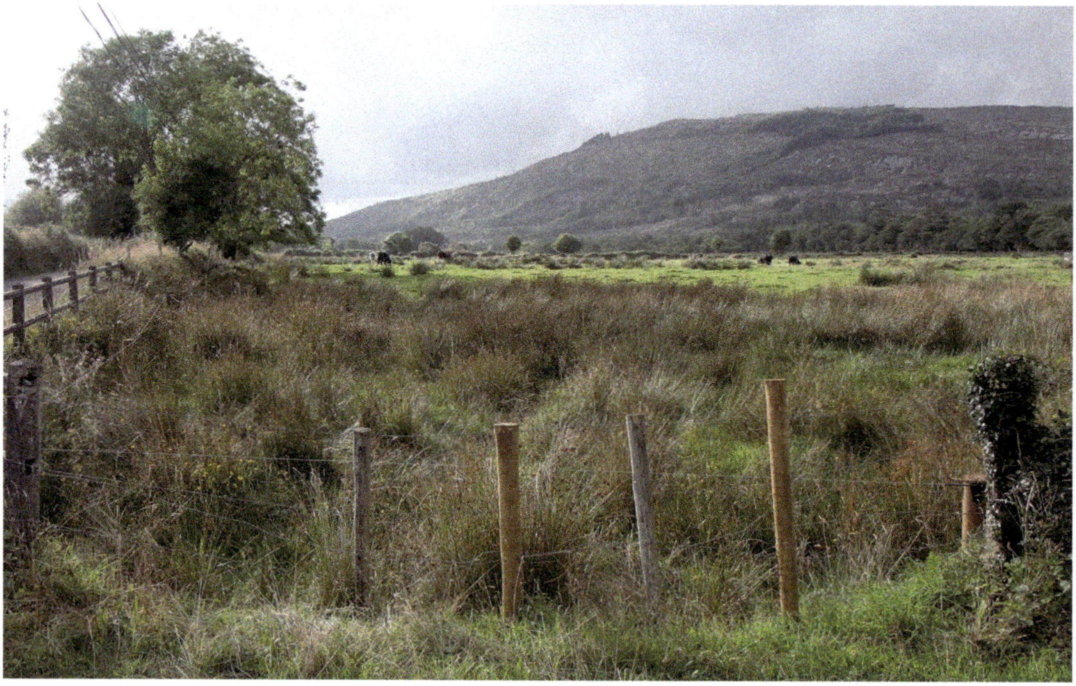

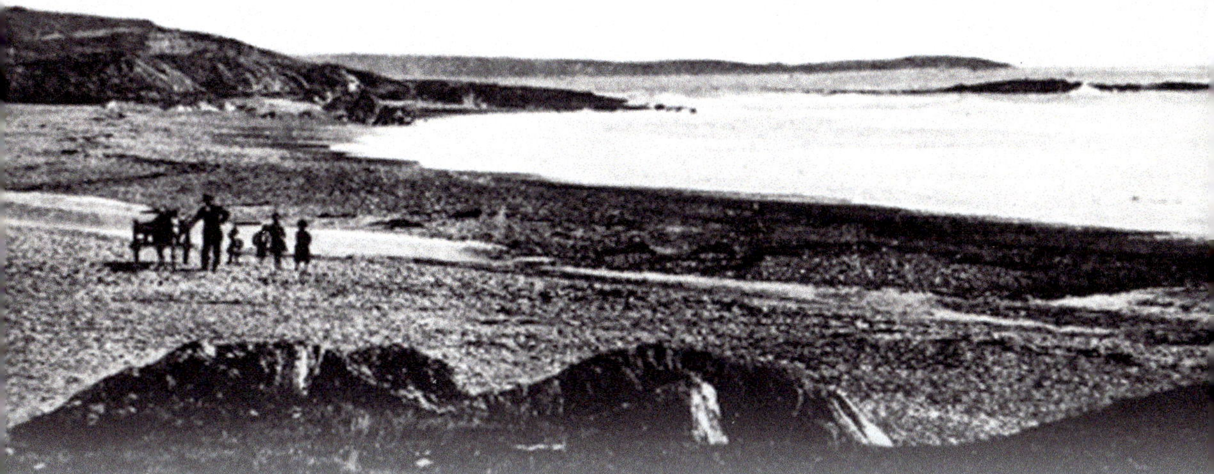

CHAPTER 2

Along the Coast

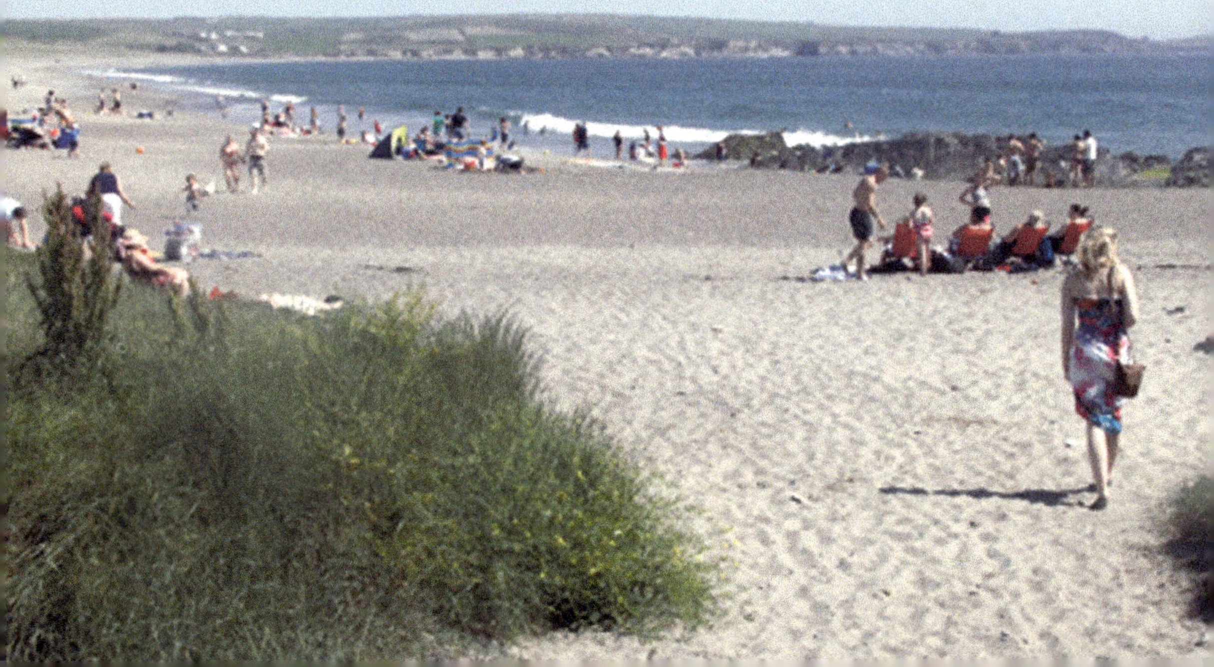

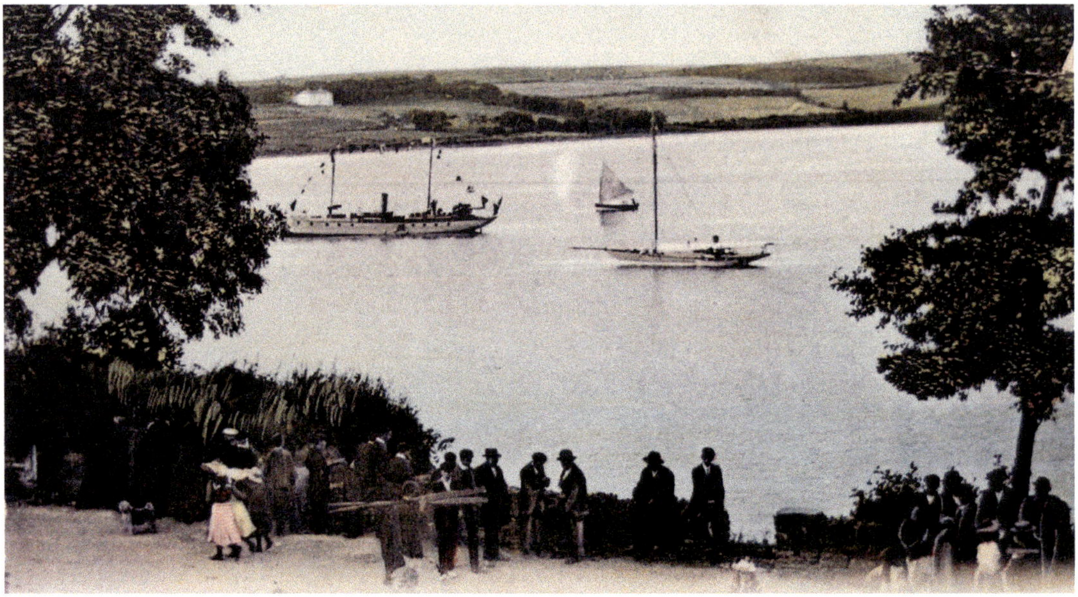

Courtmacsherry Bay

Following the Anglo-Norman invasion of 1169, large parts of Ireland were colonised. Many Anglo-Norman families settled in this area, and their surnames and place names survive to the present day. One such family were the Hodnetts; a member of that family became Gaelicised and began to use the Irish form *Seafraidh*. His descendants became MacSeafraidh, and from their court or castle, the name *Cúirt Mhic Sheafraidh*, or anglicised Courtmacsherry. The bay is also home to one of Ireland's six south-west lifeboat stations (established 1825).

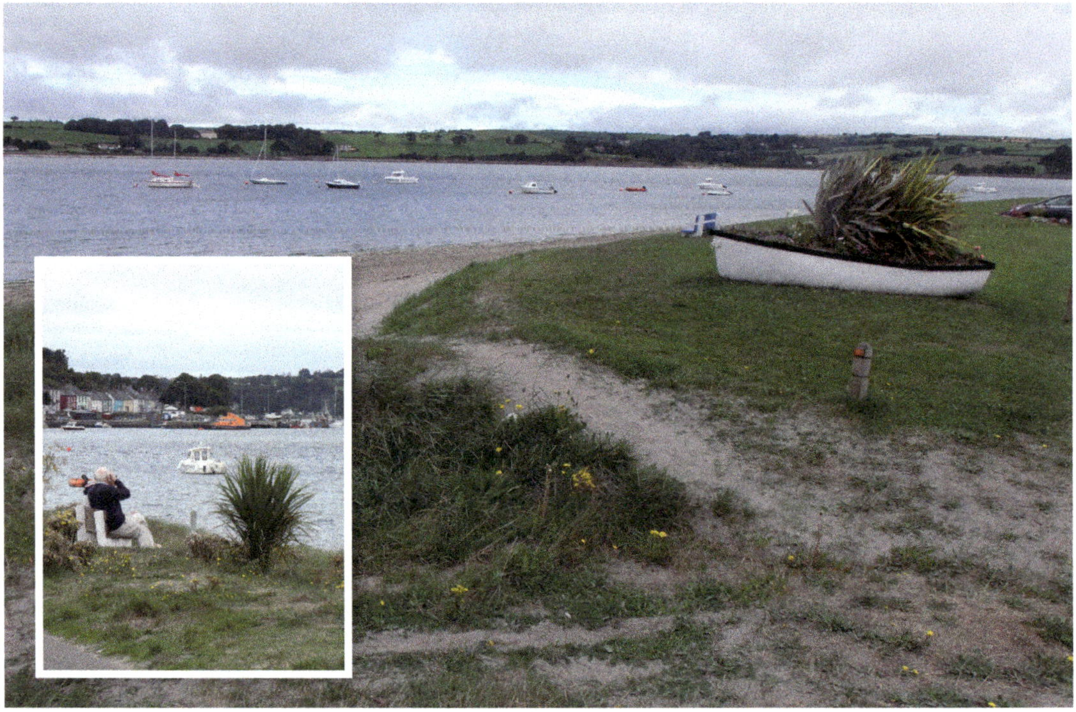

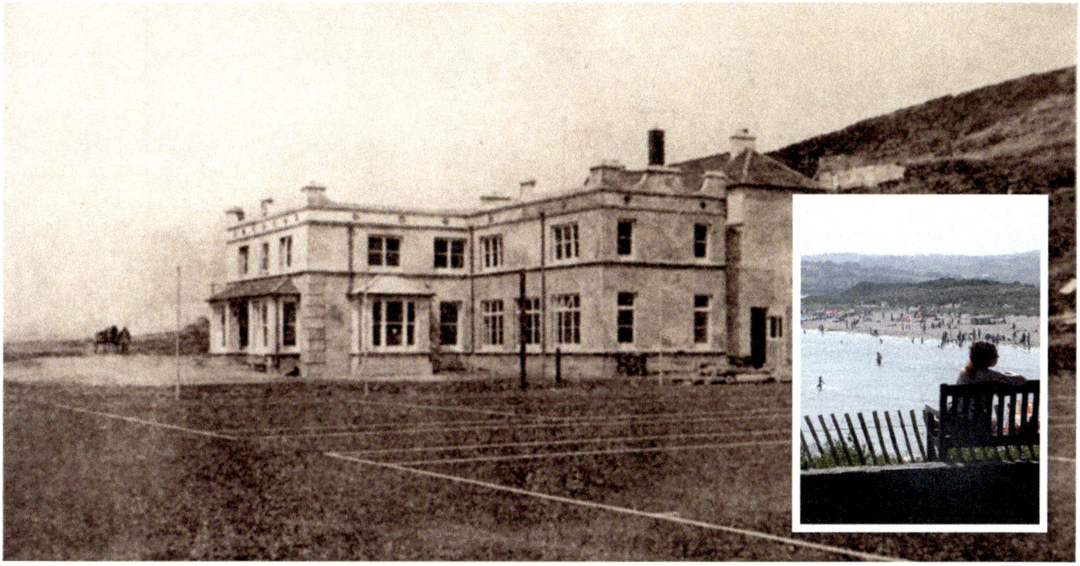

Inchidoney Hotel, Inchidoney Island

After the battle of Clonakilty in 1642 against English troops, 600 of the Irish forces fled towards this island as a place of refuge. With the tide coming in at the time, they all drowned before they could reach it. An extensive strand surrounds the base of the island, which is dry at low water. A century ago, it comprised more than 1,000 acres of rich alluvial soil, part of which was from the sea and brought it into profitable cultivation. Today, the former manor house is the site of Inchydoney Island Hotel & Spa, which commands stunning views over the Atlantic Ocean and beaches, while stretching out below is the nearby Virgin Mary sandbank (*above inset*).

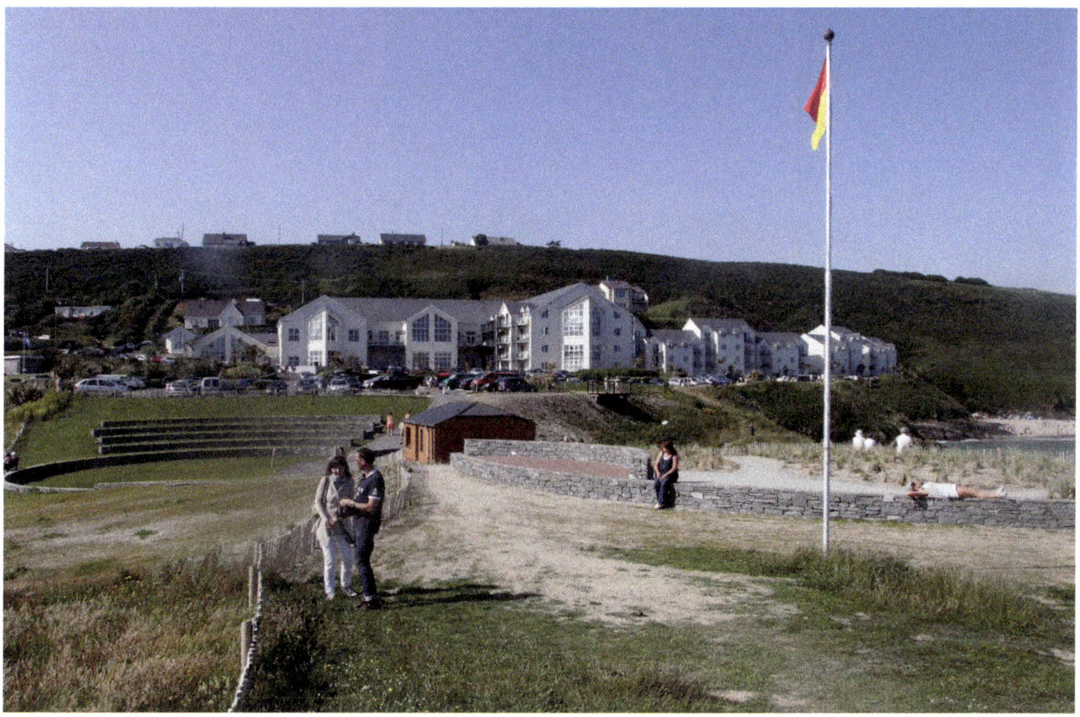

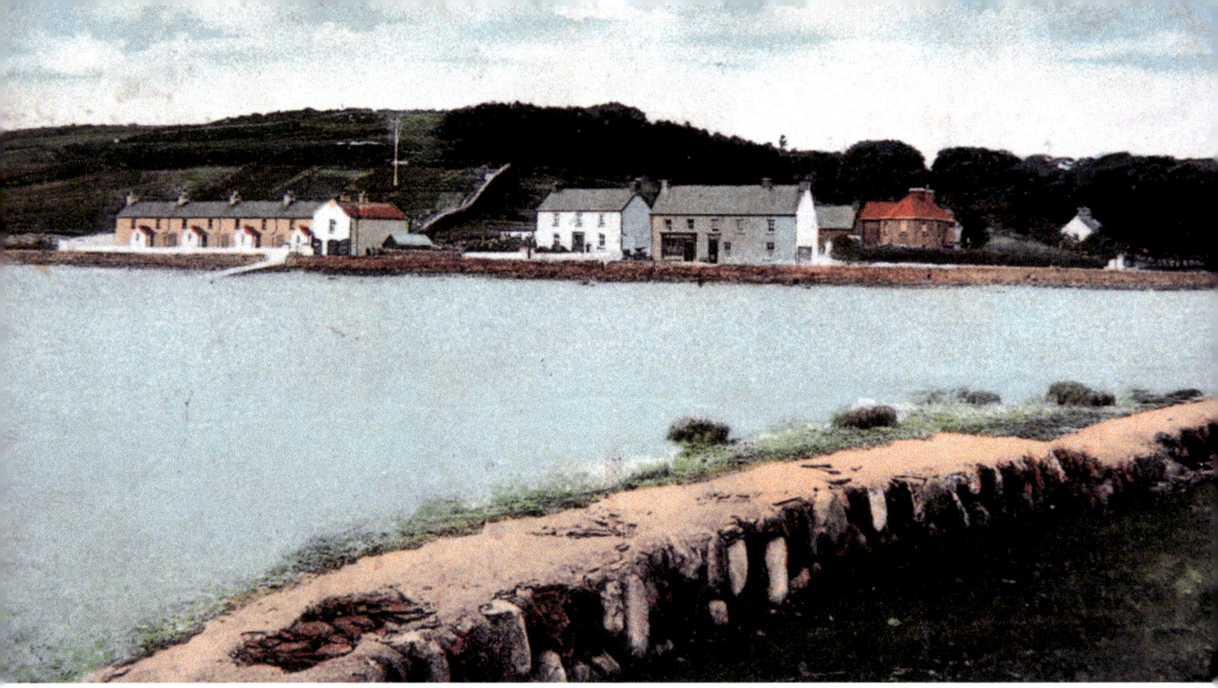

Ring Village, Clonakilty

English planter Lord Arundel, in the early part of the thirteenth century, built a very extensive and beautiful castle called Castle Arundel. Afterwards it passed to the Barrymore family, and was named *Rine*, or Ring, by them. In the nineteenth century, business continued here in grain, potatoes and flour. A total of 5,000 bushels of wheat and 1,000 tons of potatoes were annually shipped from here. To facilitate this, several large stores were built, some of which survive as ruins in this small but colourful settlement.

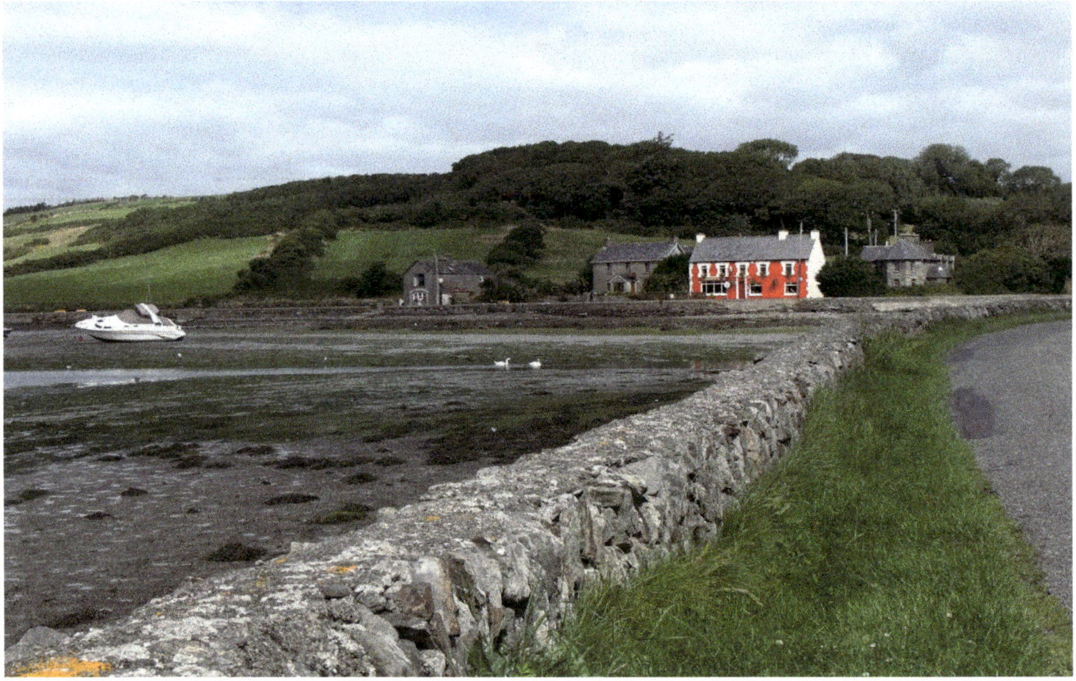

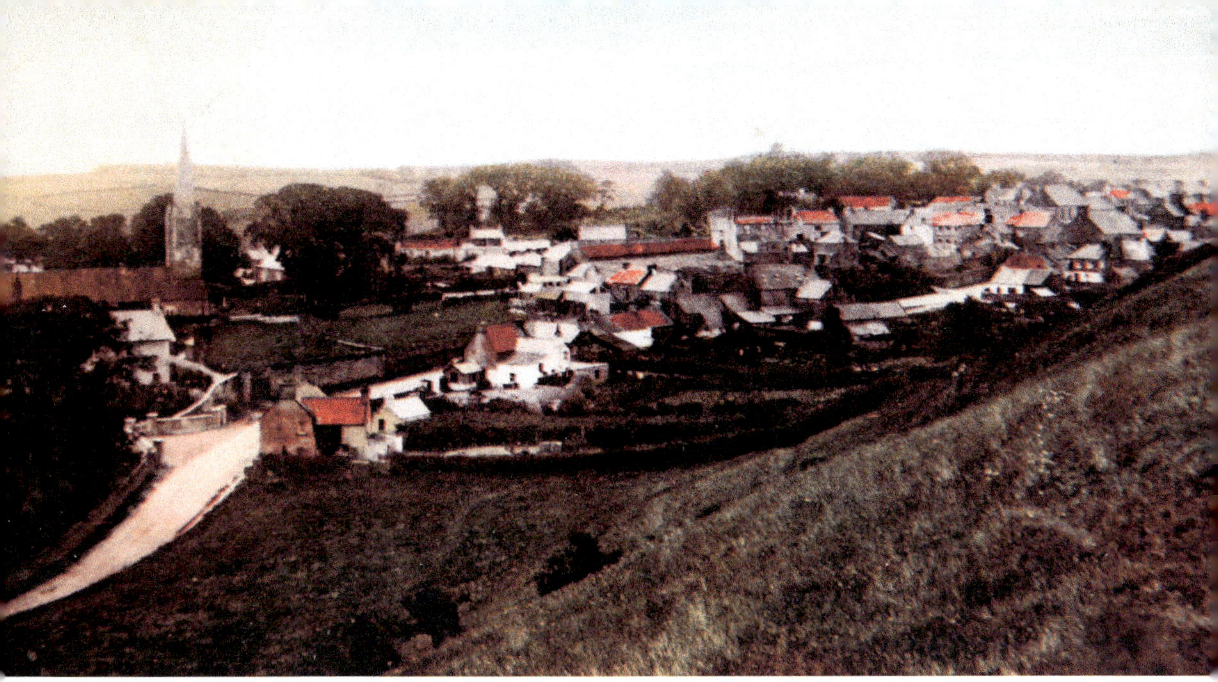

Rosscarbery

In ancient ecclesiastical records, Rosscarbery can be observed under the name *Ross Alithri*, meaning 'the Field of Pilgrims'. In the early sixth century, it became well known for the sanctity of St Faughnan, Abbot of Moelanfaidh, in the county of Waterford, who founded an abbey at this West Cork location and presided over it until his death. A town gradually rose around the monastery, which later became the seat of a diocese. In wars against the English planters, Irish clans such as the McCarthys, O'Driscolls and others bombarded the walls, and a great part of the town was destroyed and rebuilt.

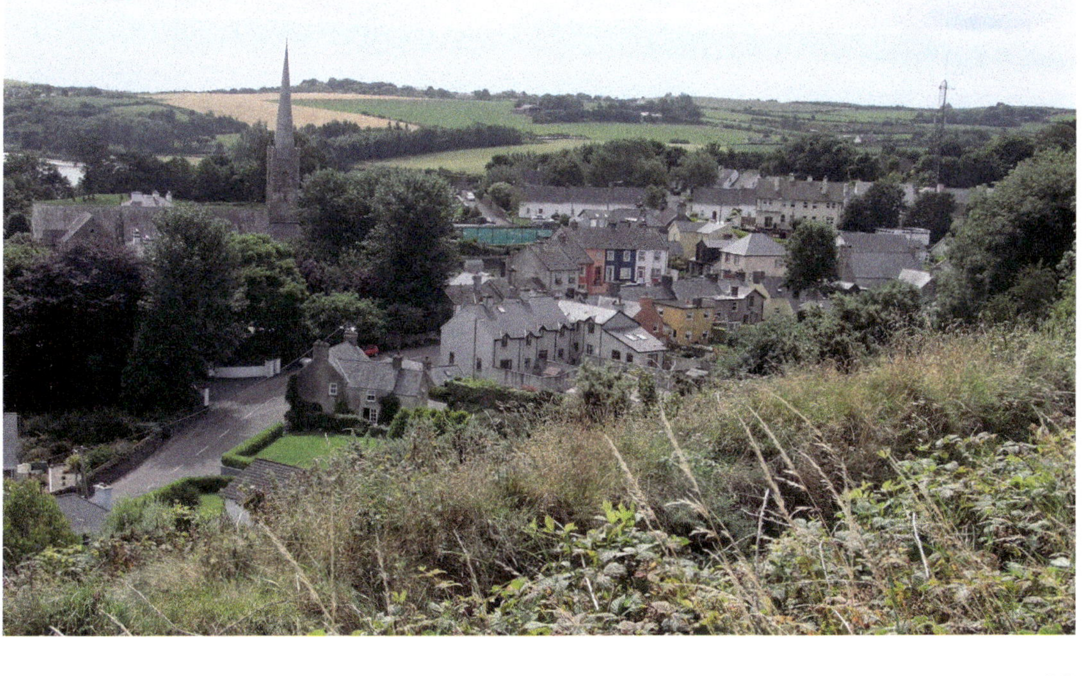

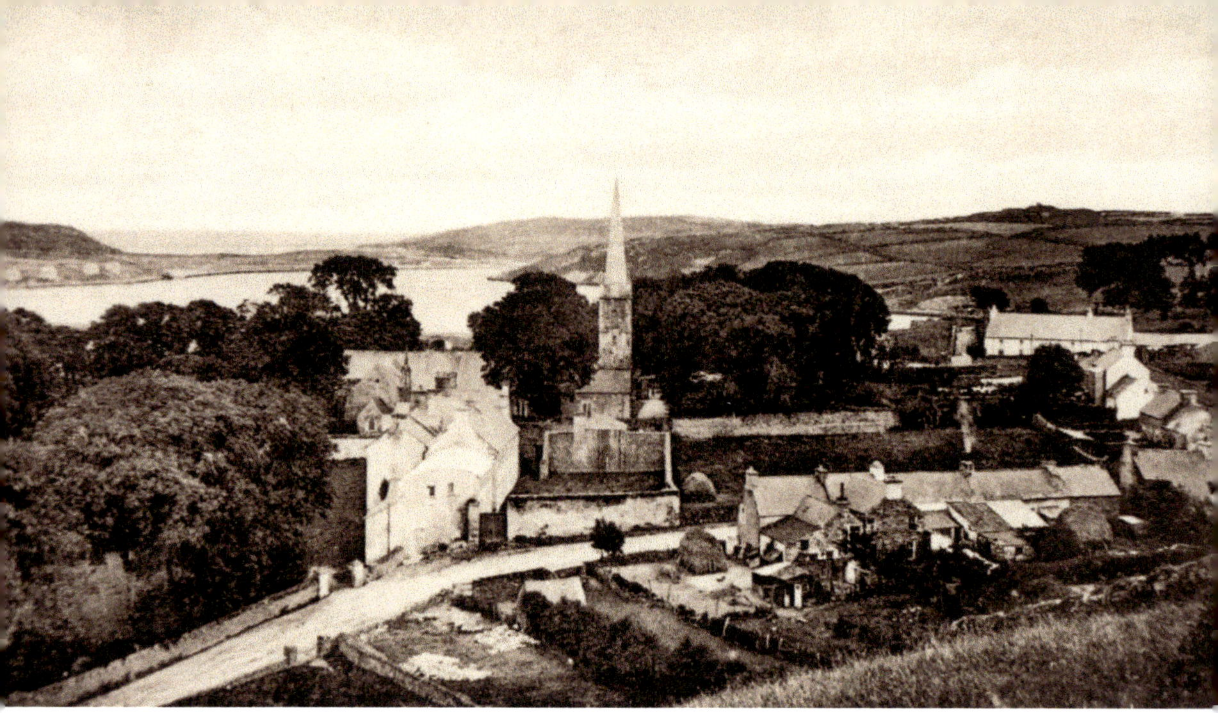

Rosscarbery Bay

Rosscarbery lies at the head of a large creek called Ross harbour and at the summit of a hill. The town has only a square and four small streets. In the nineteenth century, the inhabitants were mainly employed in agriculture and fishing, and extensive manufacture of coarse linen also took place. At one time, the extensive flour mills of Mr Lloyd were situated near the town, where more than 5,000 barrels of fine flour were made annually.

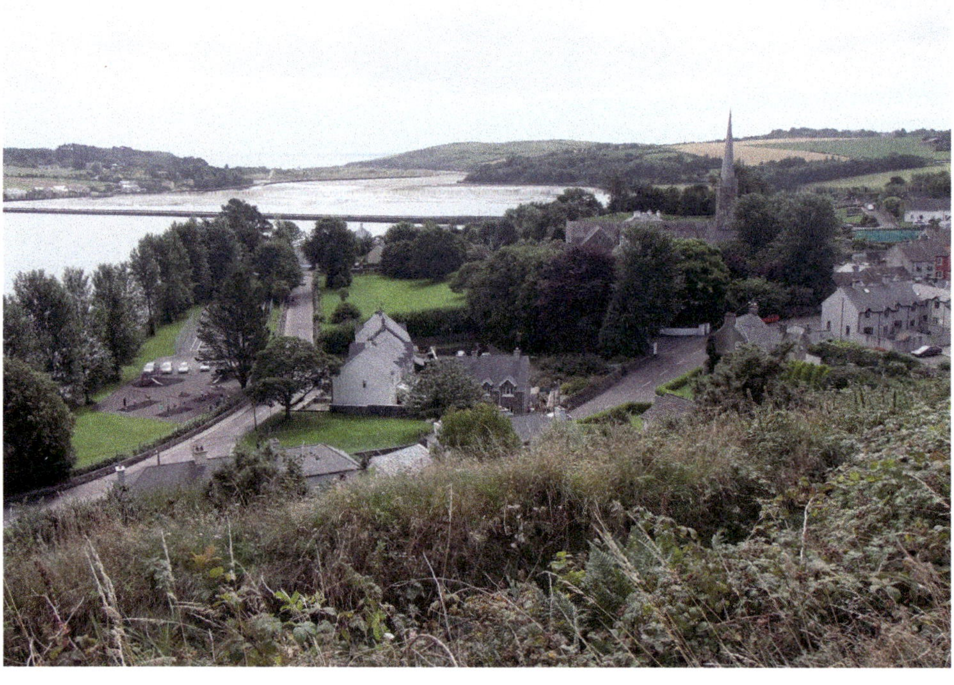

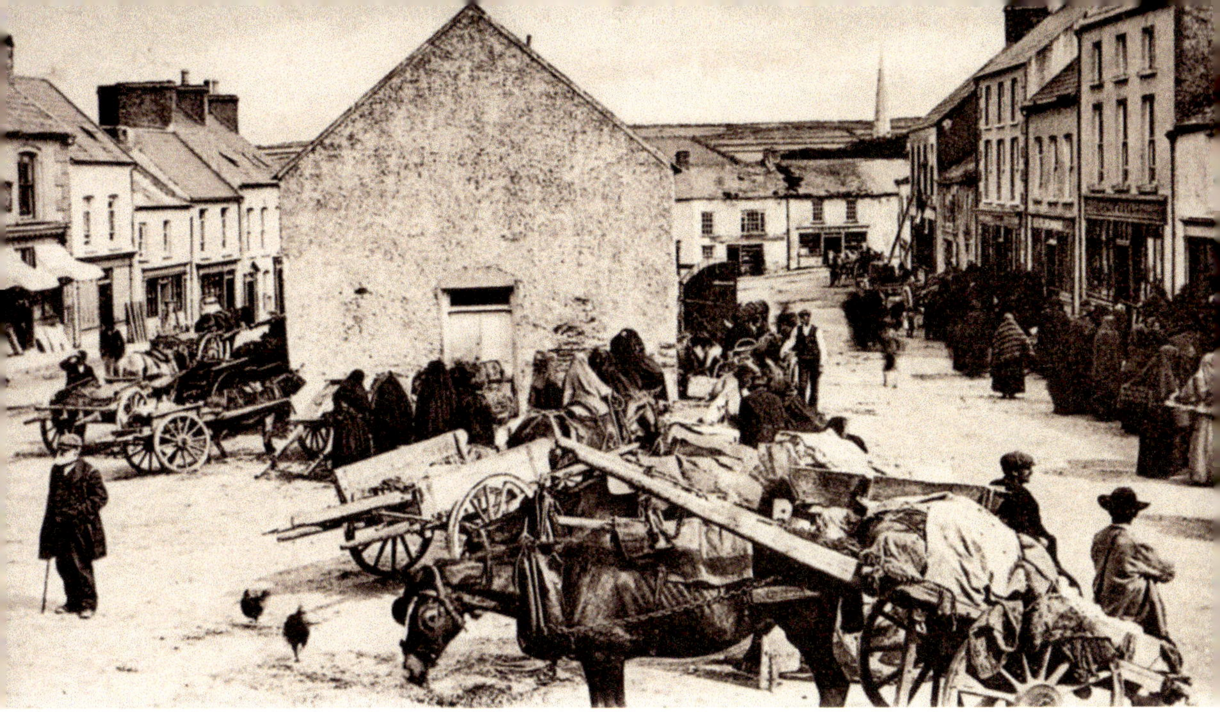

Market Day, Rosscarbery

At one time, the market in Rosscarbery was held on Wednesdays, and fairs were held on 26 August, 19 September and 19 December. The market house was an old building in the centre of the square, which has since been taken down. A constabulary police force was stationed here, there was a coastguard station at Milk Cove, which was one of the three in the district of Skibbereen. Petty sessions were held every Wednesday, and a court for the manor of Ross was held every three weeks, at which debts not exceeding 40*s* were recoverable.

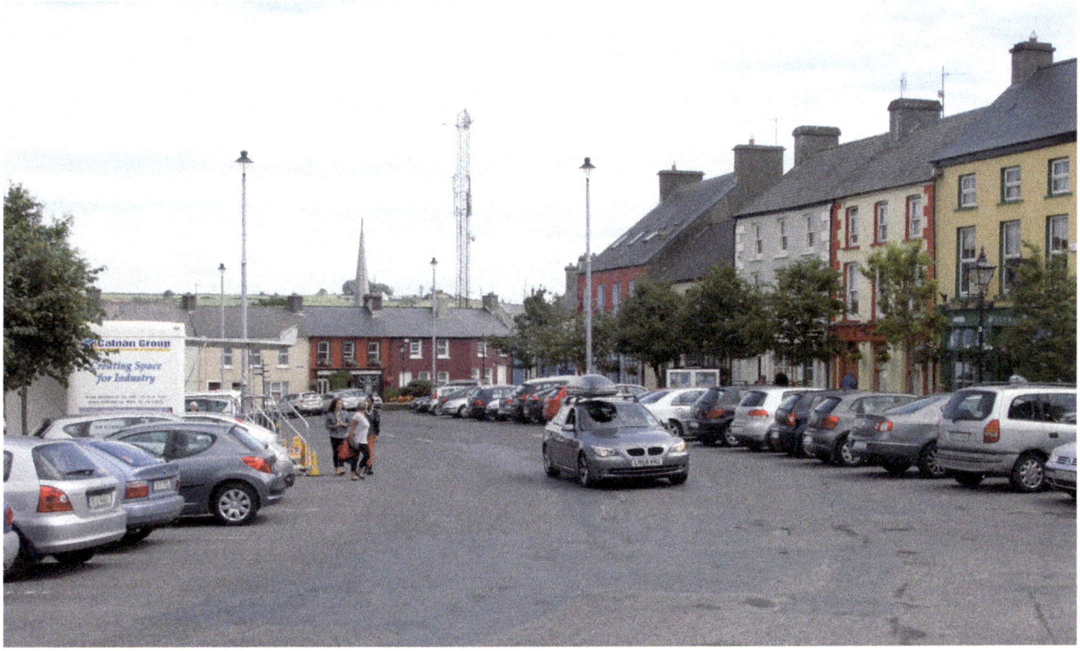

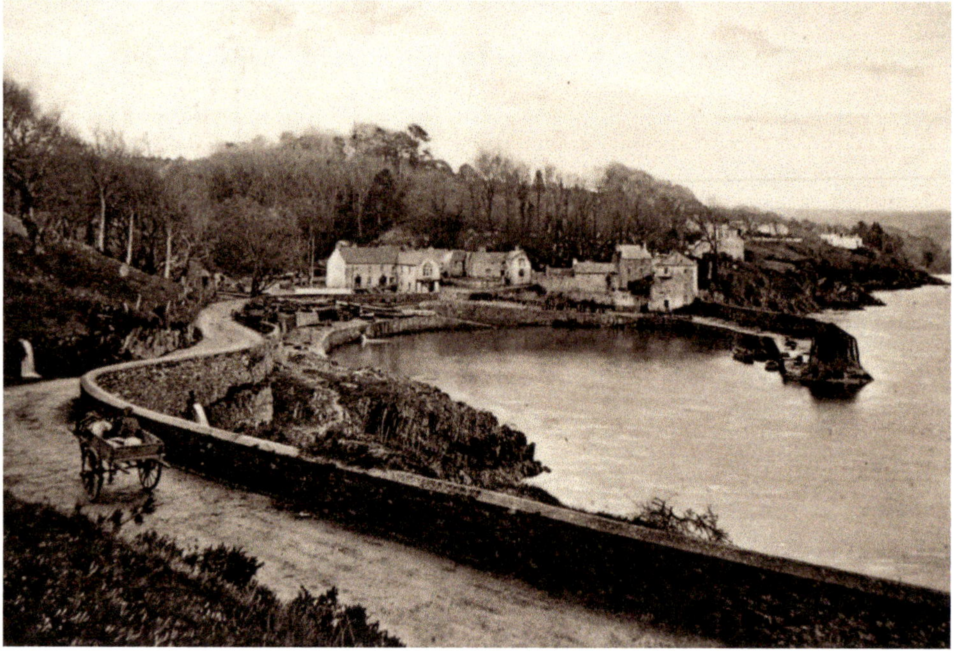

Glandore Harbour

Glandore – in Irish *Cuan Dor* – means 'harbour of oaks', or possibly 'harbour of gold'. Its position in the path of the Gulf Stream ensures its mild climate all year round. Consequently, its flora is diverse and interestingly plants can be found in bloom during their traditional out of season time. Glandore was one of the earliest settlements in West Cork. Nearby is Drombeg stone circle, which was a place of ritual dating back to the Bronze Age.

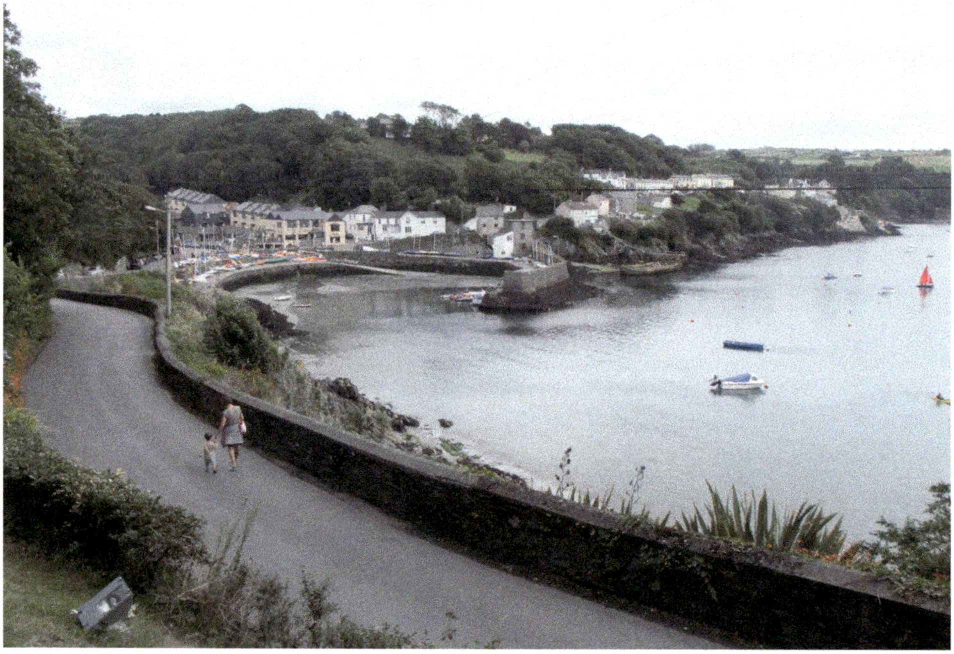

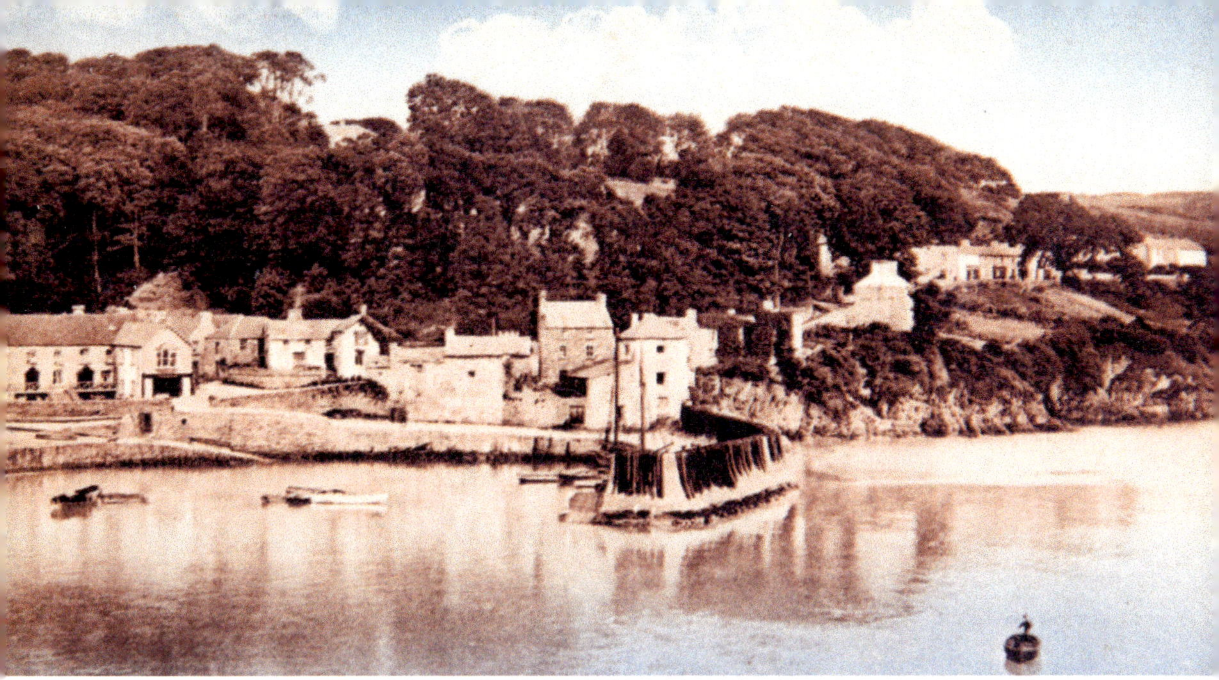

Glandore Harbour

The development of Glandore owes a lot to the arrival of James Redmond Barry MP, when he bought Glandore estate in 1823. Under Barry's encouragement and financial aid, Glandore began to improve quickly. The pier was developed and a new road was built from Glandore to Leap. He also built a new hotel, now The Glandore Inn. Barry was the MP for the area, and is credited with the development of the fishing industry along the coast, through the erection of numerous piers and the installation of navigation marks in the nearby harbour. Today this infrastructure still serves the multiple small vessels that enjoy this small bay.

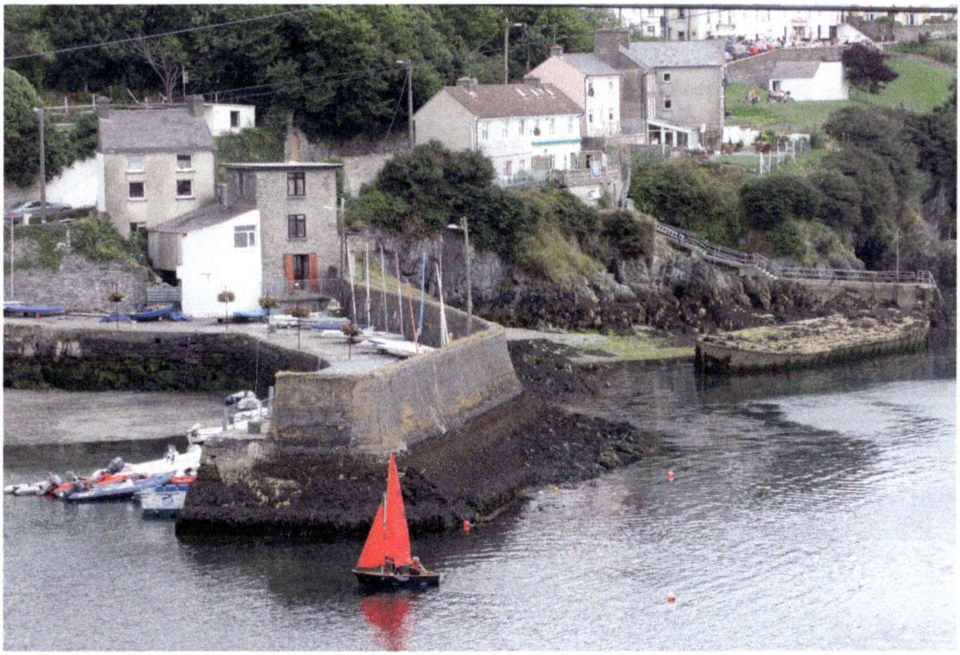

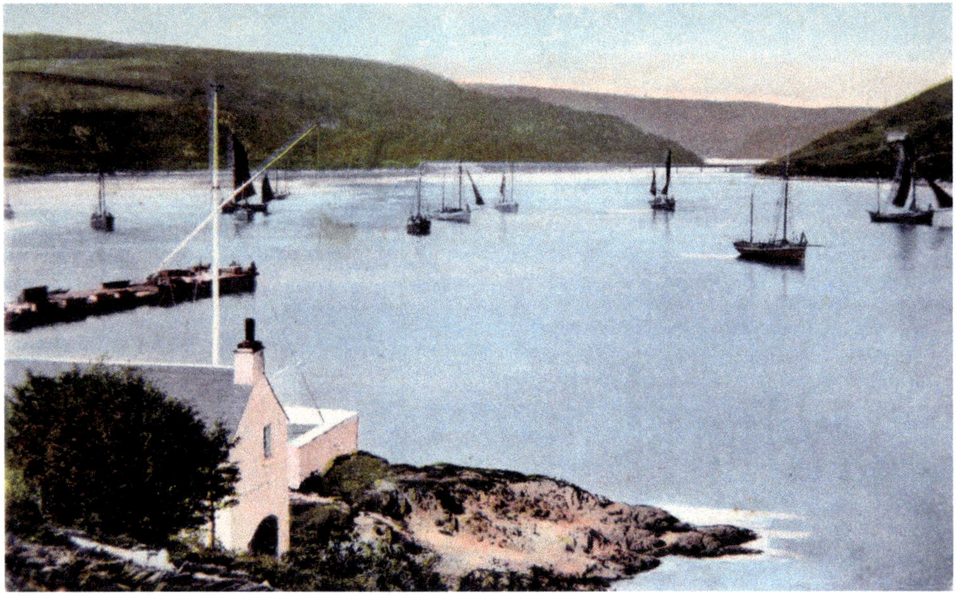

Glandore Harbour from Union Hall

Some say Union Hall existed before 1800. Some would contend that it grew up around a big house, which was built by William Somerville Limerick at the end of the eighteenth century. It was called The Hall, and later 'Union' was added to commemorate the passing of the Act of Union between Britain and Ireland in 1801. The local anchor memorial is dedicated to all seafarers. The anchor dates from the early 1700s from an unknown French ship, and it is the largest one of that era to be recovered from Irish waters. Nicknamed the 'Hook', it was of much hindrance to local fisherman as it would catch the base of boats, especially with an easterly wind and an ebb tide.

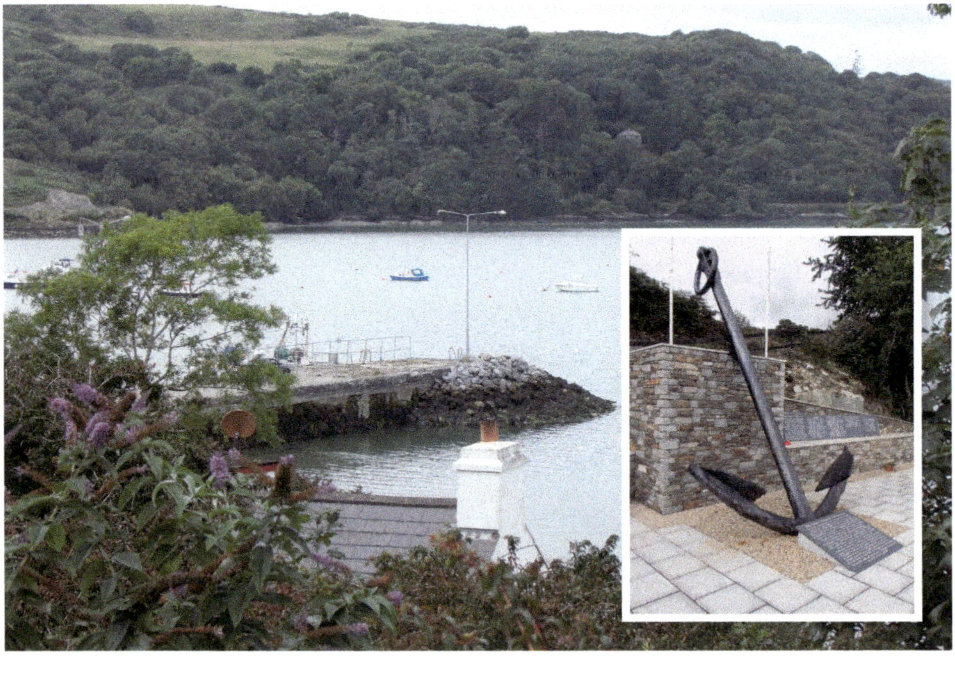

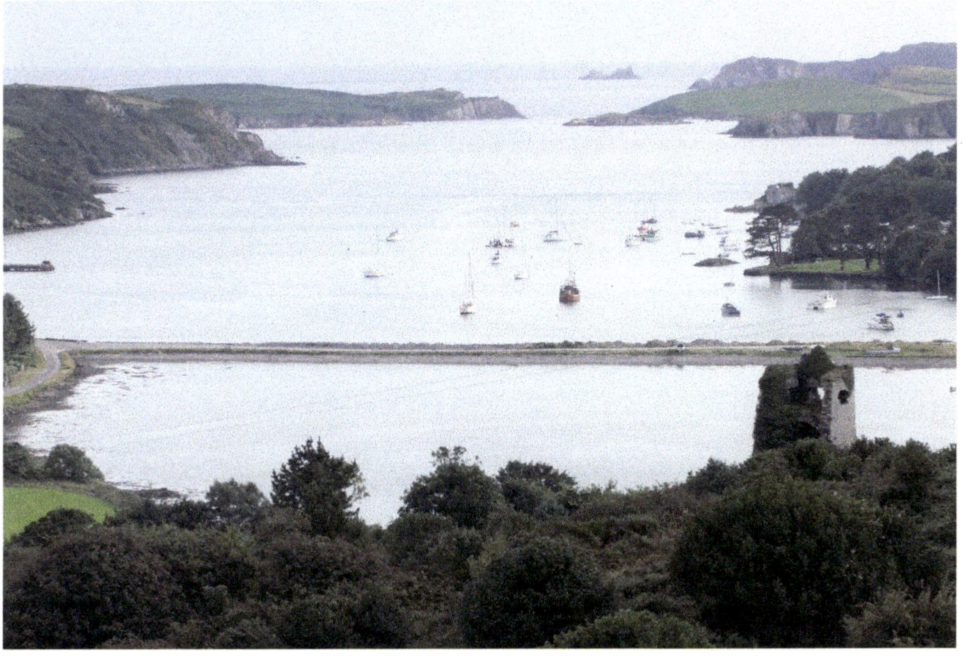

Raheen Castle, Castlehaven

This ivy-clad ruin was once the home of the Irish clan O'Donovan. Driven out of their homeland in County Limerick by the Anglo-Norman invasion, they settled in West Cork. In 1560, they built the impressive Castledonovan in Drimoleague and this smaller version of similar design near the water's edge on the east bank of Castlehaven Harbour. Donall O'Donovan III and his family escaped from Castledonovan to Raheen Castle when Castledonovan was attacked in 1641 by the forces of Oliver Cromwell. Raheen was also severely damaged by cannonballs by Oliver Cromwell's naval forces, which can still be seen in the west wall.

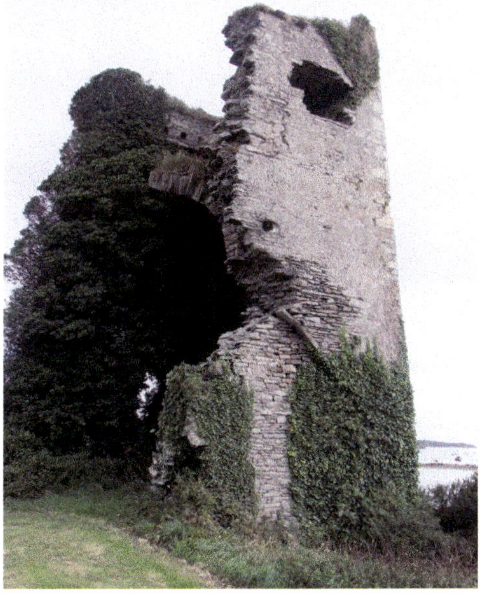

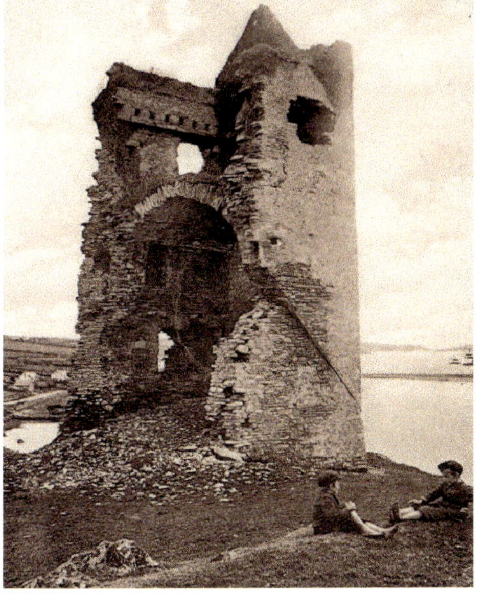

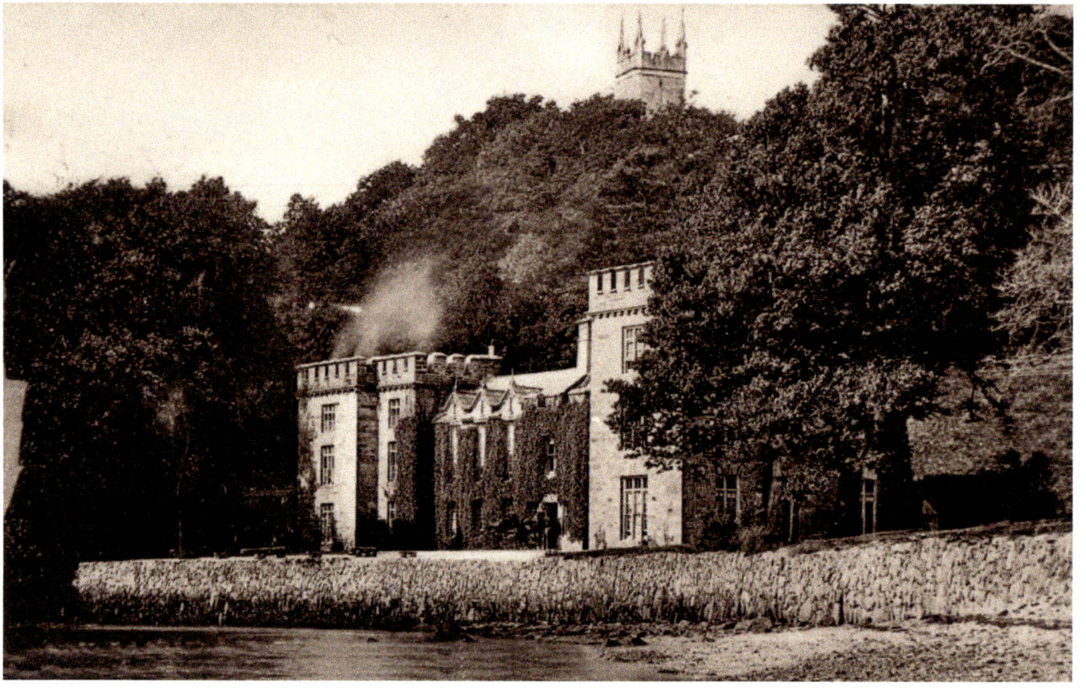

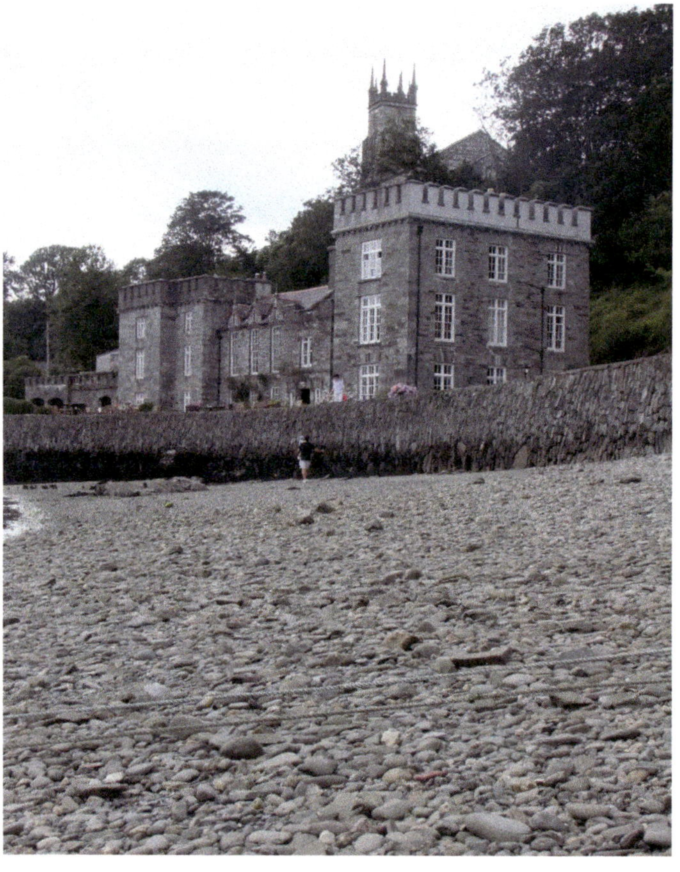

The Castle, Castletownshend

The attractive village of Castletownshend is situated on the coast around 8 km from Skibbereen. The village developed around the castle, which was built in the mid-1600s by the Townshends, and is the seat of the family. The steeply inclined main street runs down to the castle, the quayside and the harbour. Anciently it was called Glanbarrahane, named from a deep rocky glen dedicated to St Barrahane, a local fifth-century hermit saint. Another unique feature of Castletownshend are its two sycamore trees growing in the roundabout in the centre of the village. The present sycamores replaced two trees planted in the 1800s.

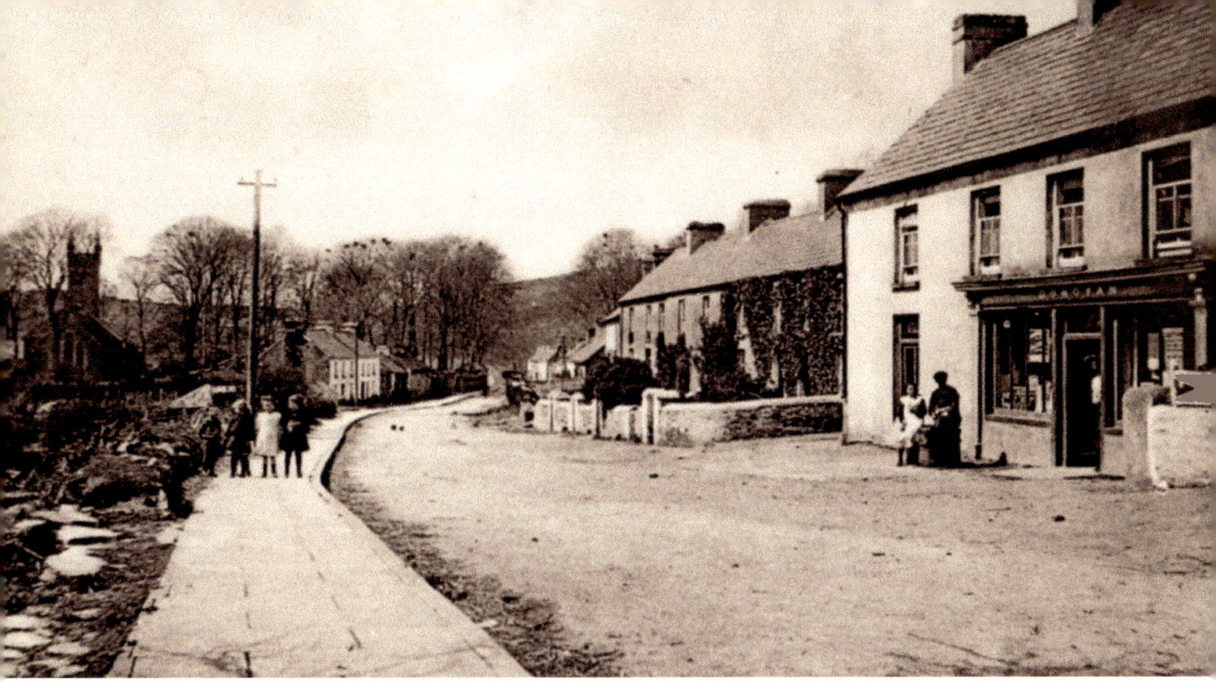

Leap

Leap in Irish is *Léim Uí Dhonnabhain*, meaning O'Donovan's Leap. It has been shortened in recent times to *An Léim* or *Léim* (Leap). At the western side of the village is a deep gorge, over which, according to legend, an O'Donovan leaped on horseback while being pursued by British soldiers. The gorge divides West from East Carbery. The local saying notes, 'beyond the Leap, beyond the Law'. A hundred years ago, Leap could boast Roman Catholic and Church of Ireland churches, as well as four public schools, a post office and two public houses.

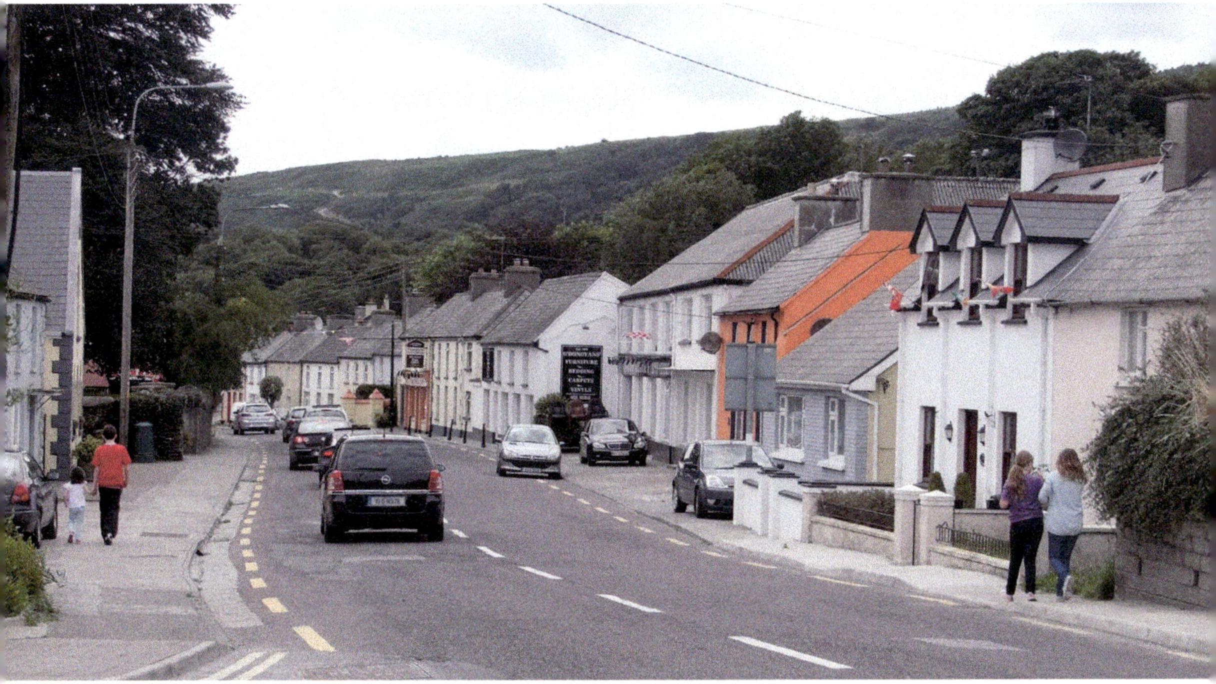

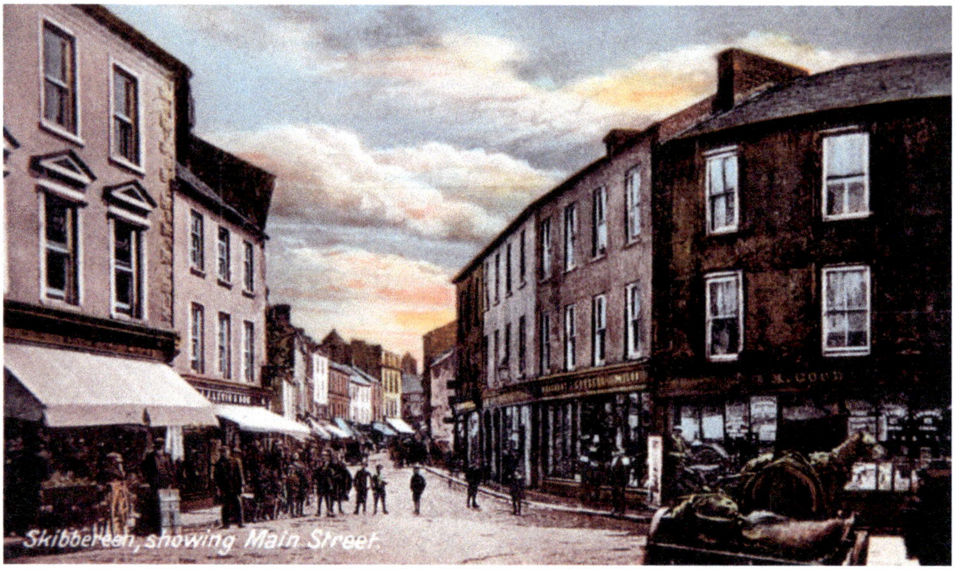

Skibbereen

Over a century ago, Skibbereen boasted considerable trade, arising from the manufacture of woollen cloth, linen, checks and handkerchiefs. It was advantageously situated for trade; the tide from the harbour of Baltimore flowed up to the town, and the river was navigable for vessels of 200 tons burden to Oldcourt, 2 miles below Skibbereen. In the town there were large storehouses for corn, and a considerable quantity of flour was also exported from the mills of Mr J. Clark. The Maid of Erin memorial (*below*), remembering the United Irishmen campaign against British rule, was unveiled on 27 November 1904 by Fenian leader and local man Jeremiah O'Donovan Rossa.

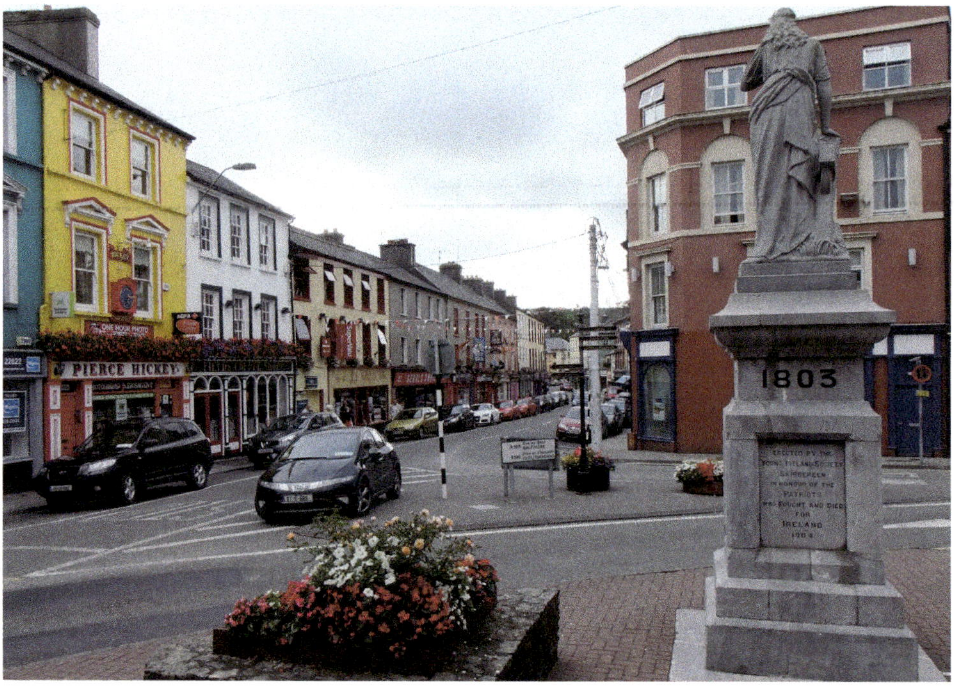

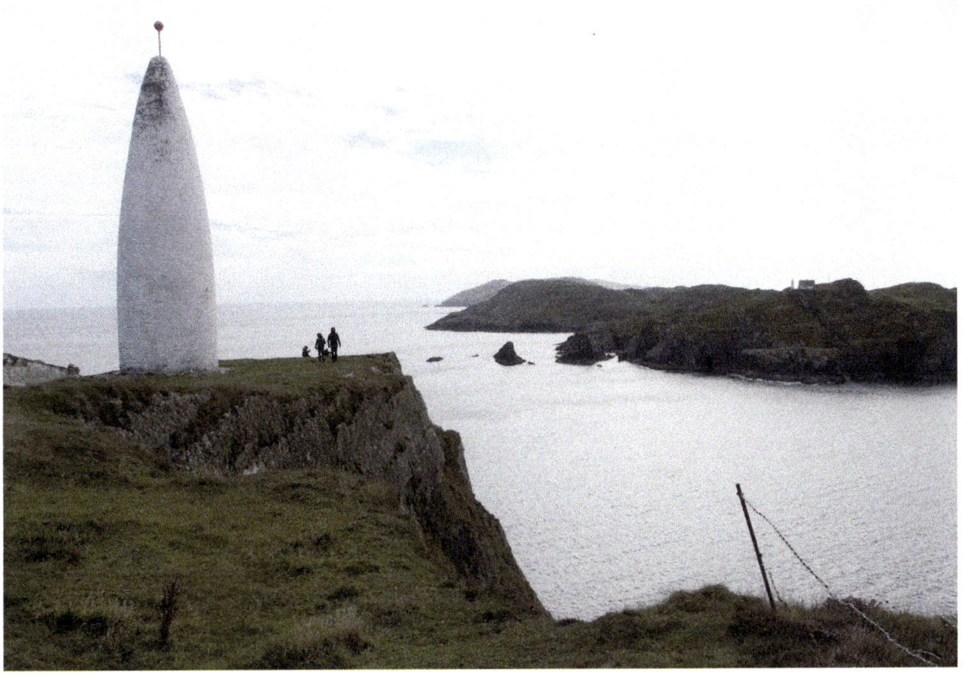

The Beacon, Baltimore Harbour

Towards the end of July 1847, Cdr James Wolfe, Royal Navy, informed the Ballast Board that he had recently completed a survey of Baltimore Harbour and noticed the destruction of the warning of rocks beacon on the eastern point of the southern entrance to the harbour. Almost a year passed before the board requested the secretary to seek permission from Lord Carbery for a piece of ground 30 feet in diameter, on which to build a new beacon (6 July 1848). The impressive conical white-painted Baltimore Beacon, sometimes called the 'pillar of salt' or 'Lott's wife', is approximately 50 feet (15.2 m) high and 15 feet (4.6 m) in diameter at the base.

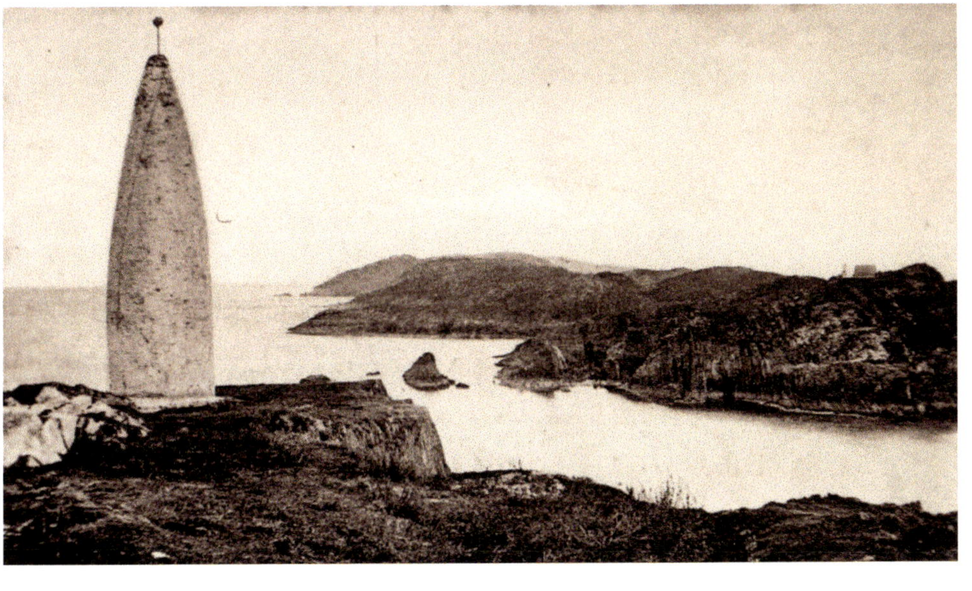

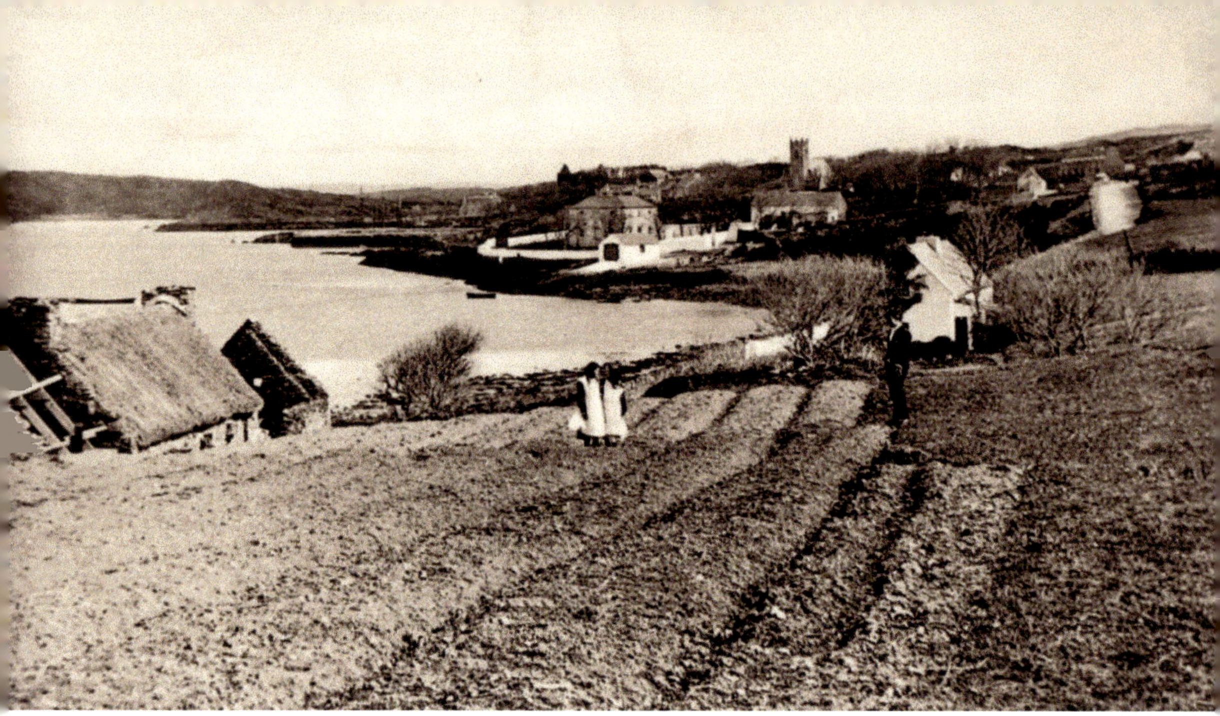

Baltimore

Baltimore's history has always been shaped by the sea. One standout event occurred in 1631 when much of the population was carried off by pirates, never to be seen again – an event known as the Sack of Baltimore. The castle of *Dún na Séad*, or Fort of the Jewels, which gives the village its Irish name, was also sacked by seaborne invaders more than once since its first establishment in 1215. Much of the view presented above is all built upon with housing, but perhaps the best view of all is from a local boat or ferry to the nearby islands.

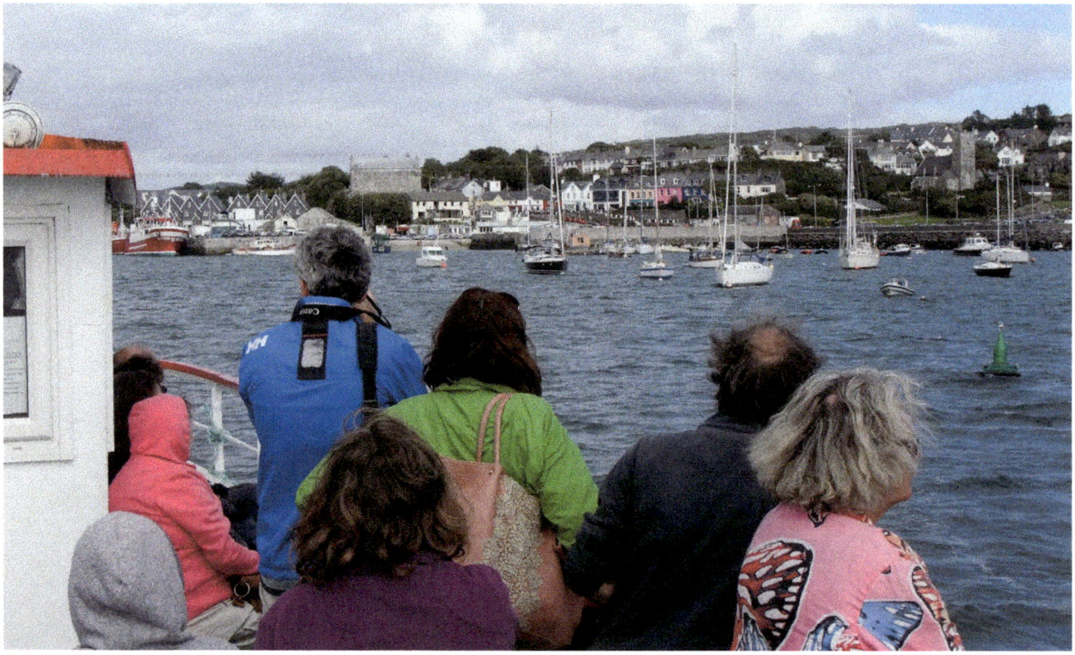

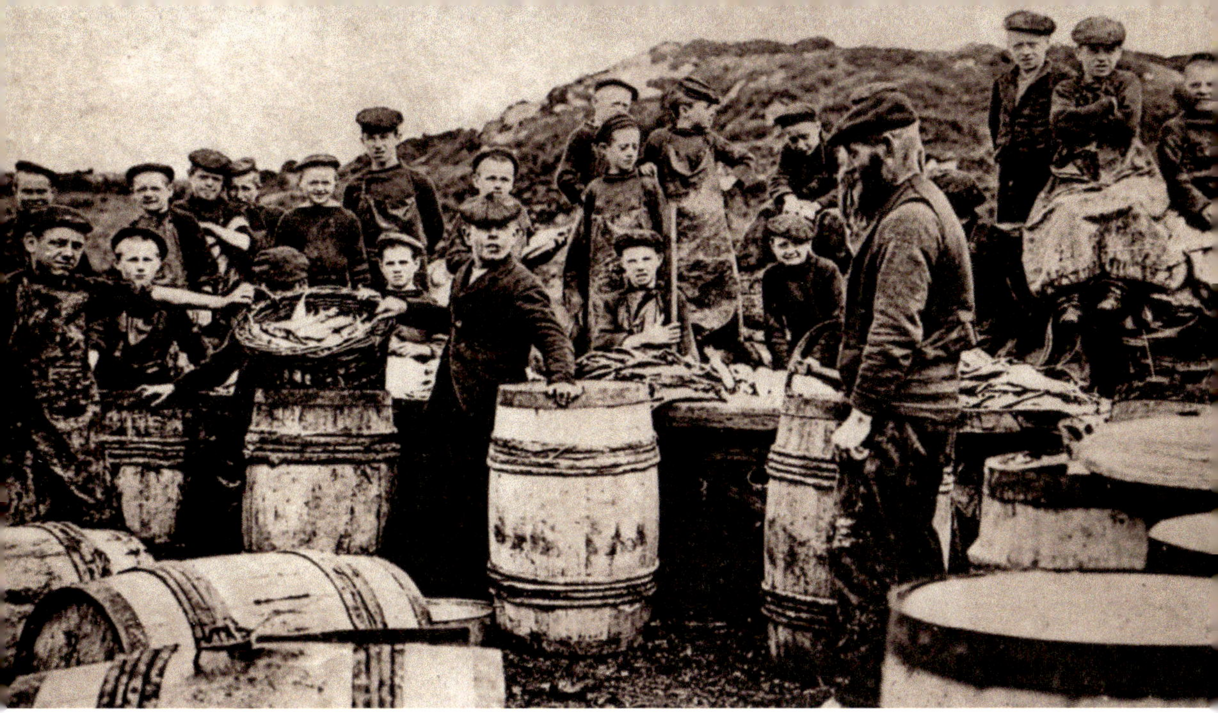

Baltimore Fish Market

Around 1900, mackerel, pilchards and herrings frequented the southern Irish coast in large quantities, and the surrounding sea abounded with fish, both round and flat, and shellfish. The mackerel and herring fisheries were chiefly worked from Kinsale, Baltimore, Union Hall, Castletownshend, Schull and Castletownbere. These places were annually visited by a large number of Manx and French fishermen for mackerel, and Scotch herring boats capturing an immense number of fish. The fishing industry also developed among the native community.

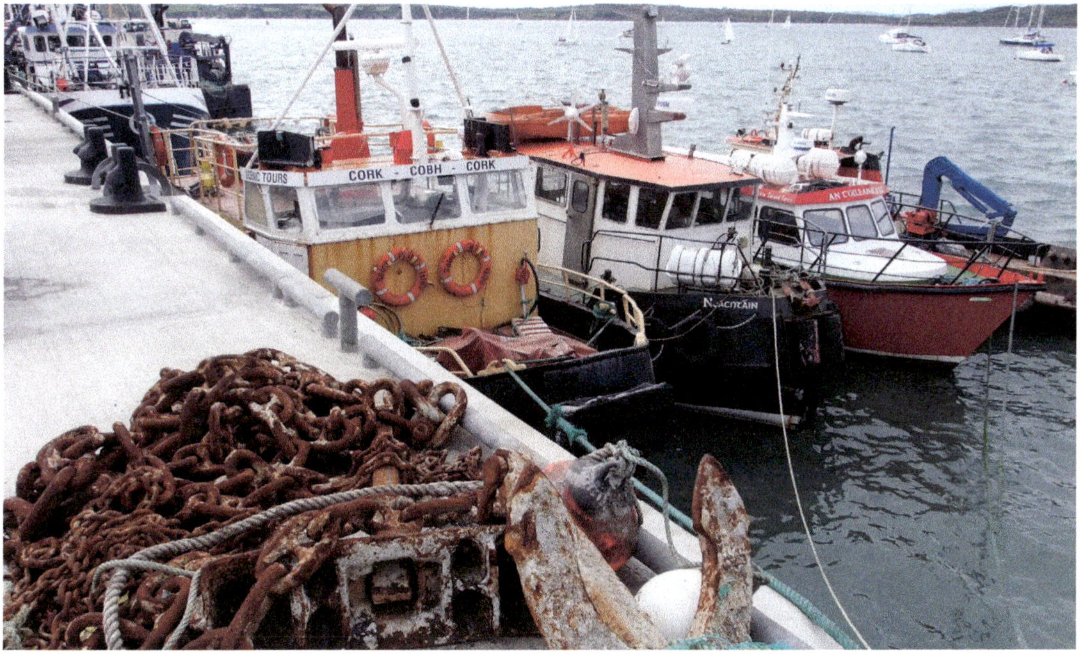

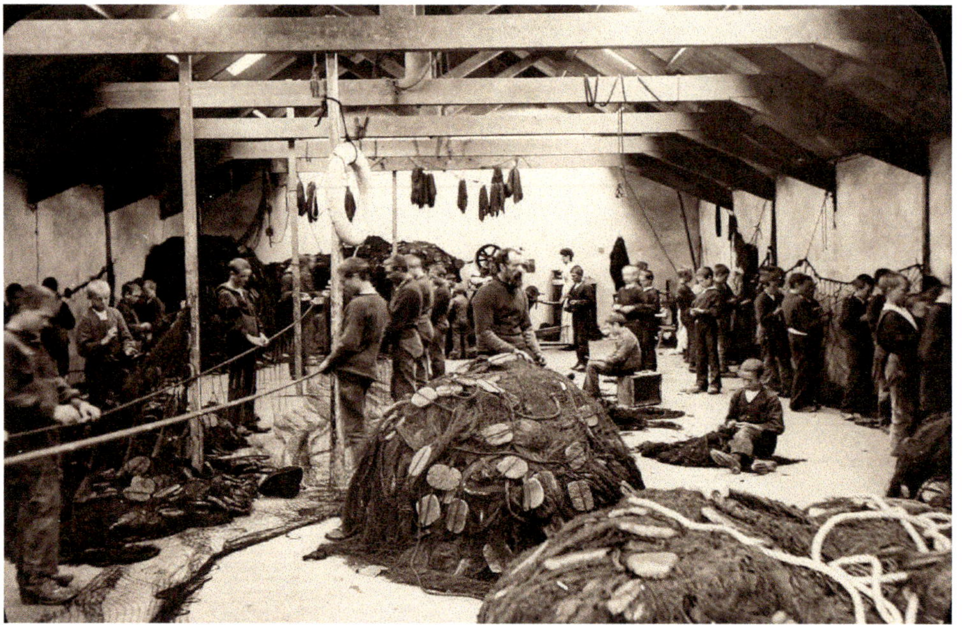

Fishing Nets, Baltimore

From 1879, Baltimore developed as a centre of an expanding mackerel fleet. Through financial support from Baroness Burdett-Coutts, parish priest Father Davis and local fishermen, the fleet expanded from approximately six to eighteen vessels. Each of the new vessels had a steam-assisted winch to haul in nets. Eleven steamers brought the spring mackerel to England on an almost daily basis. In 1887, the Baltimore Fishing School for the training of 150 boys in a fishing occupation was founded. In 1880, a new pier was built and in 1893, a new spur rail track from Skibbereen to Baltimore was opened to transport the fish to other markets in the city and county. In the early twentieth century, the movement of the fish to other feeding locations led to decline, but the fishing industry still survives in Baltimore.

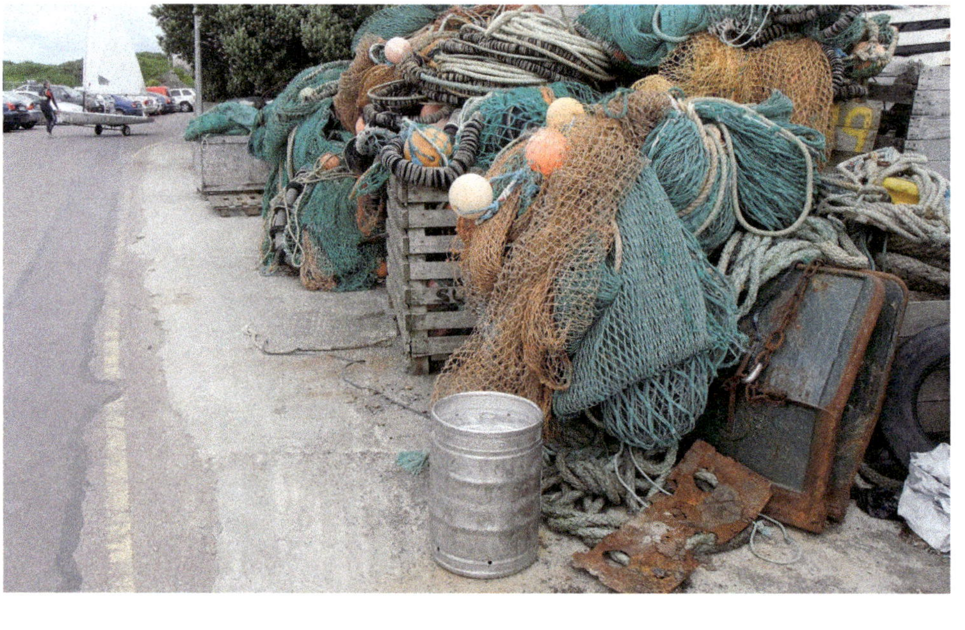

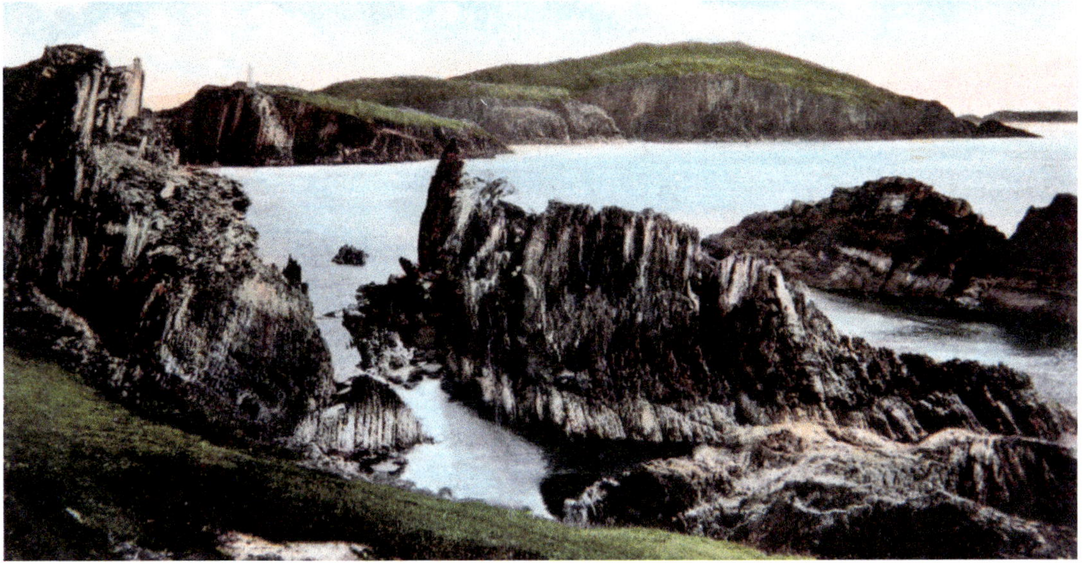

Baltimore Harbour

Across a superb natural harbour lie Carbery's Hundred Isles, including the enchanting islands of Cape Clear, Sherkin and Heir, just a short ferry ride away from Baltimore pier. Unfortunately, images of many of the islands were not published 100 years ago, save for a handful. The picture above was taken from Sherkin Island, looking towards the Baltimore Beacon. Much of the action at Baltimore takes place on the water. Activities such as sailing, diving, windsurfing and deep-sea angling are only some of the activities on offer. These give the visitor an opportunity to explore the creeks and inlets of the beautiful West Cork coastline.

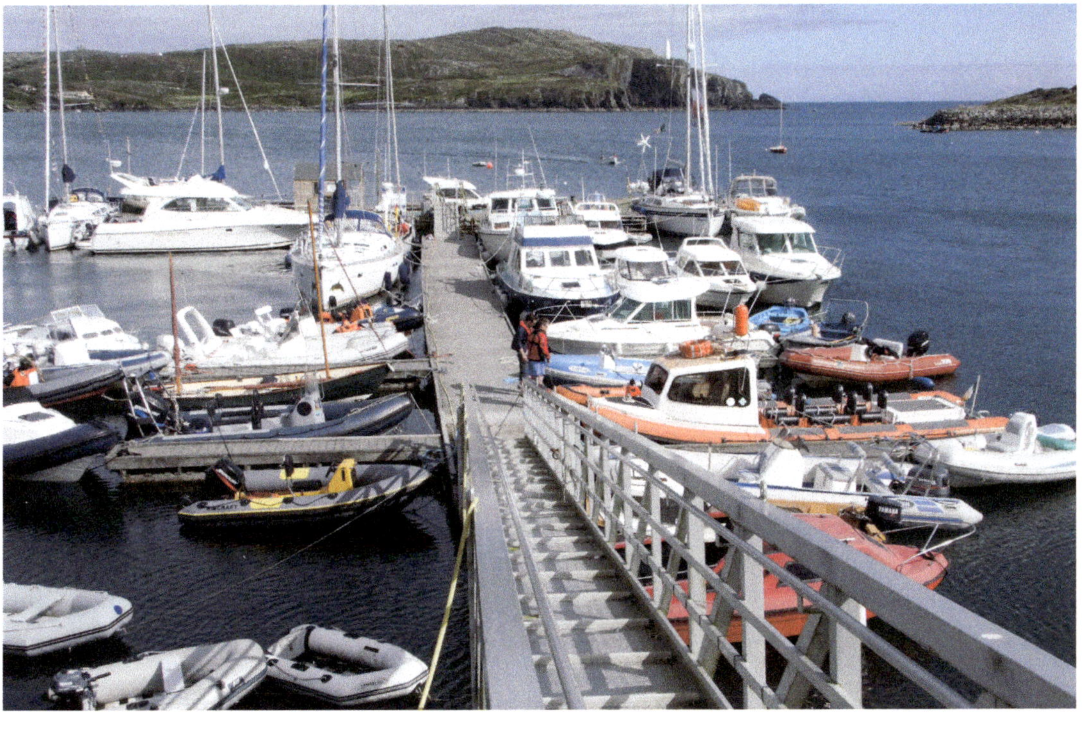

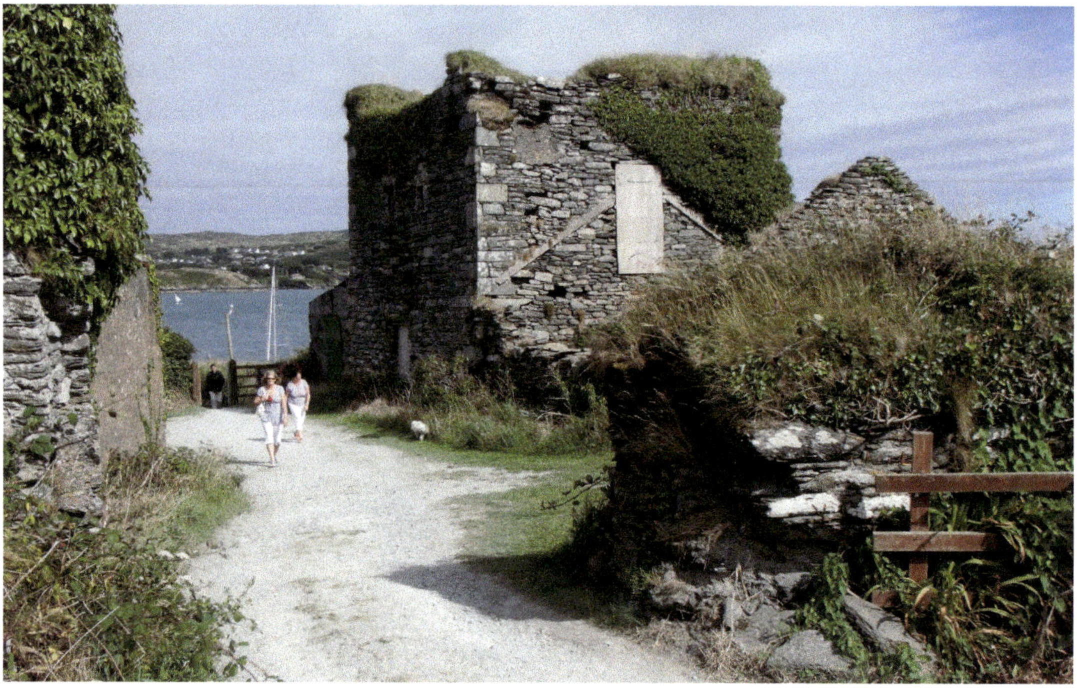

Dún na Long Castle, Sherkin Island

This castle on Sherkin Island was built on a small promontory overlooking the entrance to Baltimore Harbour in Farranacoush. An earlier castle may have been constructed on this site by the Anglo-Norman family called Sliney, and later destroyed by Gaelic forces after the Battle of Callan (1261). This battle was fought in Kilgarvan, County Kerry, between the Anglo-Normans under John Fitzgerald and the King Desmond (South Munster), Finghin McCarthy.

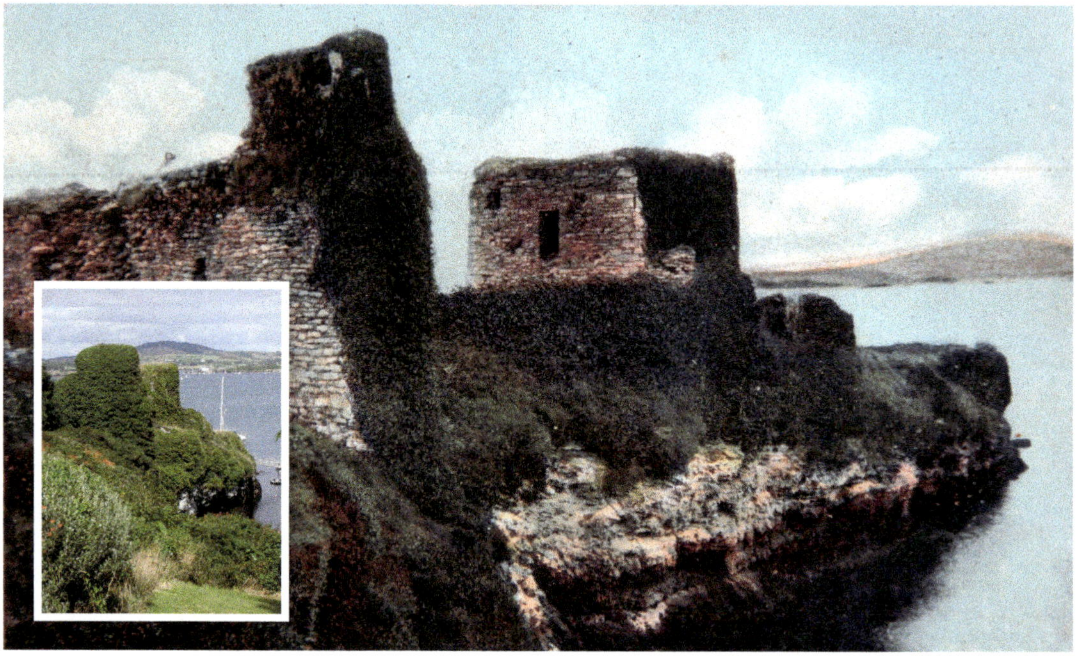

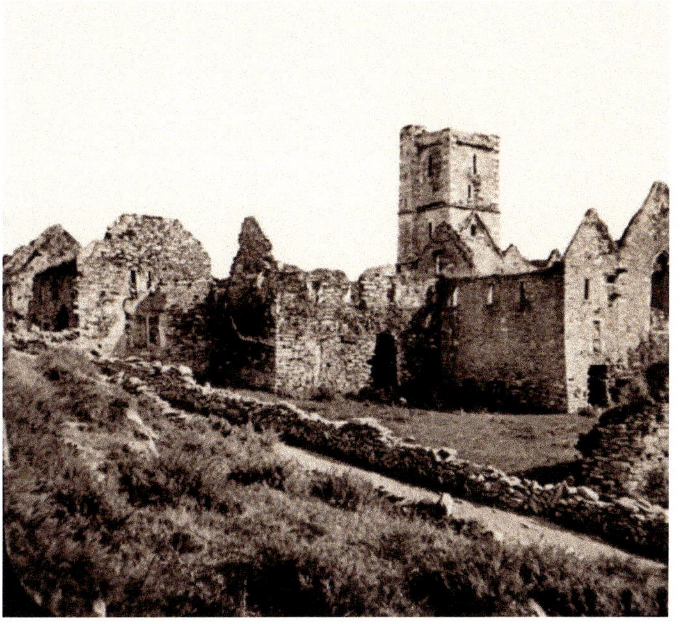

Franciscan Abbey, Sherkin Island

Locally known as 'the Abbey', it is located near the pier of Sherkin Island and was established in 1460 by Fineen O'Driscoll, the Irish chieftain of the island. The building is of moderate dimensions and smaller than its sister Franciscan houses in Timoleague and Kilcrea (near Cork City). Despite King Henry VIII's laws closing such abbeys in the 1540s, the friary continued to function but to a lesser degree. In 1601, it consisted of a croft, a cemetery and other ruined buildings, and a close containing 6 acres. In 1895, Sir Henry Beecher handed it over to the Board of Works, and it is now under the protection of the National Monuments Service.

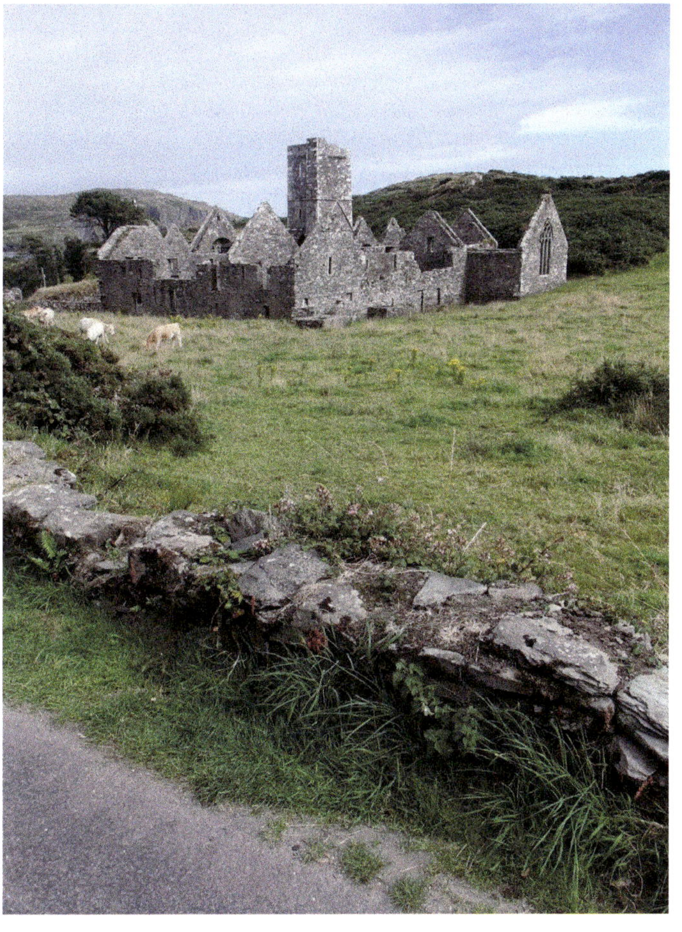

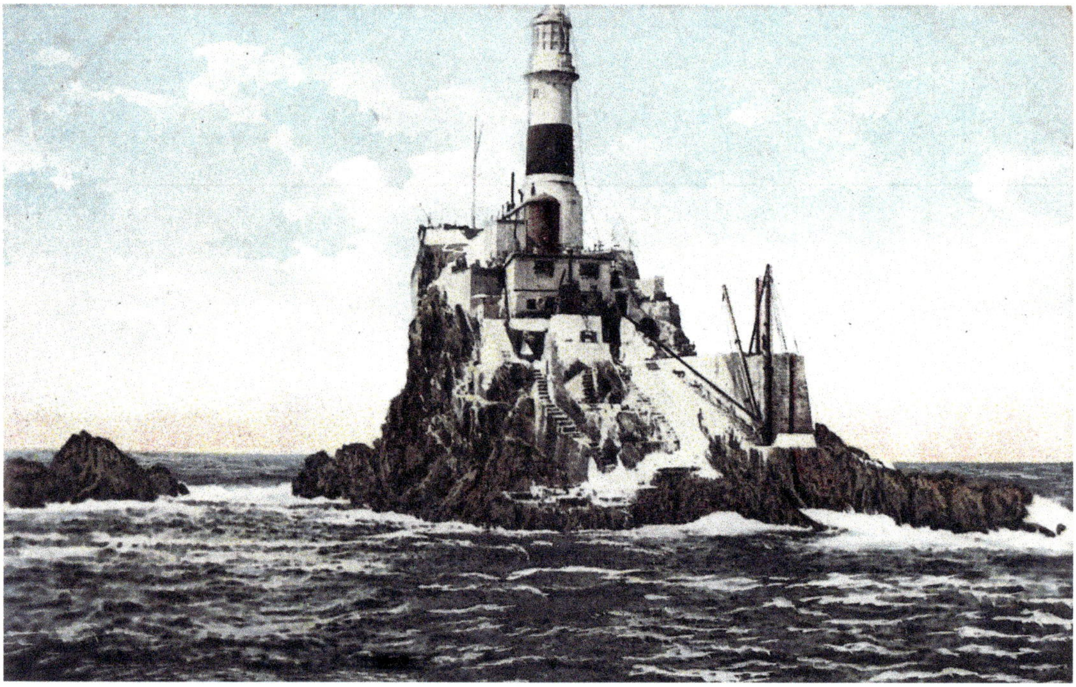

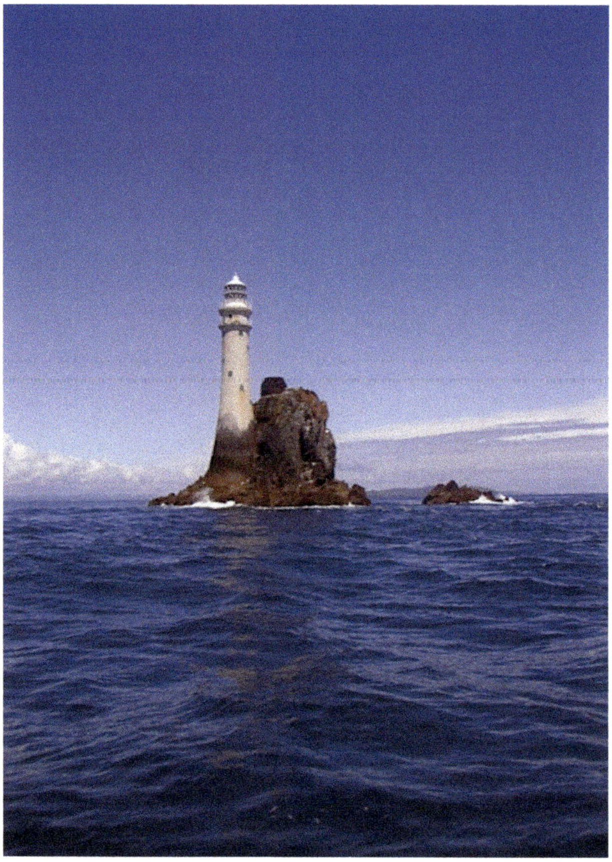

Fastnet Rock

Fastnet Rock lighthouse (from Old Norse, *Hvasstann-ait,* meaning 'sharp-tooth ait', and *Carraig Aonair* in Irish, meaning 'solitary rock')constructed in 1897, is the second to be built on the rock and is the highest in Ireland. It lies in the Atlantic Ocean, 11 km south of Baltimore and rises to about 30 m above sea level. The Fastnet lighthouse had the nickname 'Ireland's Teardrop', as it was the last part of the country seen by Irish emigrants to the United States in the nineteenth century as they sailed past it. Guglielmo Marconi came here to try and send his first radio message across the Atlantic. The present-day picture was taken by Cork musician and sailor Gerry Kelly.

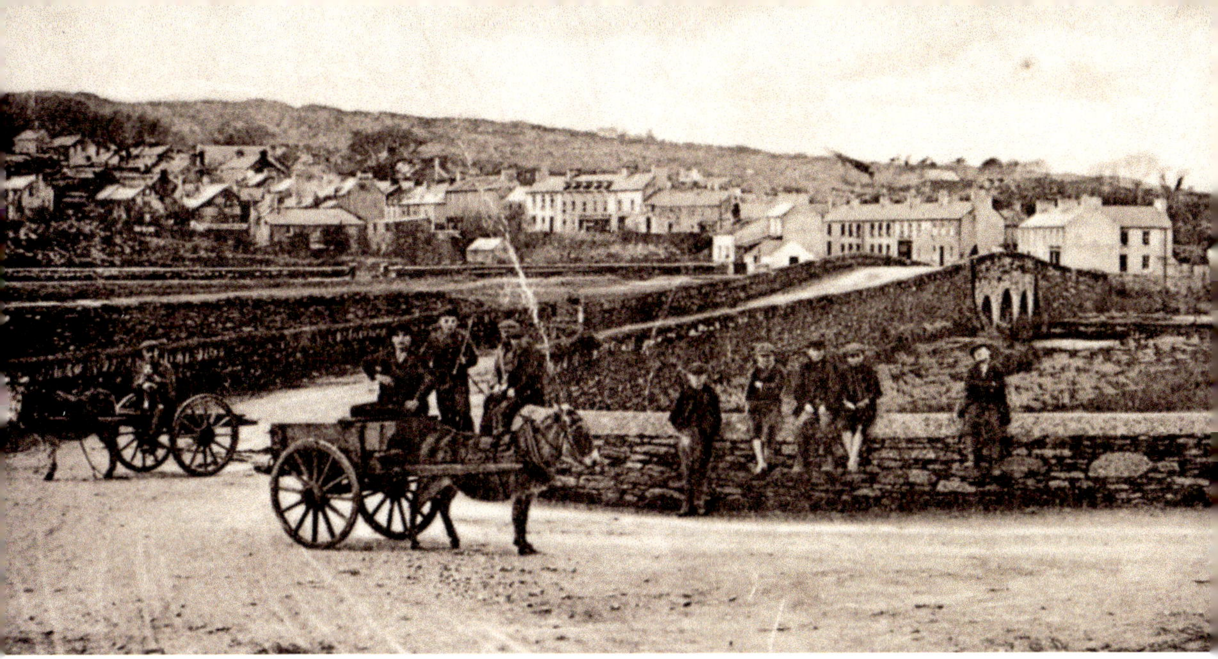

Ballydehob

There is evidence of a settlement where the village of Ballydehob now stands from as early as the fourteenth century. It was known as *Béal Atha Dá Chab,* as the river that flows into the nearby estuary divides into two a short distance upstream – hence the name Atha, meaning a ford. In 1602, soldiers led by Sir George Carew, Lord President of Munster, descended on the area in a successful bid to break the power of the Irish chieftains.

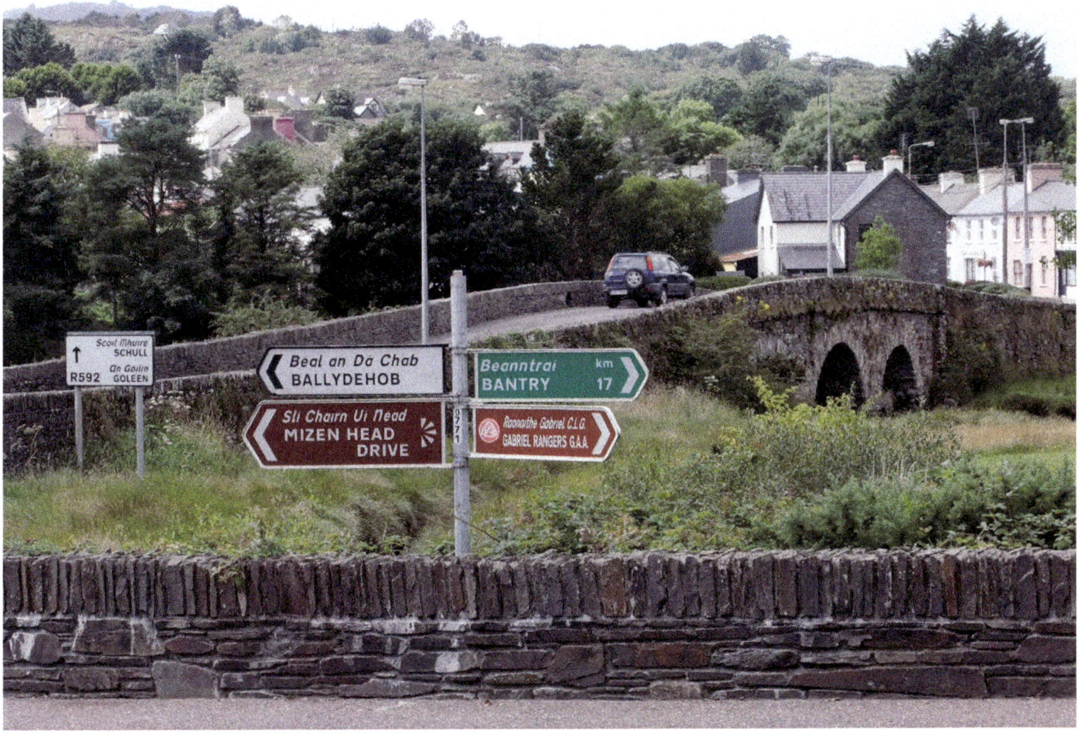

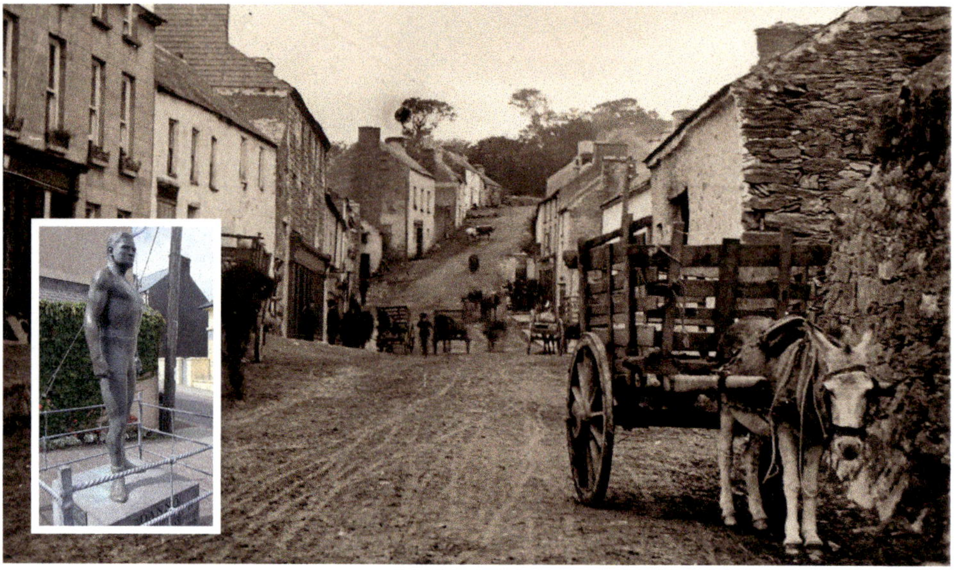

Ballydehob

The seventeenth century saw the arrival of a number settlers, mainly from England, but many were also Protestants (Huguenots) fleeing persecution in Catholic France. The Swantons from Norfolk emerged as the most prominent family in the area and, by the late eighteenth century, they had even changed the name of Ballydehob to Swanton's Town. The natives, however, resisted the dominance of foreigners. A garrison of twelve British soldiers attempted to uphold the law. Robert Swanton, the leader of the group, enlisted the help of the garrison to take over Ballydehob. A group of six local men, who were trained in arms, issued a challenge to the garrison and 'Black-hearted Bob', and a pitched battle was fought on Staball Hill (the hill seen in the centre of both photographs). The year was 1642. The village's most famous former inhabitant was the wrestler Danno O'Mahony (*statue, above inset*). He won the NWA World title from Jim Londos in Boston on 30 June 1935, and was known as the 'Irish Whip' in celebration of his famous throwing technique. He was also a champion hammer thrower.

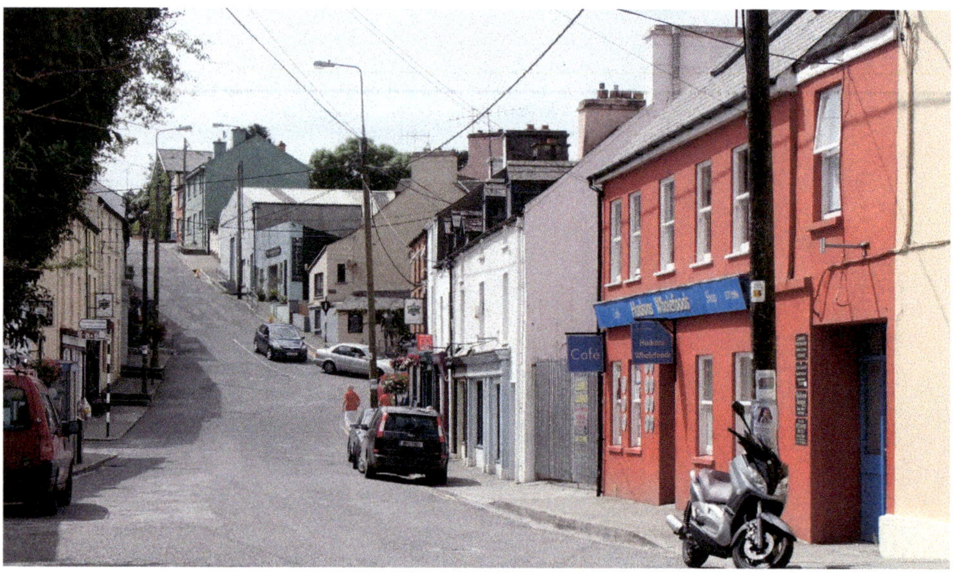

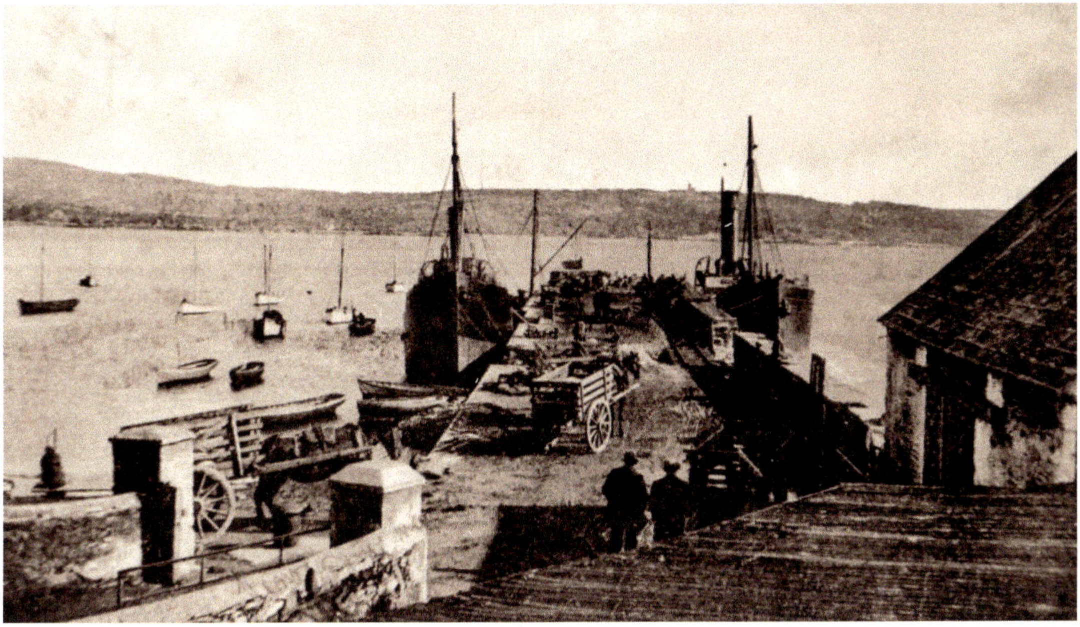

Schull Harbour

Sheltered from the northerly winds by Mount Gabriel, Schull village commands a beautiful view of the adjacent harbour. The name is derived from *Scoil Mhuire*, or Our Lady's School. South and west lie the islands of Cape Clear, Long Island and several smaller ones. Every August, the Schull Regatta takes place, as it has since the nineteenth century. At one time, a railway line also operated to this pier, giving the multiple fisherman access to regional fish markets and to Cork City.

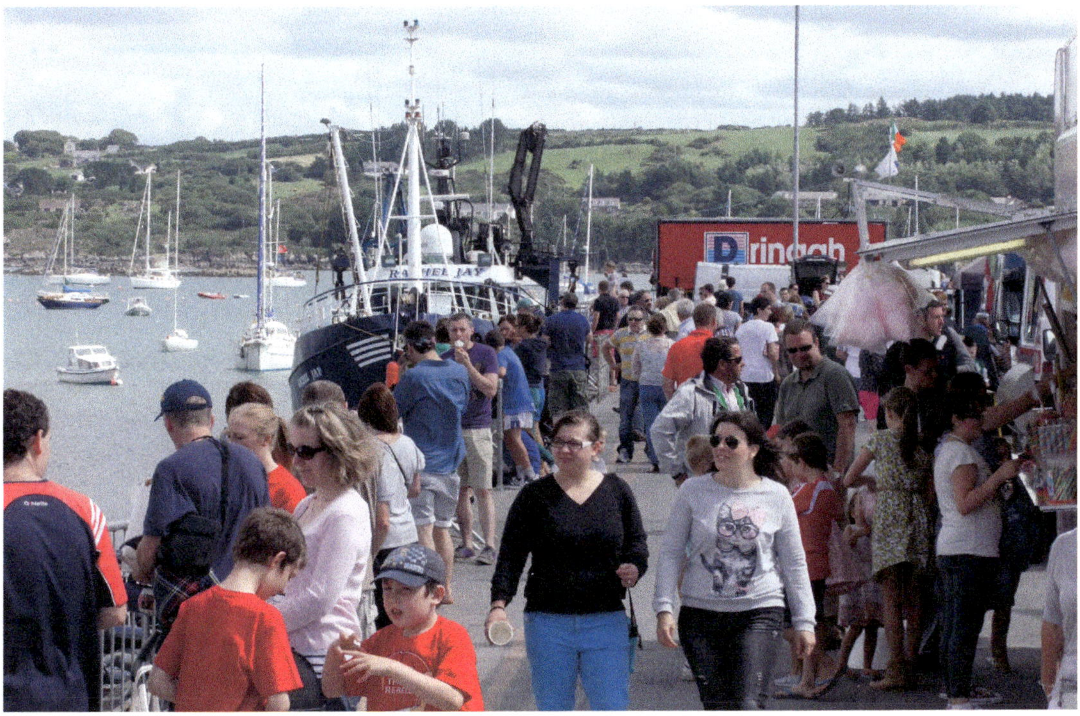

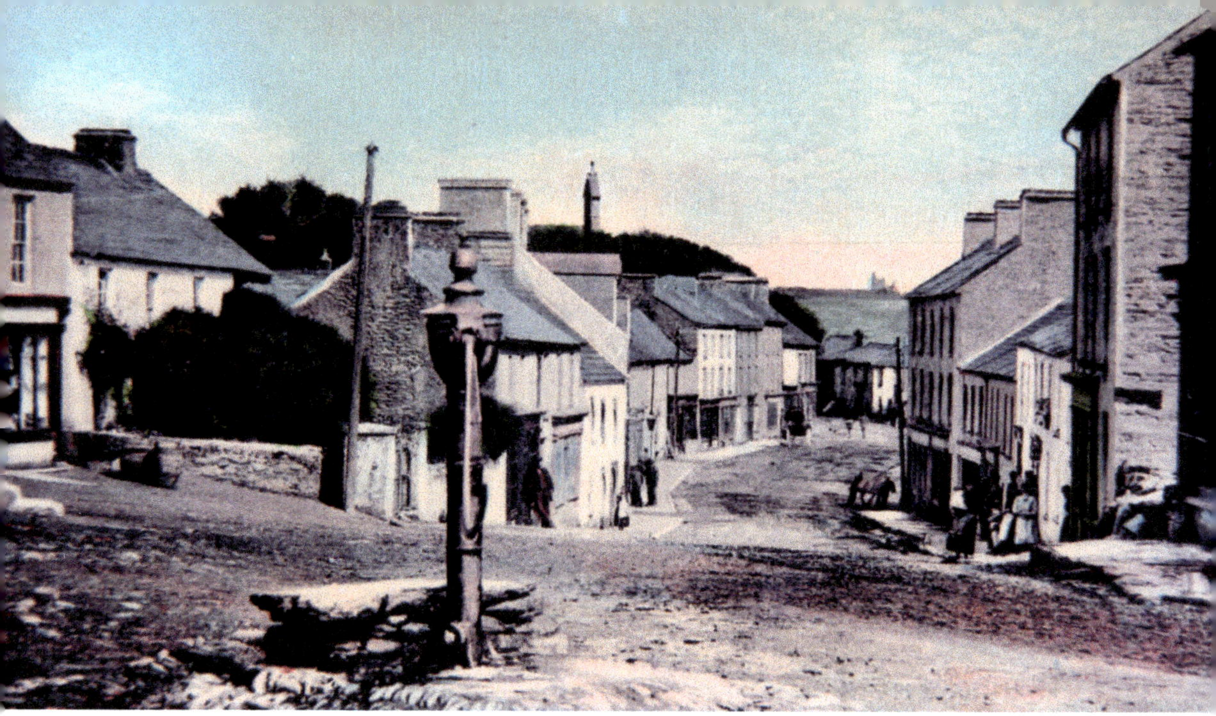

Main Street, Schull

The 1841 census figures for Schull were 17,314. Ten years later, arising from the Great Famine and emigration, the figures stood at 11,000. By 1890, the figure stood at 7,381. These drops haunt not only Schull but the various local histories the West Cork region. Nevertheless, in 1913, Schull could boast an array of community infrastructure from churches (Catholic, Church of Ireland and Methodist) to national schools, a telegraph office, petty session courts, constabulary barracks, a coastguard station and a small railway station.

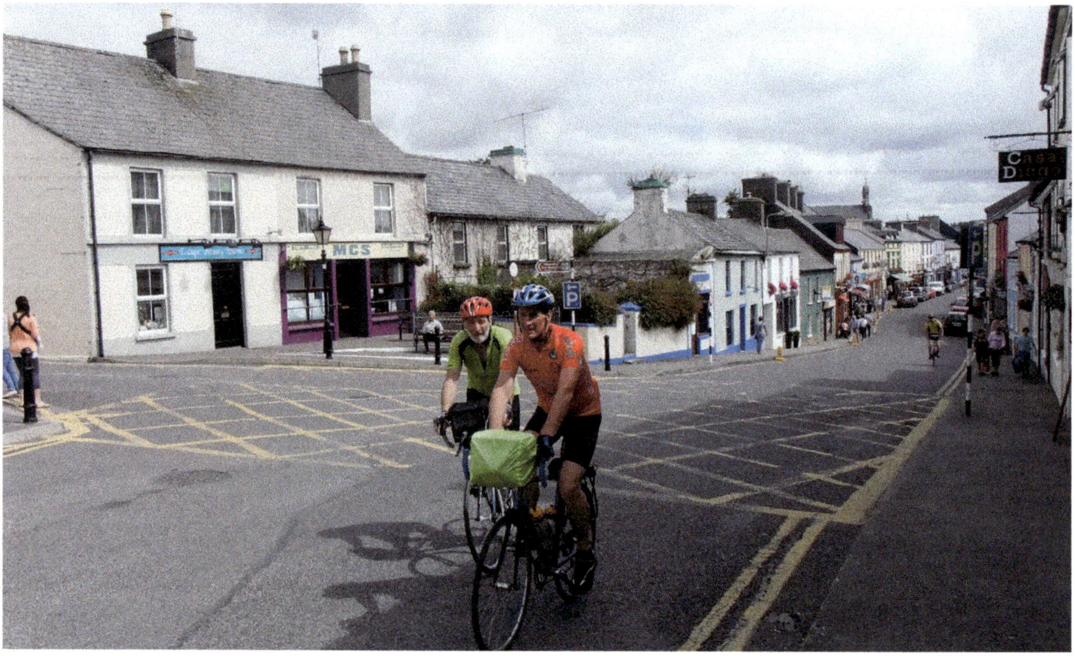

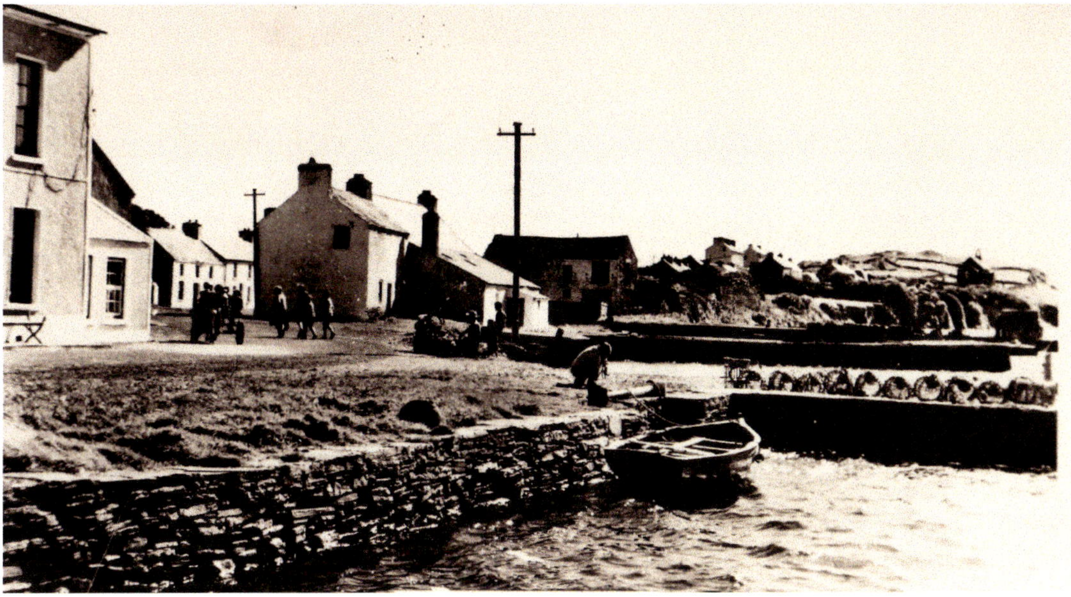

Crookhaven

The Irish name of Crookhaven is *Cruachan*. It lies on the peninsula of the Mizen, or *Ivagha* in Irish. Cruachan possibly means 'the little rick' or 'little hillock'. The English name of Crookhaven is generally believed to derive from Sir Thomas Crooke, who is also associated with the English settlement in Baltimore in the early 1600s. Over the centuries, ships stocked up with provisions here before tackling the Atlantic Ocean. At the beginning of the twentieth century it was said that you could cross the harbour on the decks of boats. 700 people lived and worked in the village against the twenty-nine permanent inhabitants who reside here today. Nearby is the old Roadstone Quarry, which provided metalling for the roads in Wales until 1945.

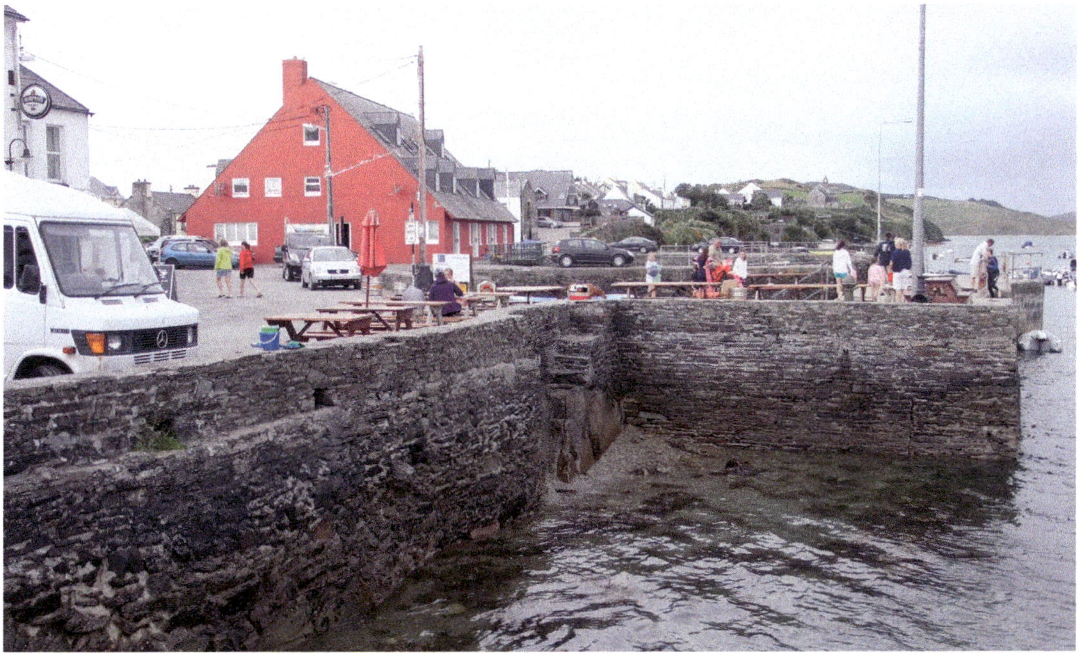

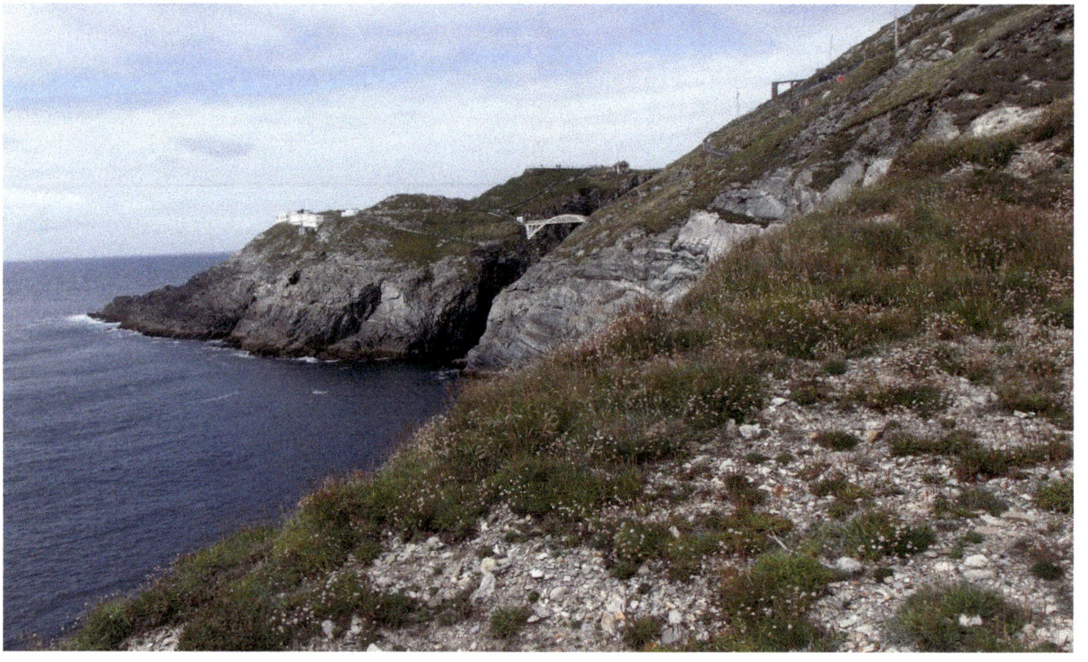

Mizen Head

At Ireland's most south-westerly point lies Mizen Head Fog Signal Station, which was sanctioned in 1906 by the Irish Lights Board to combat the high loss of life and shipping on the rocks. Until 1993, the station was manned by three keepers. In April 1993, the station was automated. In 1992, Mizen Tourism Co-operative Society Ltd, a community rural development initiative, was formed to create a visitor attraction, which explores Ireland's geological and maritime environments. There is also the impressive, recently revamped arched bridge to cross in order to get to the lighthouse.

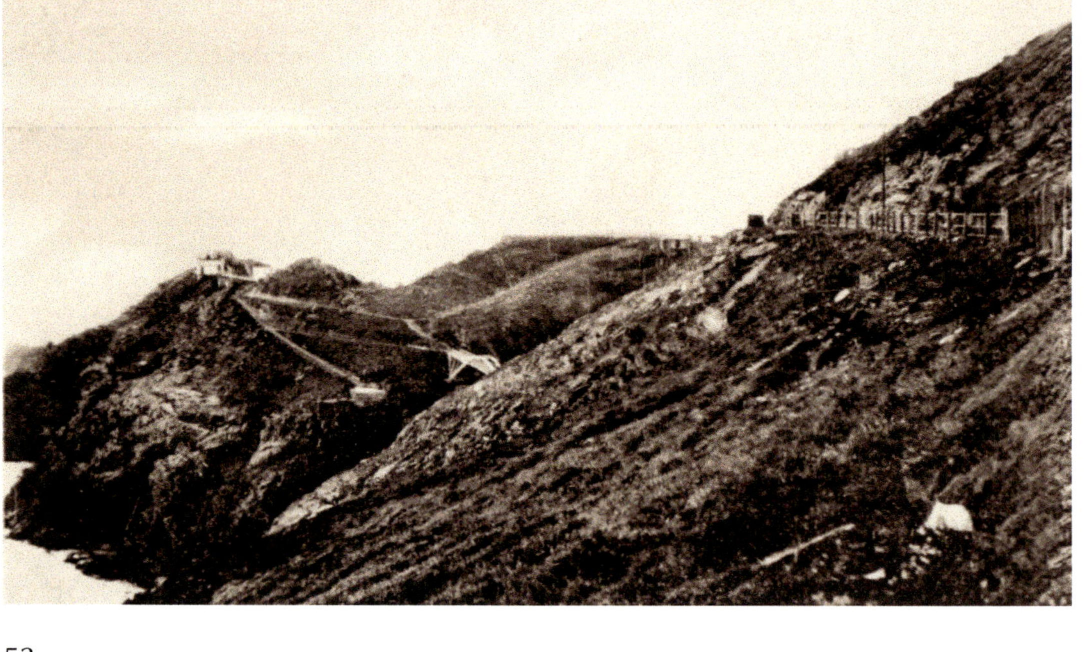

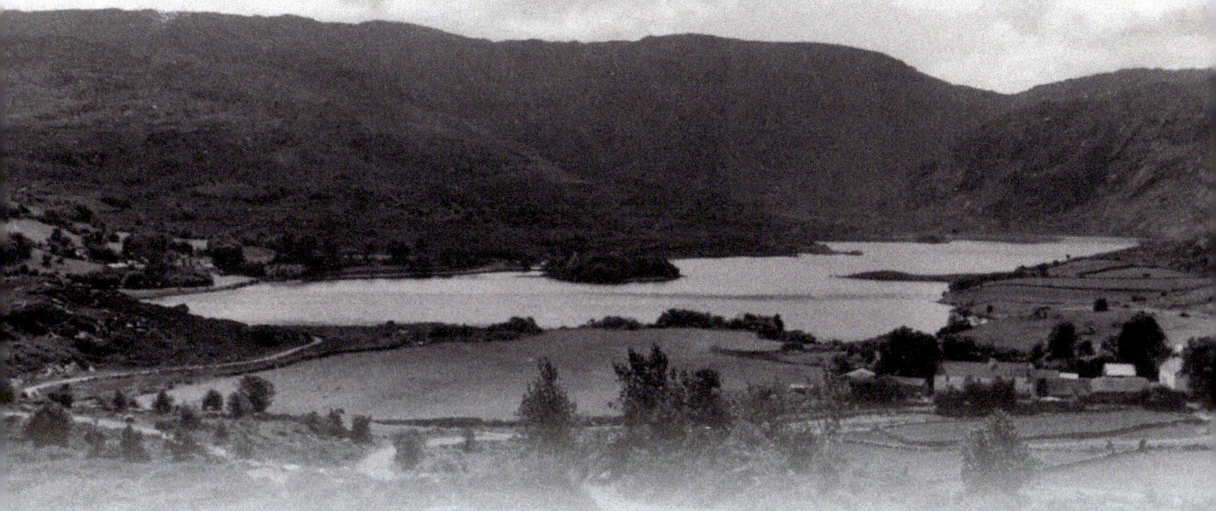

CHAPTER 3

A Pilgrim's Way – The Heart of Gougane Barra

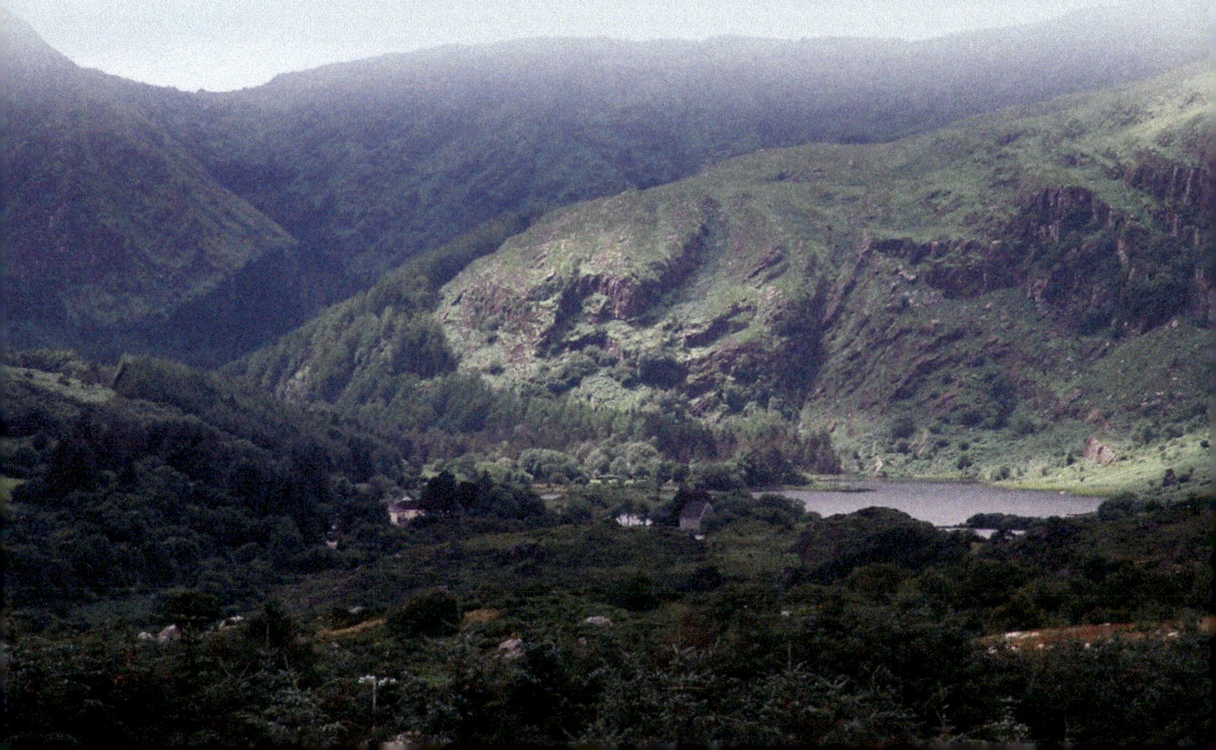

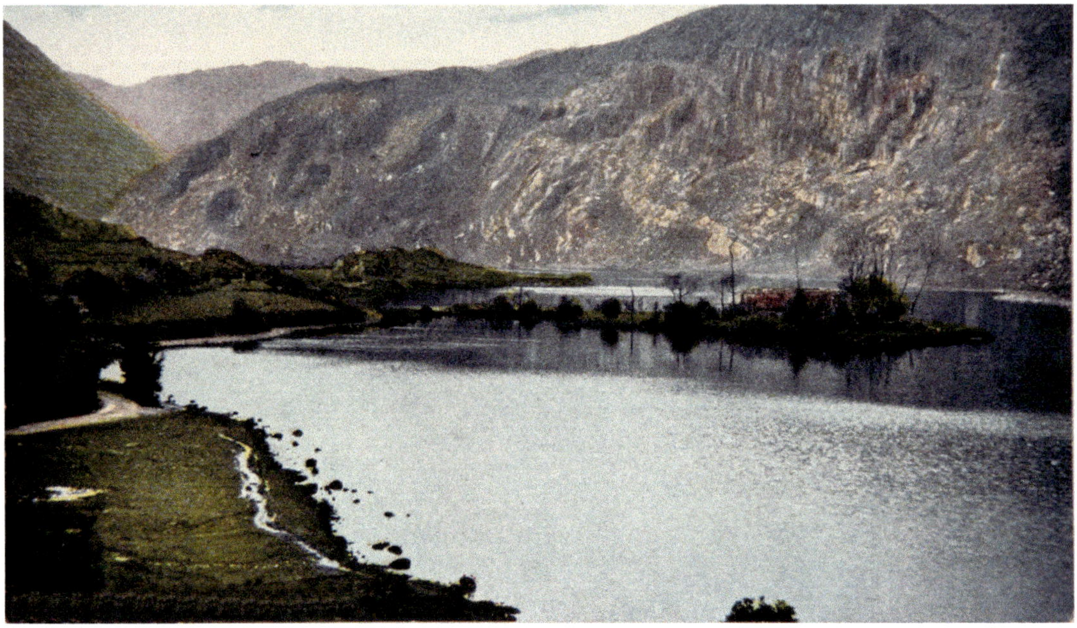

Gougane Barra

The source of the River Lee in the Shehy Mountains is revered as the site of one of the first monasteries of the patron saint of Cork City, St Finbarr. The Roman Catholic pilgrimage island in the middle of the lake has been added to in time by various religious supporters of the collective memory of the saint. Eighteenth-century pilgrimage cells and an oratory built in 1901 are two of the more striking memorials on this island, which has a stone and earth causeway to it.

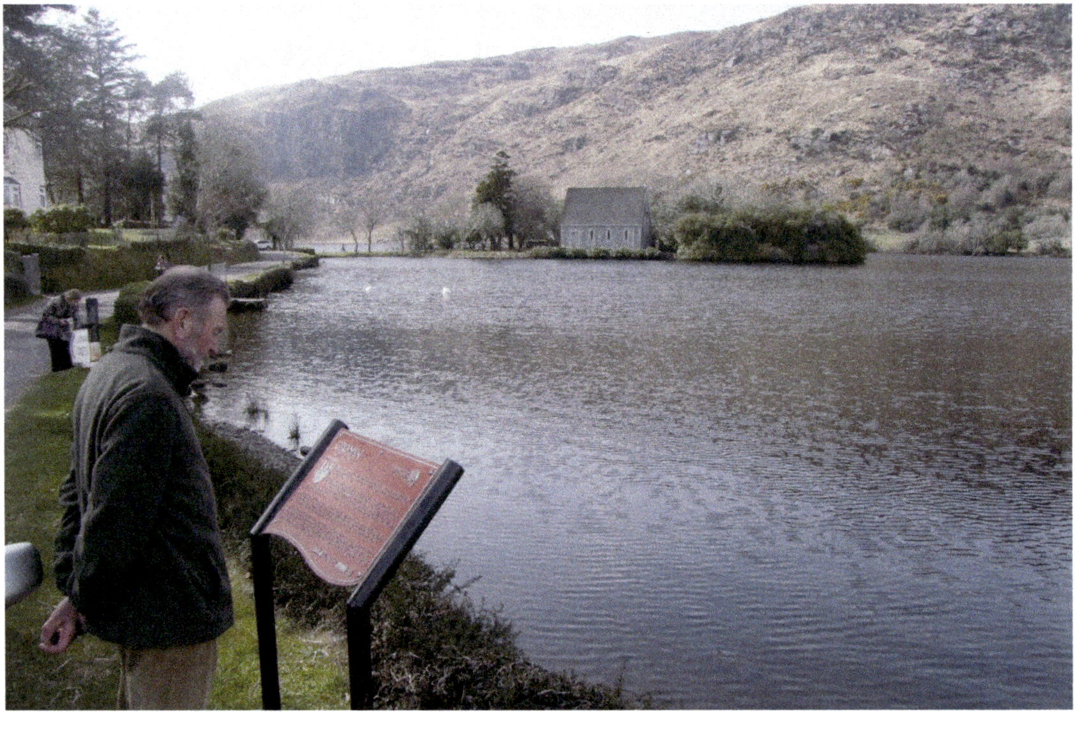

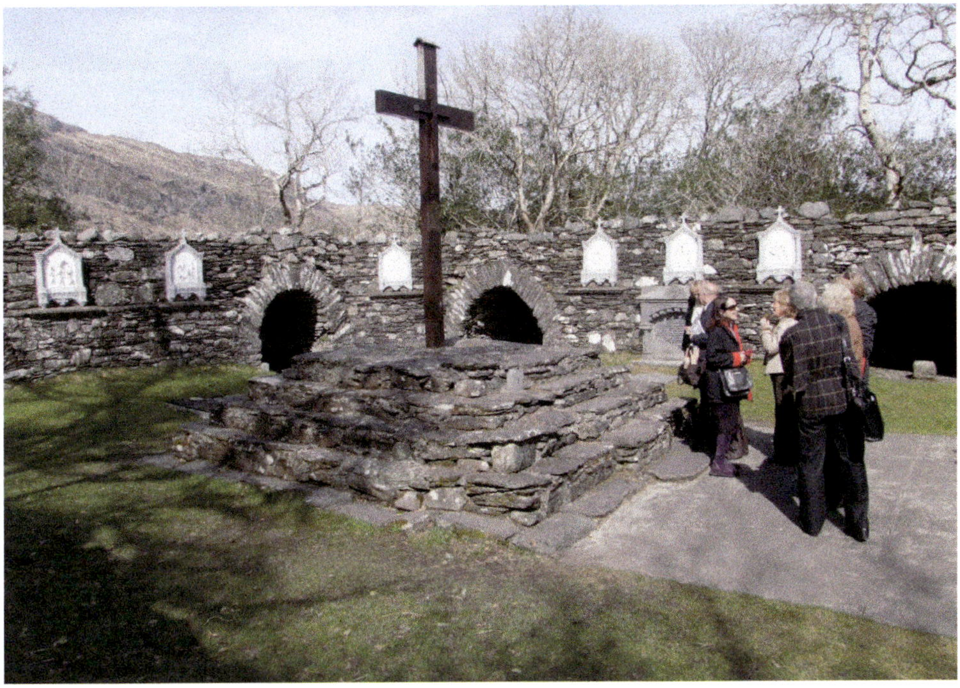

Pilgrims at Gougane Barra

The first to engage with the memory of St Finbarr was the Catholic priest Father Denis O'Mahony. His advent in the late seventeenth century to the site brought his own thoughts on how to mark the story of Finbarr. Father O'Mahony introduced a memorial, a series of cells and gardens on the pilgrimage island. He chose to physically enhance the symbolism of the island site. The cells complex has been revamped and repaired through the centuries. Today, the island is in the ownership of the diocese of Cork and Ross.

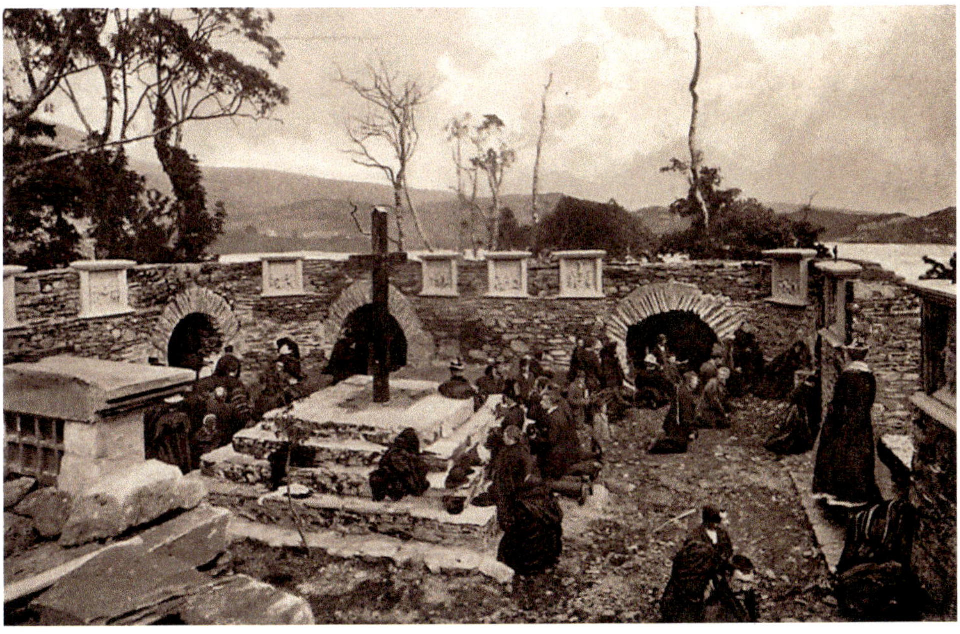

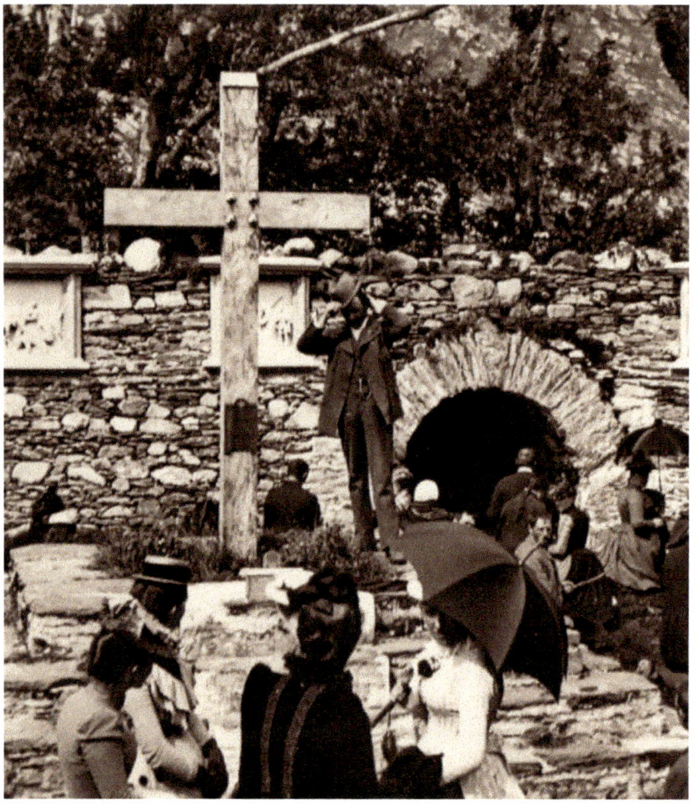

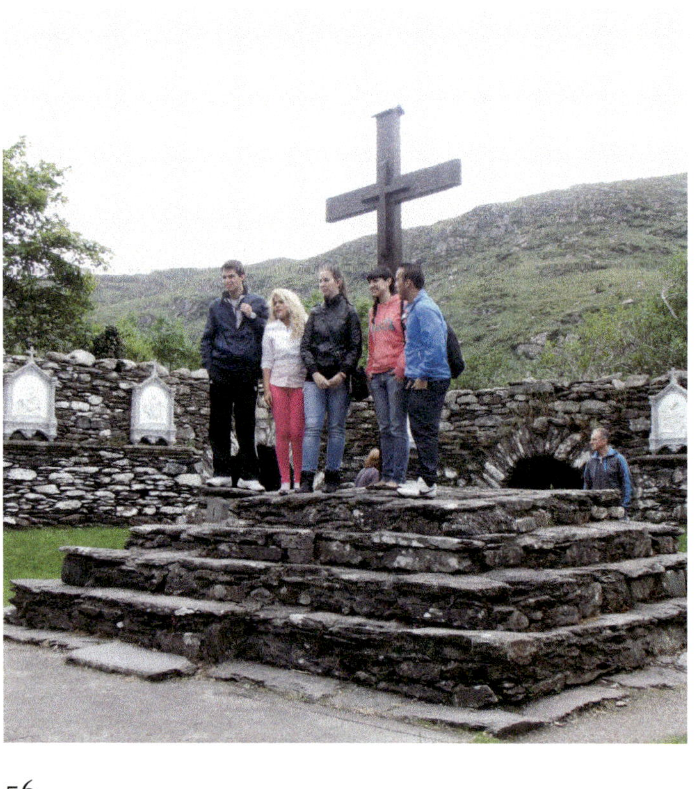

Cells Complex, Gougane Barra

Local parish priest Father Patrick Hurley pursued a repair agenda for the pilgrimage site in the 1890s. He also wished to improve the lives of local people by encouraging industrial pursuits. He prompted an industrial revival amongst local people. He also brought lecturers into the area to share their ideas of cultivation in difficult landscapes for growing crops and dairy farming. In addition, Father Hurley established a lace-making industry in the district. Significantly, he succeeded in getting the local district council to build new roads in the area. He then encouraged the Tourist Development Company to run coaches to Glengarriff and Killarney, via Macroom and Gougane Barra, putting the pilgrimage site firmly on a regional tourist route.

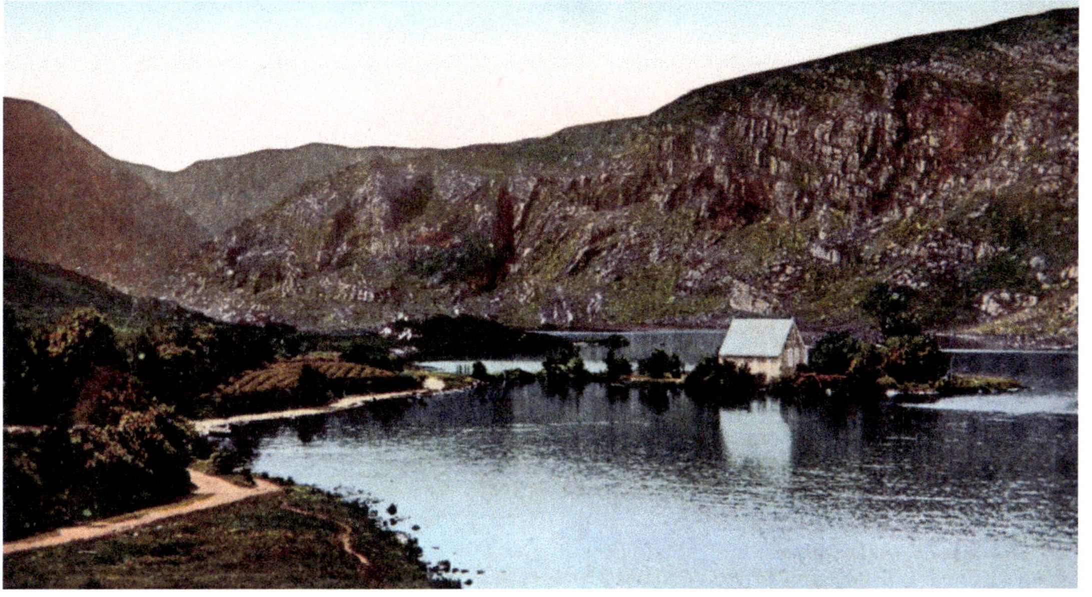

Gougane Barra, Post-Revamp, *c.* 1901

St Finbarr's Oratory (built around 1900/01) owes its origin to the local parish priest Father Patrick Hurley, who financed the erection of it to two wealthy Irish Americans in America (one living in Chicago). The new oratory replaced Father Denis O'Mahony's oratory, which was nearly 200 years old. The oratory is built in Hiberno-Byzantine style and modelled after the chapel of Cormac on the Rock of Cashel.

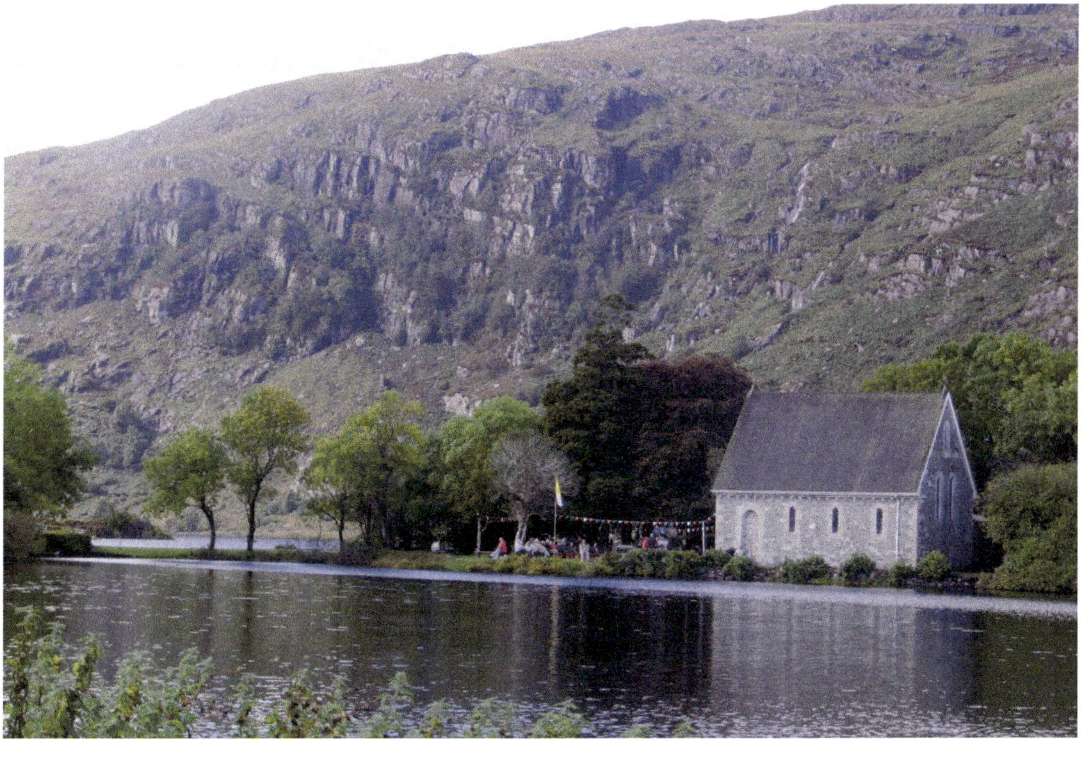

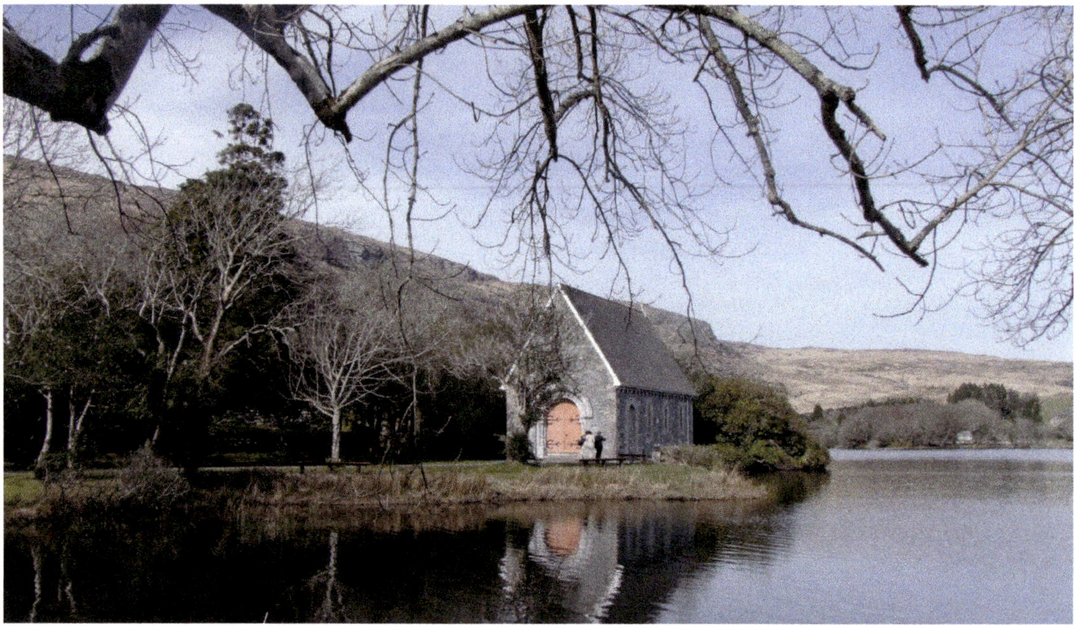

St Finbarr's Oratory, Gougane Barra

Mr Samuel F. Hynes, Cork, designed the new oratory, and the artist was Mr M. J. C. Buckley, who had offices in Cork and Bruges, Belgium. Hynes was an architect of great experience, and had been involved in the rebuilding or design of additions to several Cork churches. The walling of Gougane Barra oratory is of mountain stone and is relieved by dressings of limestone, while the roof, like the chapel of Cormac, is of stone, necessitated by the heavy rains that prevail in mountain districts. The original plan was to have a round tower at the entrance to the oratory, but it was never completed.

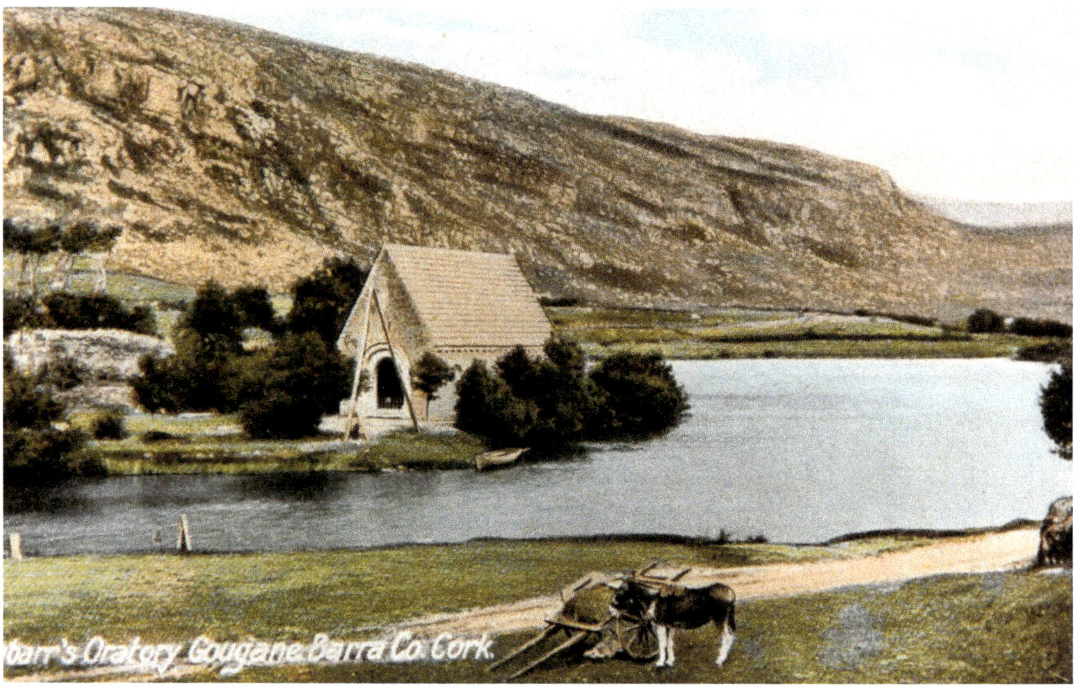

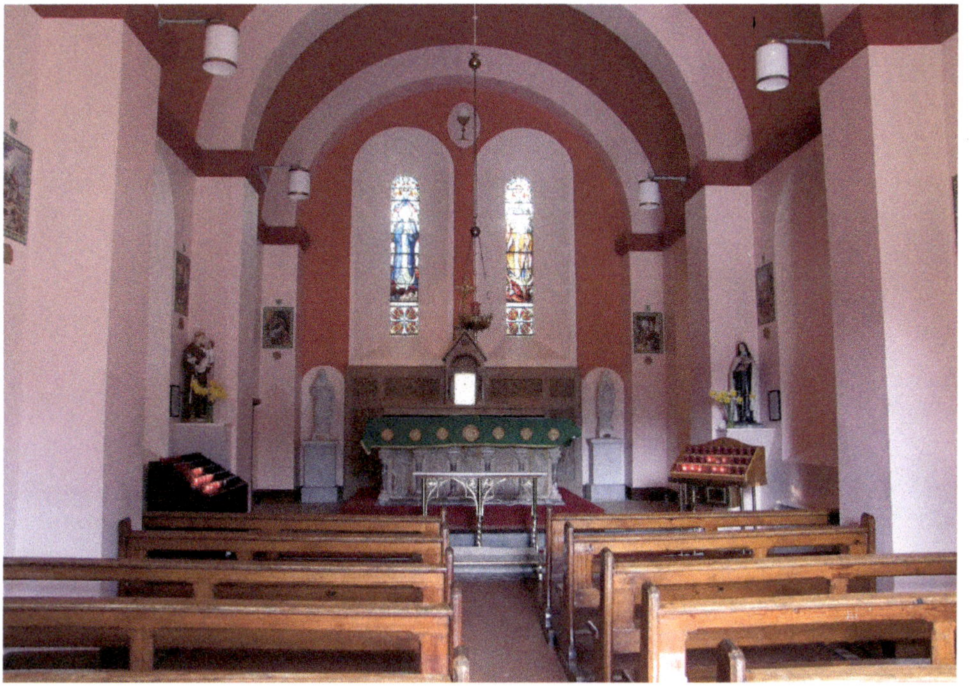

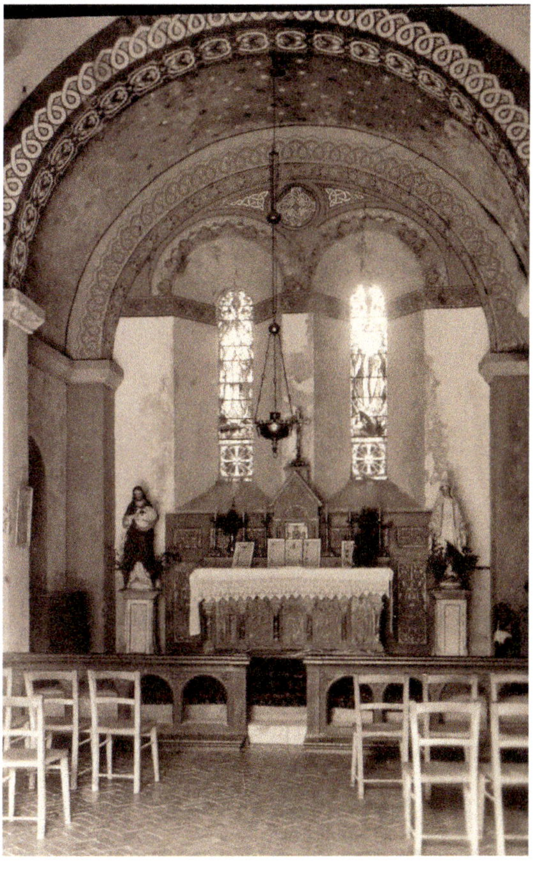

St Finbarr's Oratory, Gougane Barra

The western end of the oratory is ornamented by a boldly excised doorway of limestone. At the head of the label mould is a cut head of St Finbarr. The interior of Gougane oratory is richly embellished with stories of the early spread of Christianity and the extent of the early Roman Empire. The majority of the marble that is used is made principally of St Maximin creamy-toned marble from the Jura. Eight stained-glass windows decorate the interior. Each contains the figure of some saint connected with St Finbarr's life or the parish. In the two lights over the altar is a figure of the Blessed Virgin, and beside it on the right is a figure of St Finbarr.

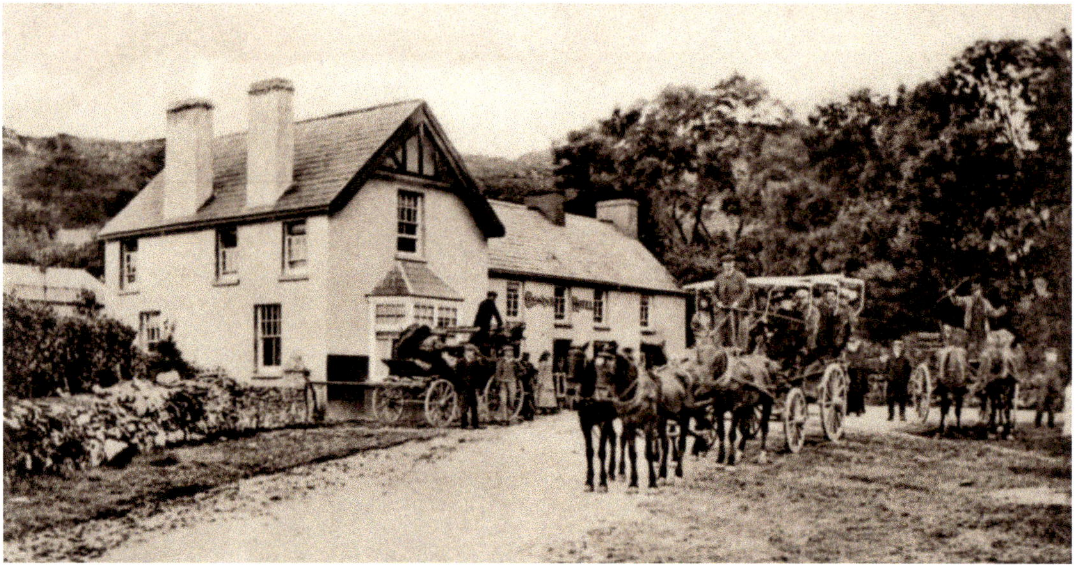

Cronin's Hotel, Gougane Barra

With a focus on the tourist market, Cronin's Hotel was designed by local man Cornelius Cronin around 1897, and built by direct labour under his supervision. Inspired by the growth of tourist traffic in the locality, there was also fishing and shooting to be had there to attract visitors. By a family arrangement in 1935, Cornelius got a portion of the holding owned by his late father. On that portion, the applicant built a new fourteen-room hotel at a cost of £2,000. Today the business is still going strong.

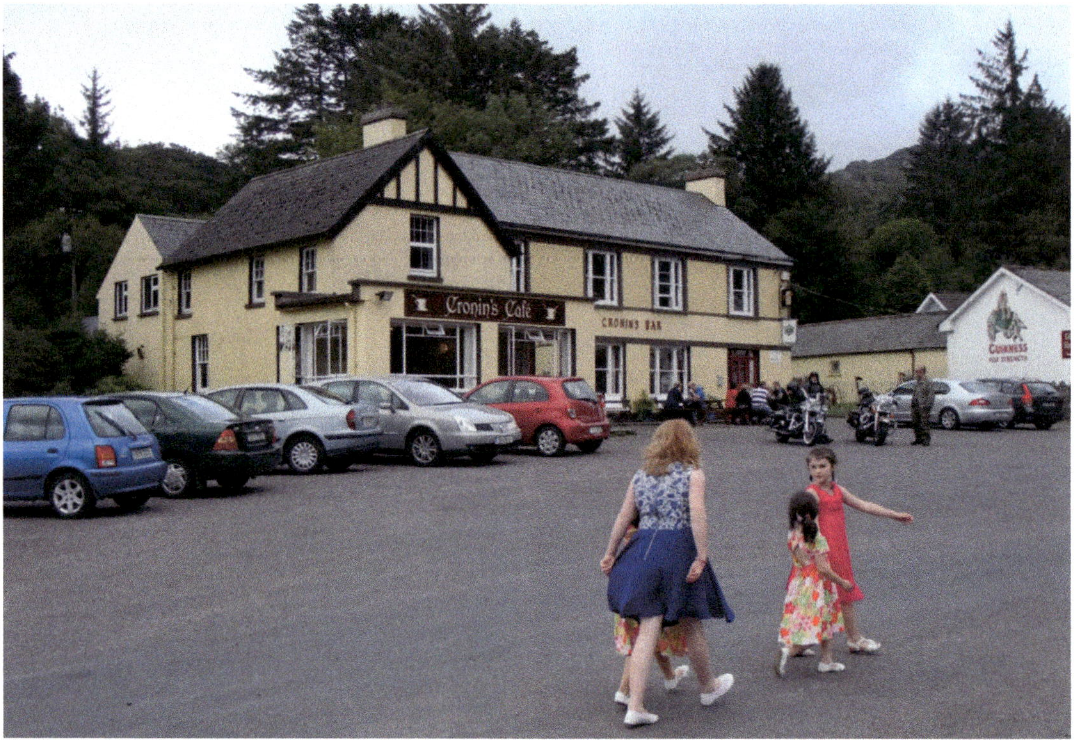

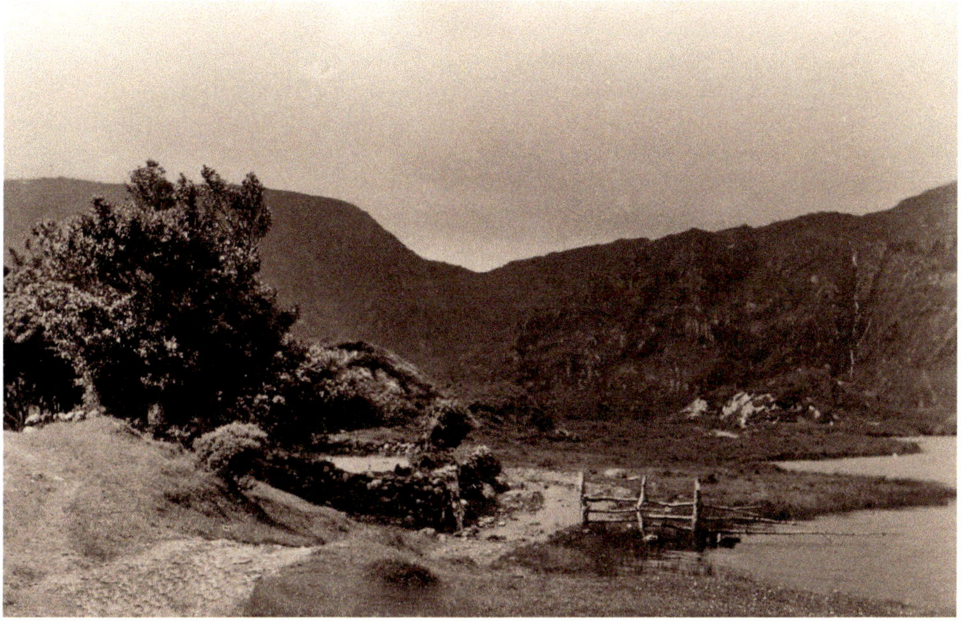

Forest Park, Gougane Barra

An important Irish government-supported project in Gougane Barra was that of the Irish Free State Forestry Programme in the late 1930s. Plantings were largely of Sitka spruce, Lodgepole pine, Japanese larch and some Scots pine. Having reached maturity, some of these areas were in time harvested and restocked with a wider variety of species. However, one of the finest stands of Sitka spruce in the country still exists in the valley, with trees reaching 38 m high and carrying a volume of up to 3 cubic meters each. The forest area became an Irish National Park in 1966.

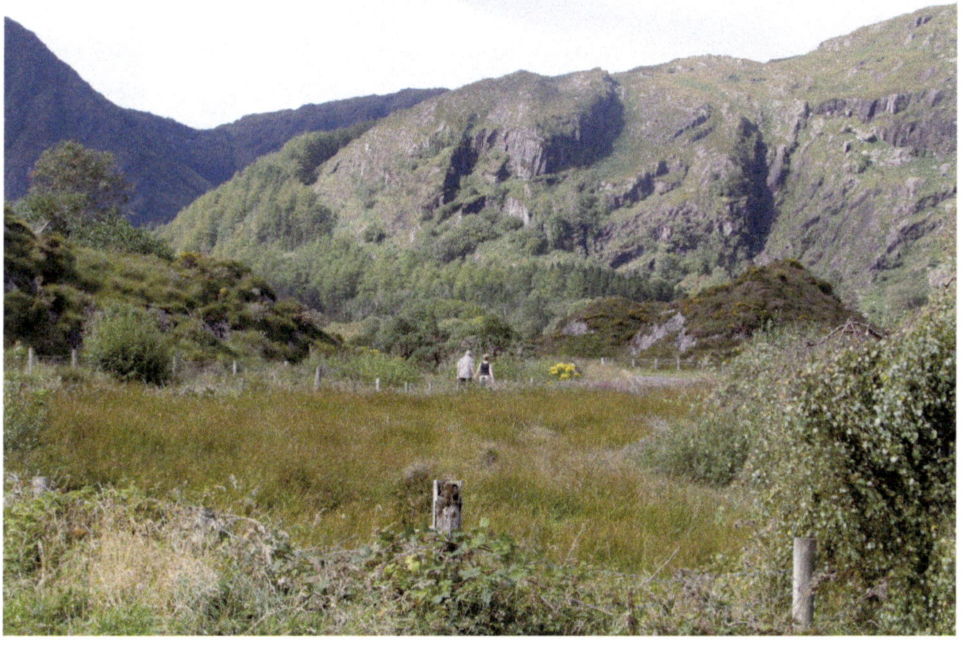

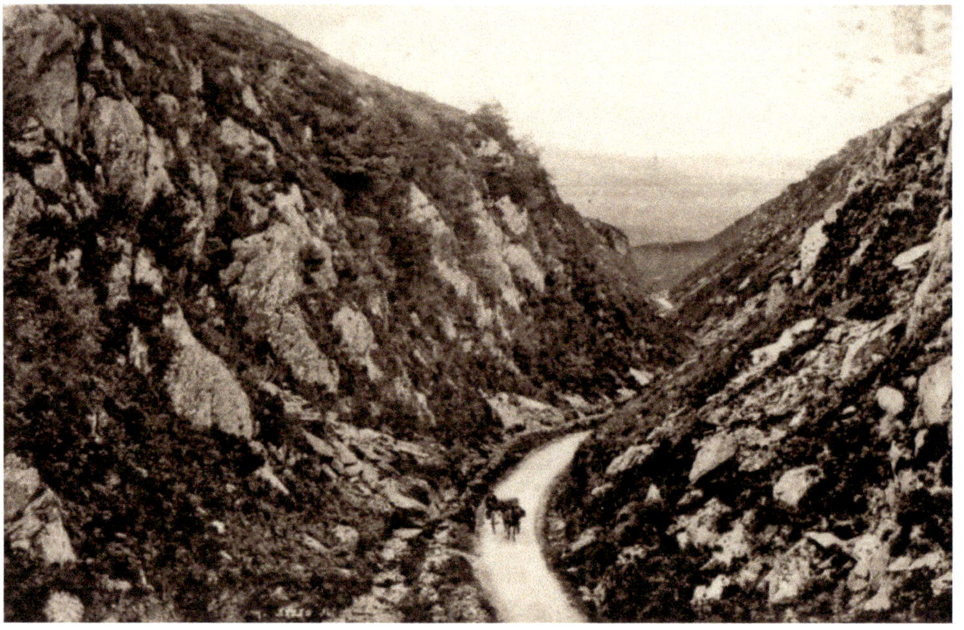

Pass of Keimaneigh

Adjacent to Gougane Barra is the wild and rugged Pass of Keimaneigh, which lies on the main road between Macroom and Bantry in West Cork. It is a wild and rugged place in the extreme western end of the parish of Iveleary (*Inchigeela*). Sheer cliffs rise on both sides of the pass to a height of 100 feet above the road. In historic terms, the pass is remembered for a number of skirmishes between locals and gentry that took place in January 1822. They arose resulting from protesting tenant farmers and labourers who were experiencing much economic hardship in the 1810s and 1820s. The Keimaneigh area was used as a base for random attacks condemning rent oppression.

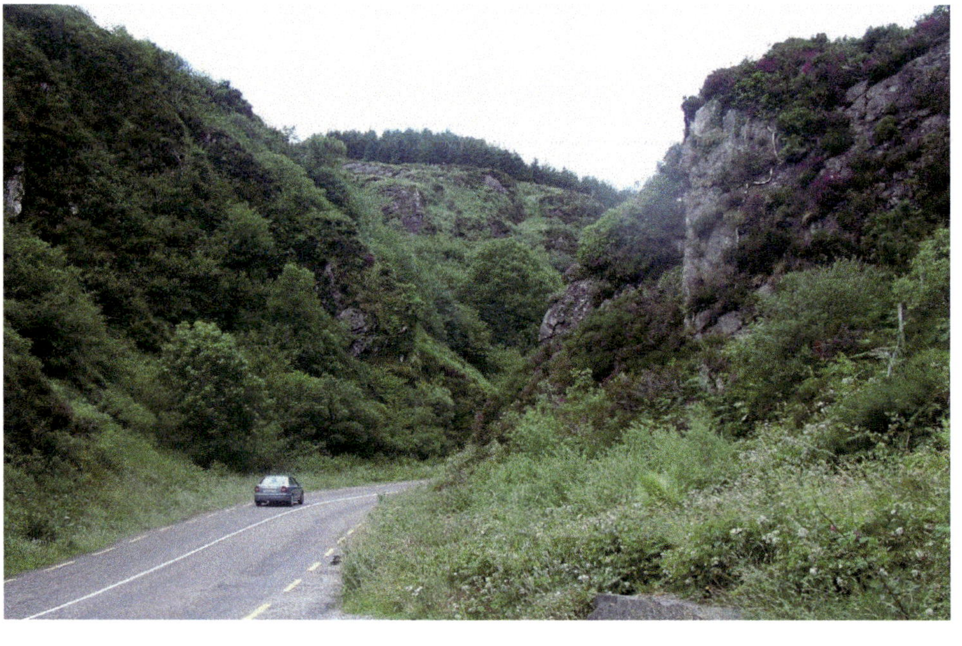

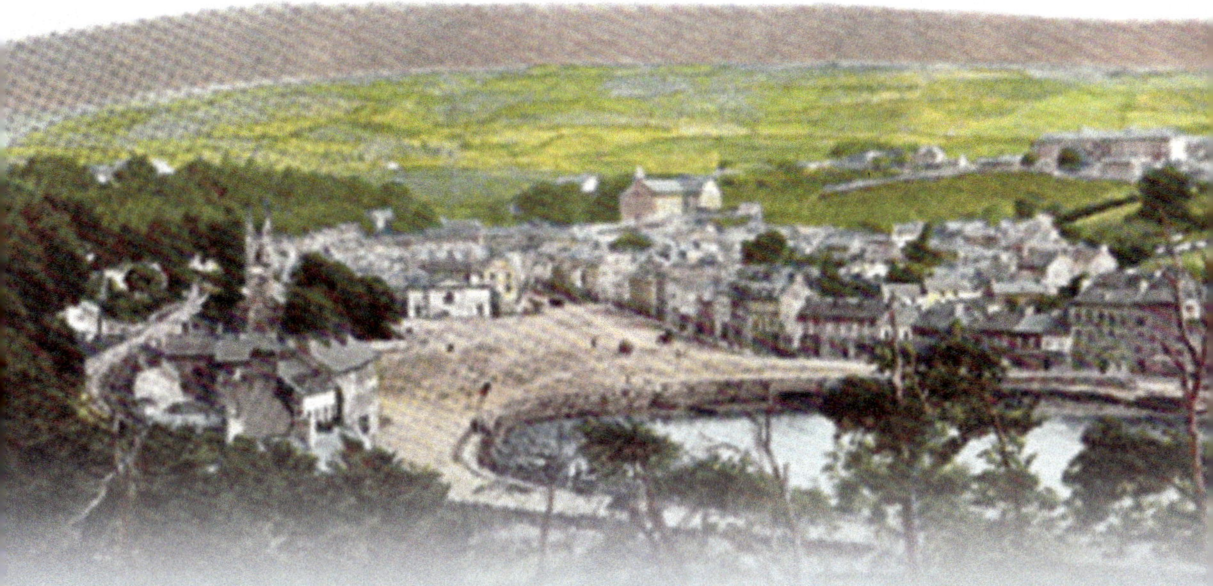

CHAPTER 4

Bantry & Beyond – The Borders of a County

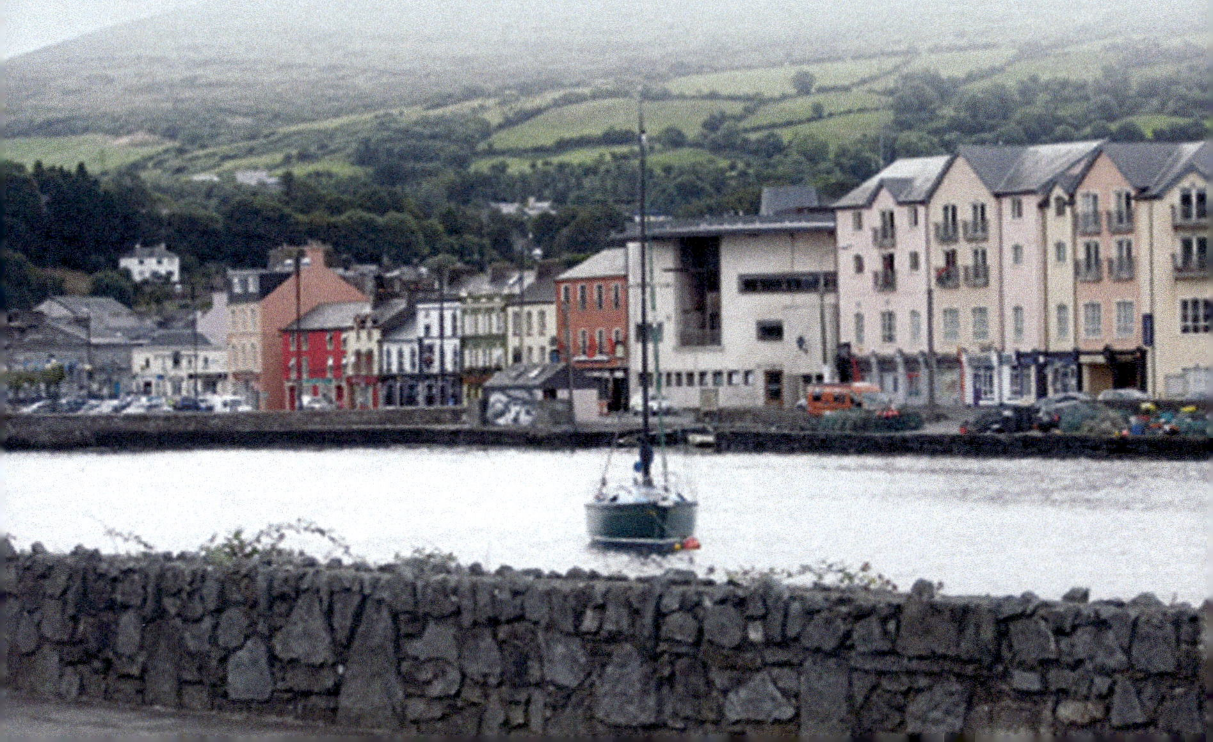

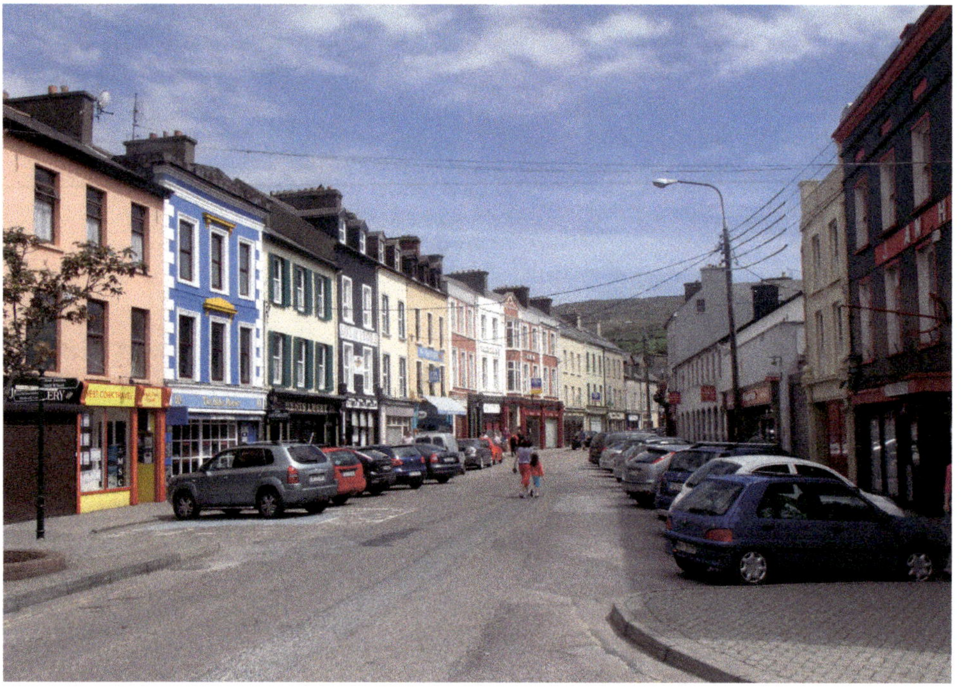

New Street, Bantry

Bantry Bay is one of the finest and safest harbours in Europe, and is situated in a strategic position on the edge of the Atlantic Ocean. Being very deep with few dangerous rocks or sandbanks, and sheltered from most winds by the mountains surrounding it, it has been used from earliest times as a haven by fishermen and merchant ships. For centuries, fleets of English, Spanish, French and Dutch ships fished in the bay, paying harbour dues and fishing tax to the Irish clan O'Sullivan, who controlled the bay. In addition, ships sailed from Bantry loaded with recruits for the French, Spanish, Austrian and Dutch armies.

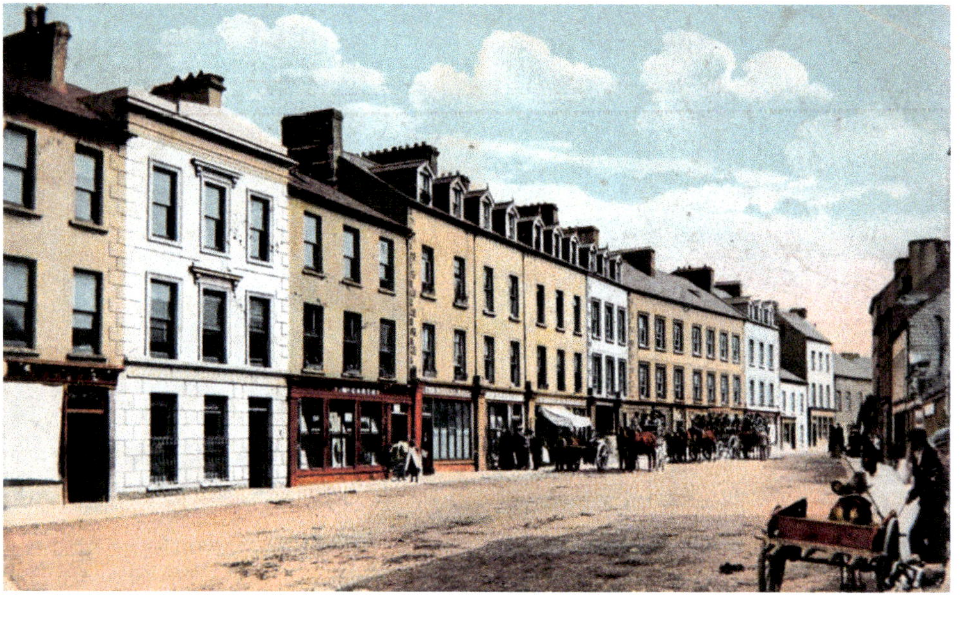

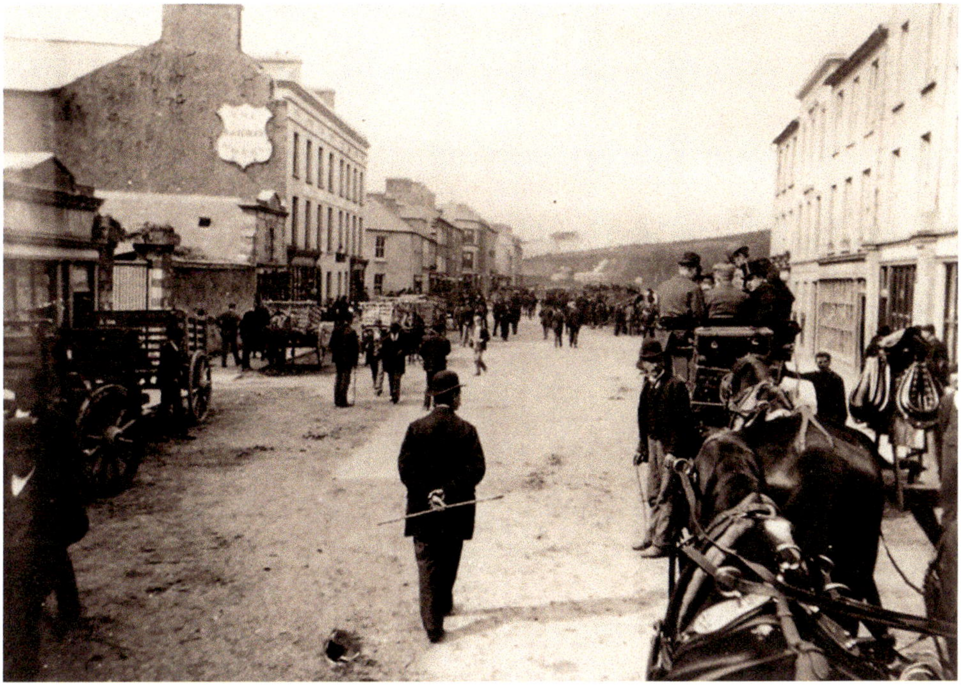

New Street, Bantry

The trade of Bantry port was once considerable, and the town gained commercial importance as a result – hence the investment in creating new streetscapes and quaysides. At one time, the manufacture of coarse linen and cotton thrived here, creating employment for several hundred people. These linens, called 'vitries', were striped pieces used primarily for bagging, and annual sales regularly exceeded £4,000. Items such as butter, pork and beef were shipped from the port in large quantities, and, from around 1775, many cargoes of butter were exported annually to Portugal.

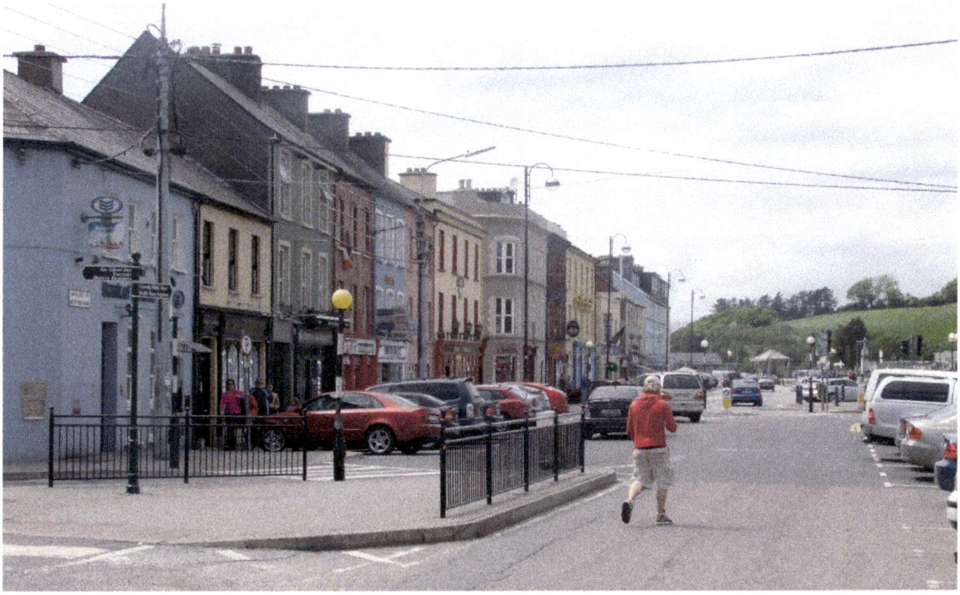

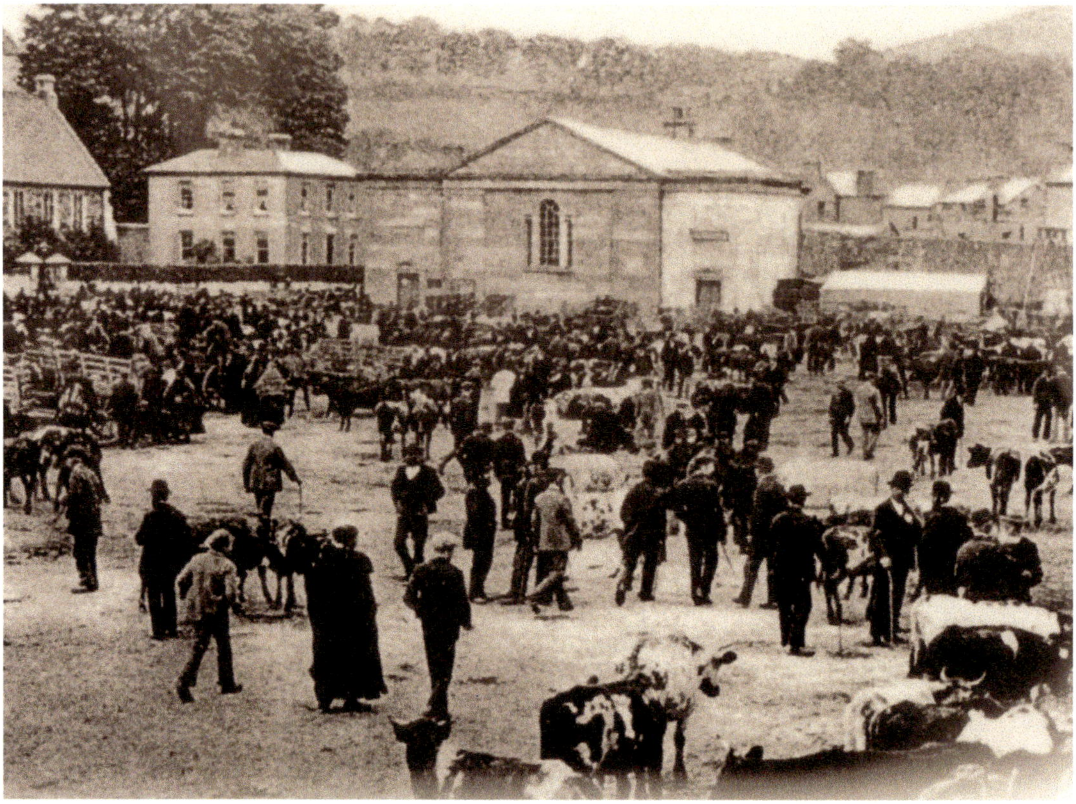

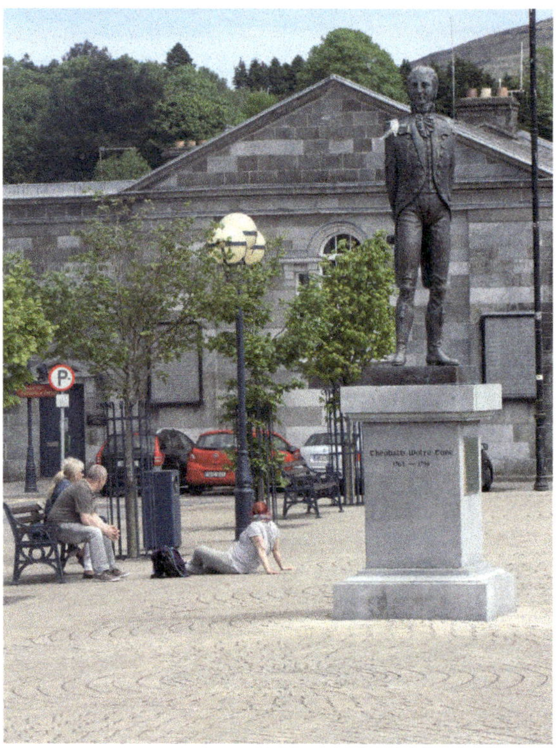

Wolfe Tone Square, Bantry

On 15 December 1796, Bantry once again became the destination of a French fleet. 43 ships and 15,000 men set sail from Brest in support of the Irish patriot, Wolfe Tone, a founding member of the United Irishmen. Tone was determined to establish an Irish Republic by armed rebellion. Easterly storms off the Irish coast dispersed the fleet and, while some succeeded in anchoring in Bantry Bay, most were scattered on the Atlantic. On 27 January 1797, the order was given to abandon the attempted invasion, and the few remaining ships in the bay that were seaworthy sailed for France. A statue of Wolfe Tone stands in the former market square today and information panels recount the story.

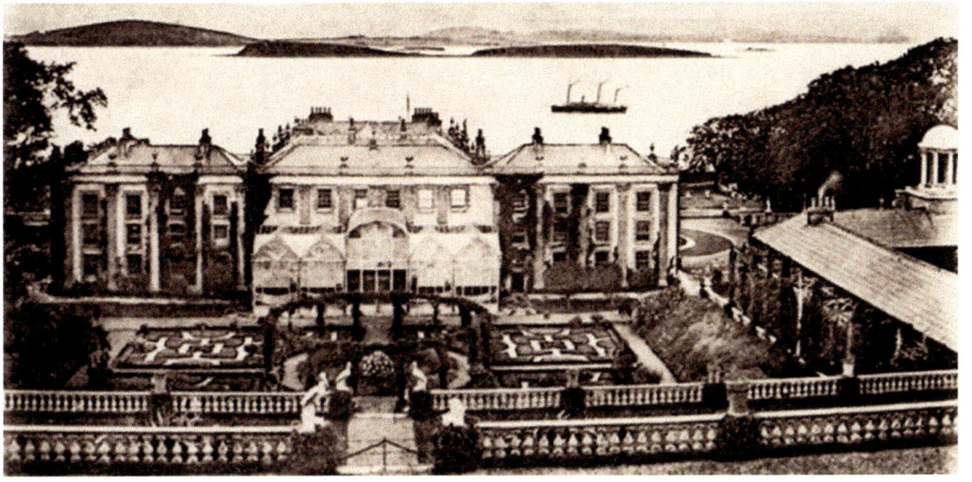

Bantry House

Blackrock, Seafield House, or Bantry House, as it is has variously been called during its history, has been the home of the White family for two centuries. The first representative of the family of whom there is any record at Bantry was Captain Richard White, son of Simon White of Knocksentry, near Limerick, who settled on Whiddy Island in Bantry Bay towards the end of the seventeenth century. He subsequently acquired property from the Earl of Anglesey, to whom extensive grants of land in the area had been made under the Acts of Settlement.

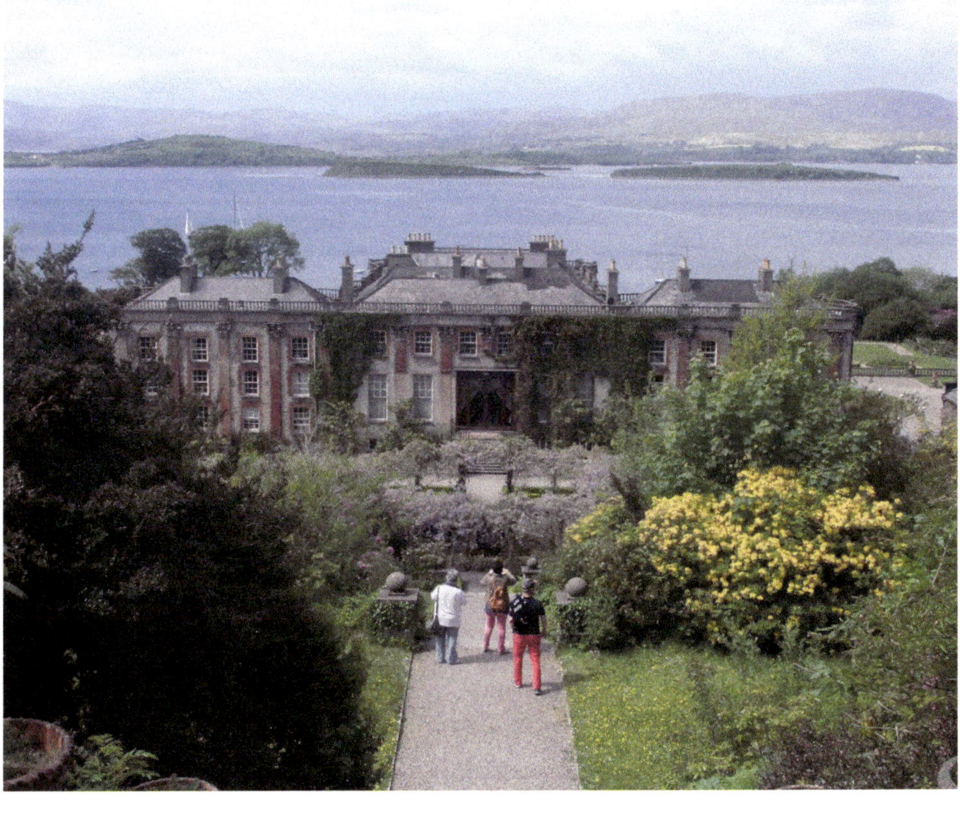

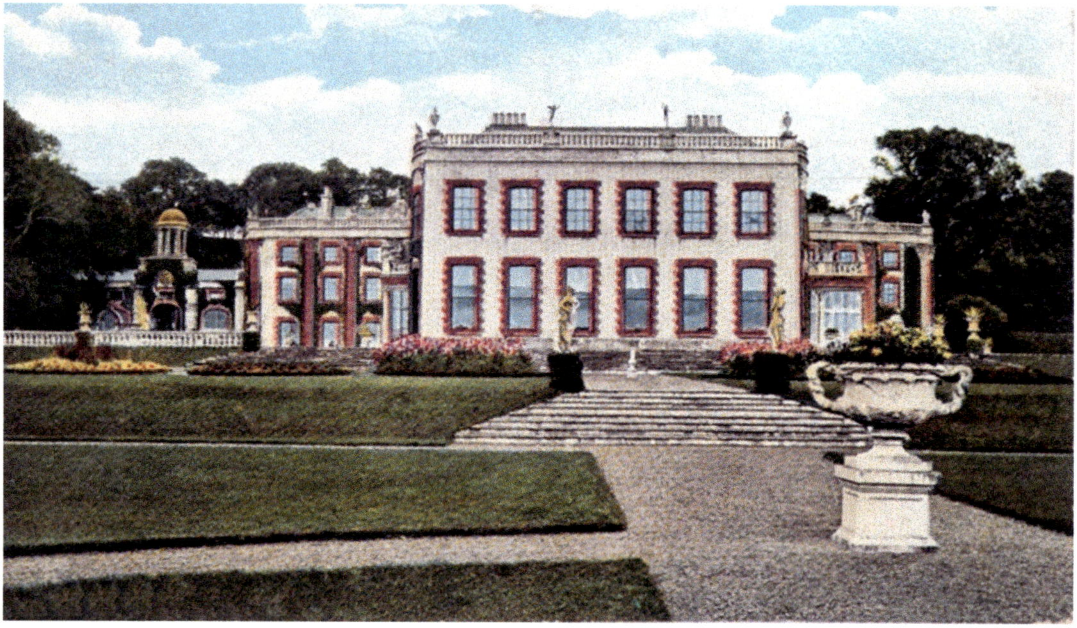

Bantry House

Bantry house was originally a typical example of a mid-eighteenth century Georgian country residence, and it was not until around the middle of the nineteenth century, when extensive alterations and additions were made by the 2nd Lord Bantry, that it assumed its present size and character. New blocks and wings were added. By the mid-nineteenth century, some twenty years later, it had become a mansion worthy of accommodating the furniture and art treasures collected by Lord Bantry during his travels in Europe. Today, the house is open to the public to explore its rich artistic and architectural heritage.

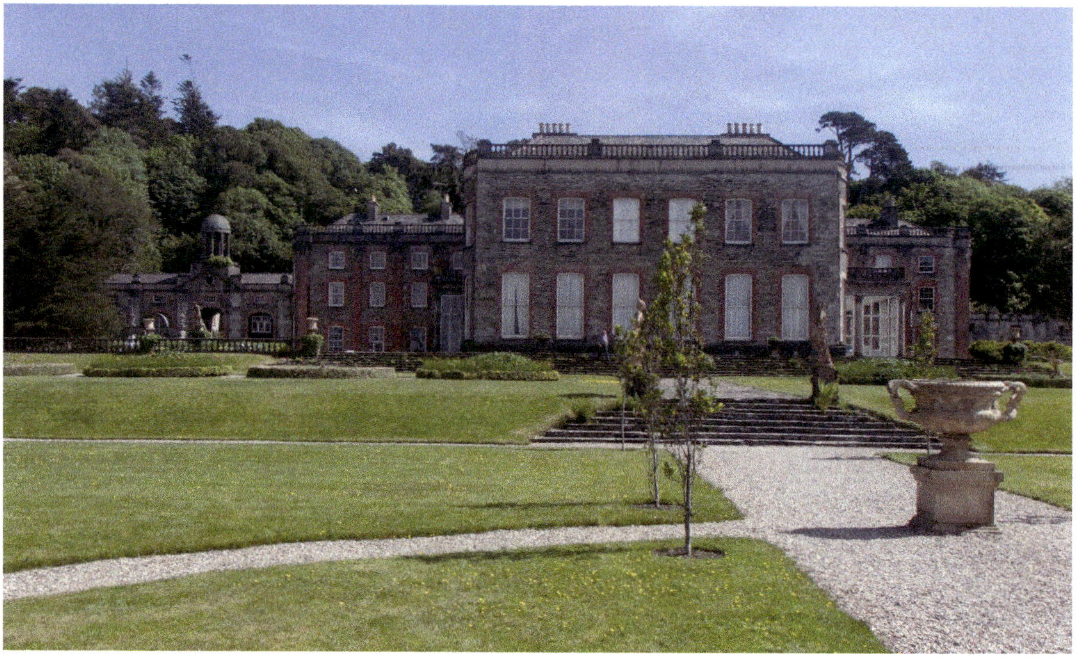

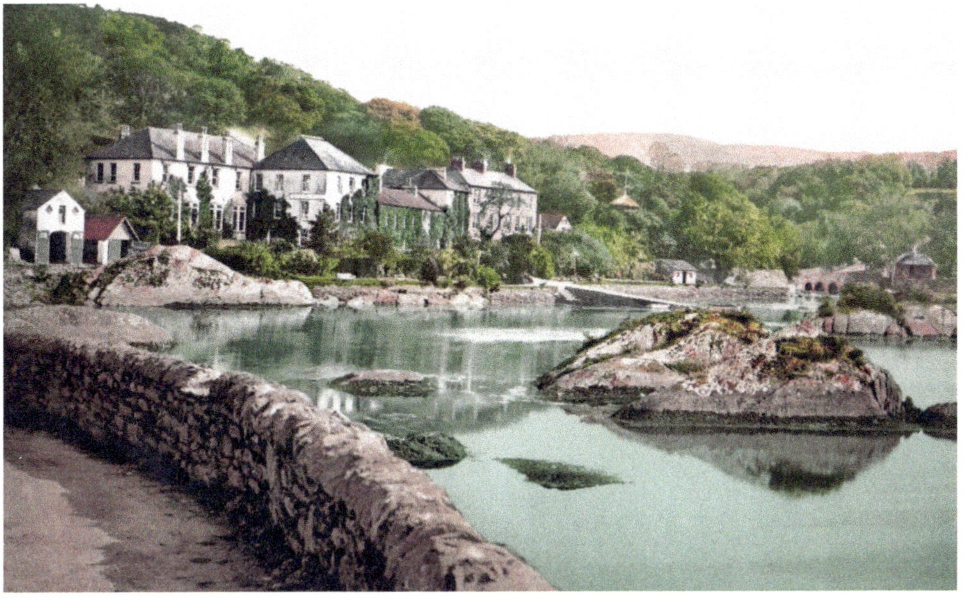

Eccles Hotel, Glengarriff

Glengarriff – translated from the Irish/Gaelic *An Gleann Garbh* meaning 'The Rugged Glen' – has been famous as a holiday destination since the 1700s, and boomed in the Victorian times as an important stop along the Prince of Wales Grand Tour route. In 1835, Thomas Eccles rented land and buildings comprising just over 28 acres from the Earl of Bantry for the sum of £16 and 12*s*. As part of this he opened an inn. John Eccles, son of Thomas, carried out major reconstruction of the inn in 1890, and also changed the name from Glengarriff Inn to the Eccles Hotel. Writer George Bernard Shaw (1856–1950) stayed in the hotel in 1910/11, and is reputed to have written extensively during his time here. During the 1920s, William Butler Yeats (poet and playwright) was a regular visitor to the Eccles Hotel.

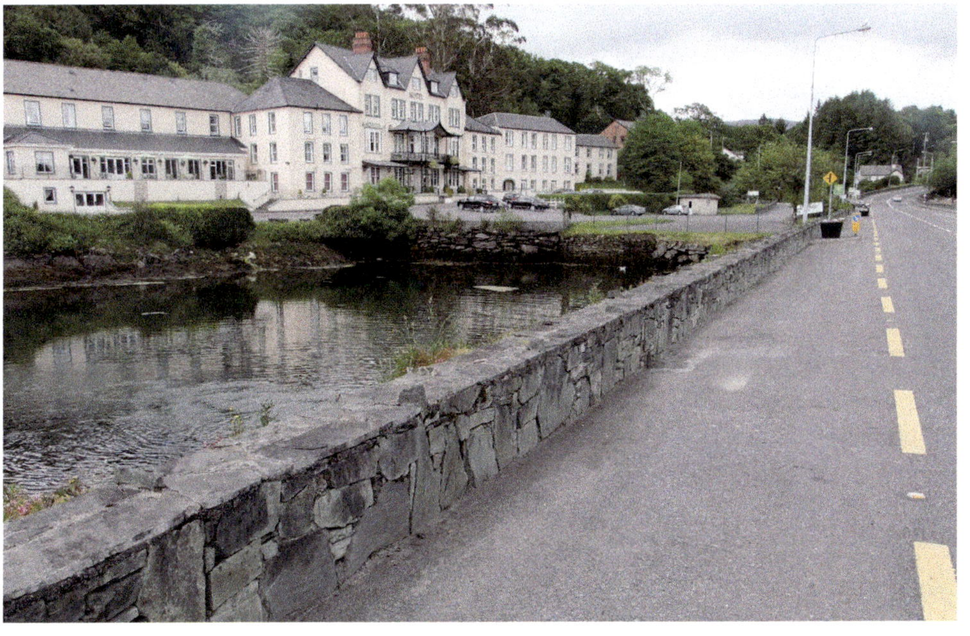

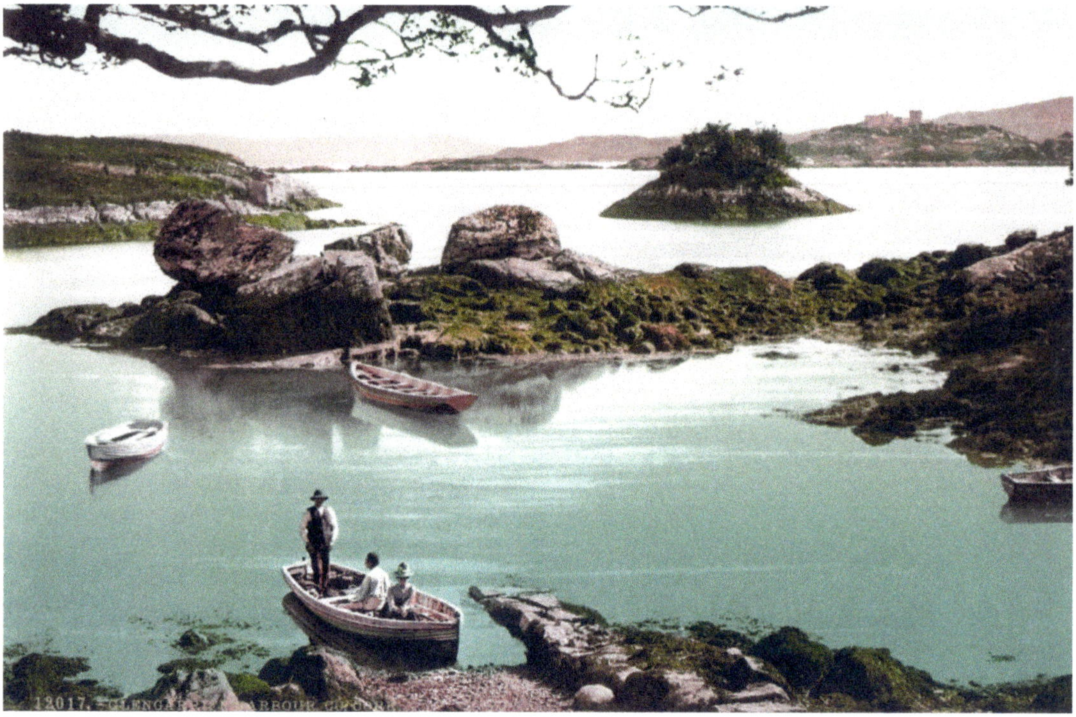

Glengarriff Bay

'In the midst of rocks, and mountains, thrown together in the greatest, are finely contrasted the richness of luxuriant woods and verdant glades, shaded with thriving plantations, intermixed with evergreens and flowering shrubs. The hotels are good, splendidly situated on the bay, and supply every accommodation for tourists and visitors. Glengarriff is a celebrated health resort, happily sheltered, and warmed by the Gulf Stream.' (*Guide to the Most Picturesque Tour of Western Europe,* 1898).

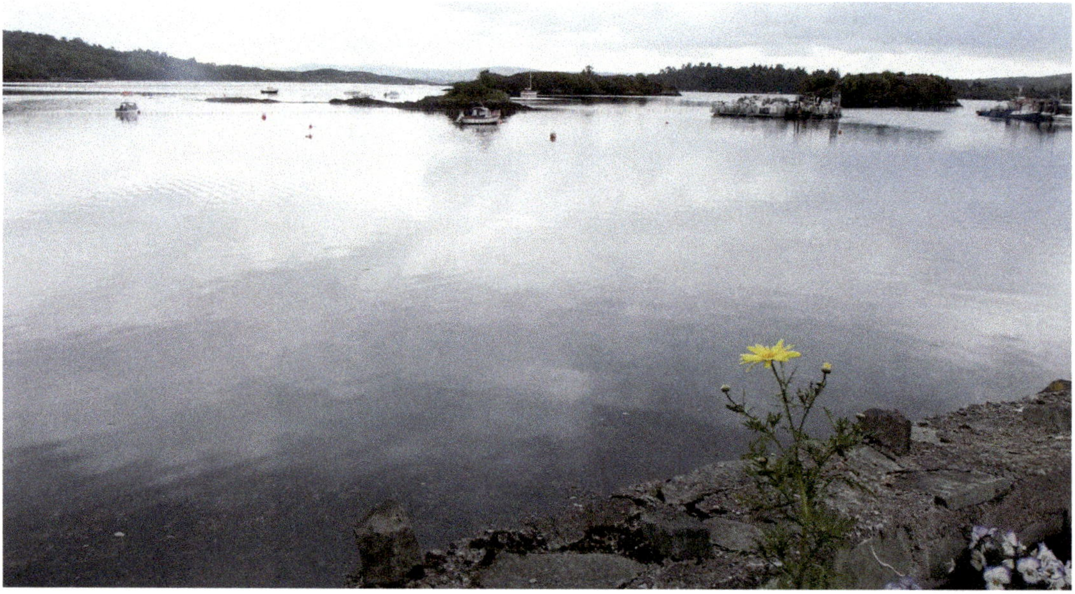

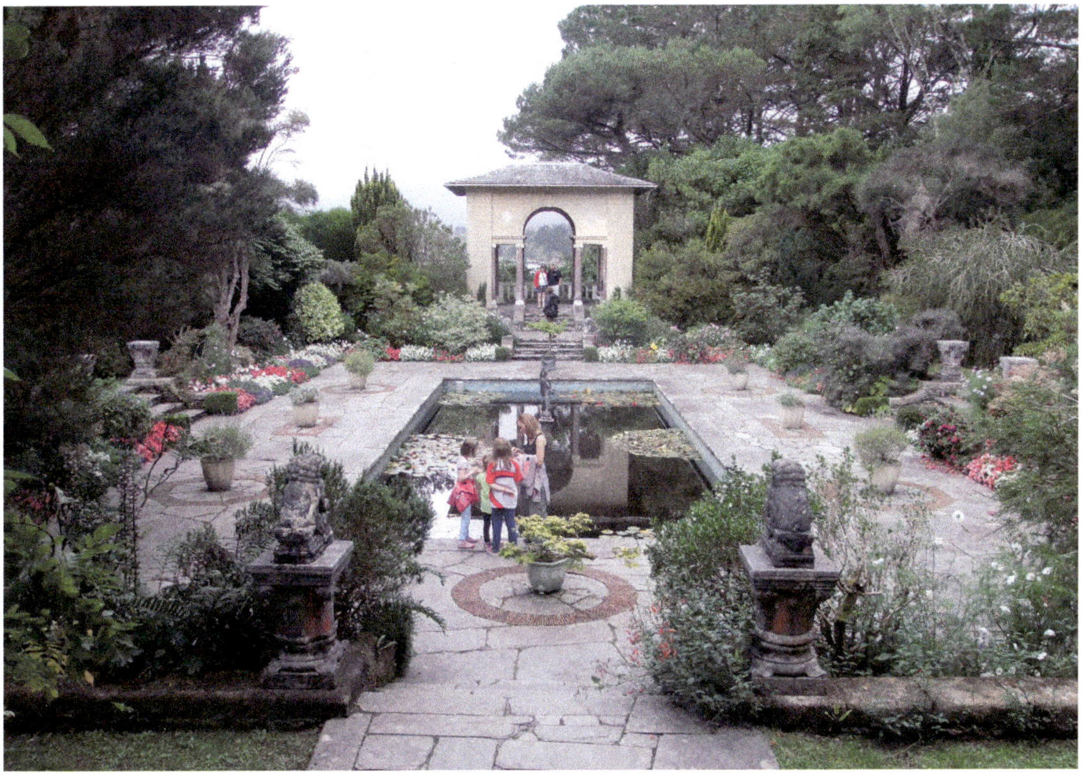

Garinish Island

Garinish Island is located in the sheltered harbour of Glengarriff. The island's official name on maps is *Ilnacullin* (island of holly). The island is 15 hectares (37 acres) in size. In 1910, John Annan Bryce MP, at the behest of his wife Violet, purchased Garinish Island from the British War Office, who had built a Martello tower on the island following the unsuccessful French invasion of 1796. The Bryces were guided by the eminent English architect and garden designer, Harold Peto, to develop the island into a world-renowned island garden of rare beauty.

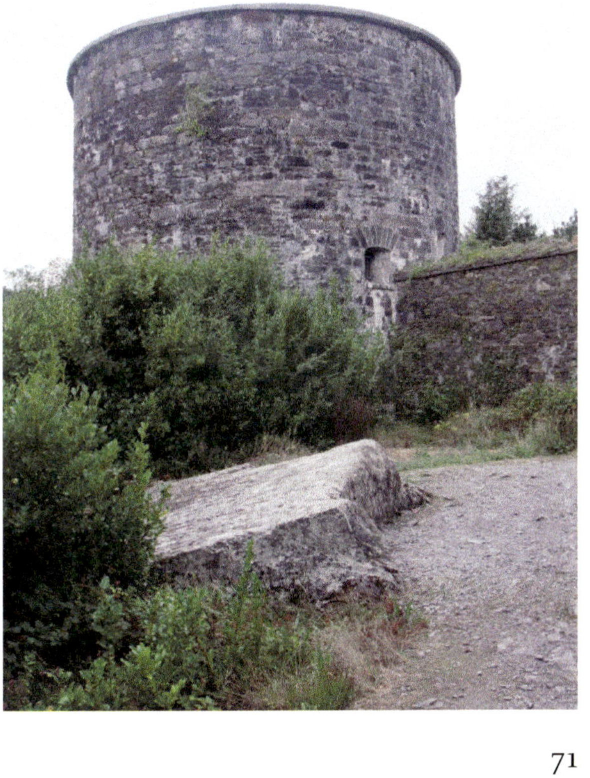

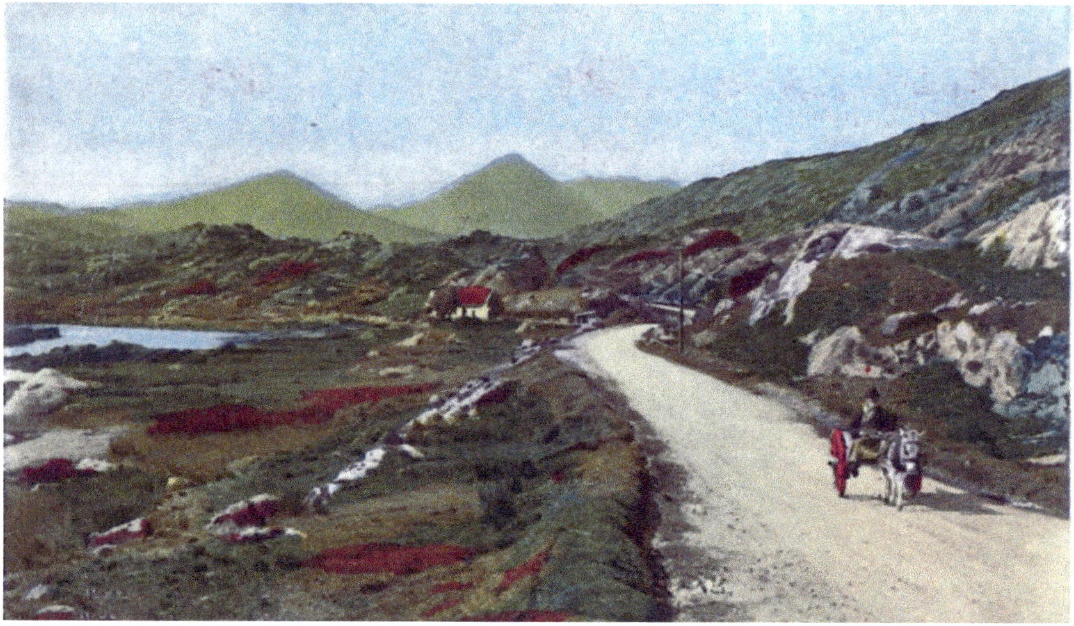

Glengarriff Mountain Road

'As we proceed the road for some distance is pleasantly diversified, but soon becomes by miniature lakes, streams, barren mountainous districts, and craggy precipices. The grandeur and beauty of this drive will justify the traveller in saying with a celebrated writer, that the attractions of Ireland are kept too silent – in fact, that there is a "conspiracy of silence" by which the loveliness of the island is kept away from tourists.' ('Glengarriff' section in *Guide to the Most Picturesque Tour of Western Europe,* 1898).

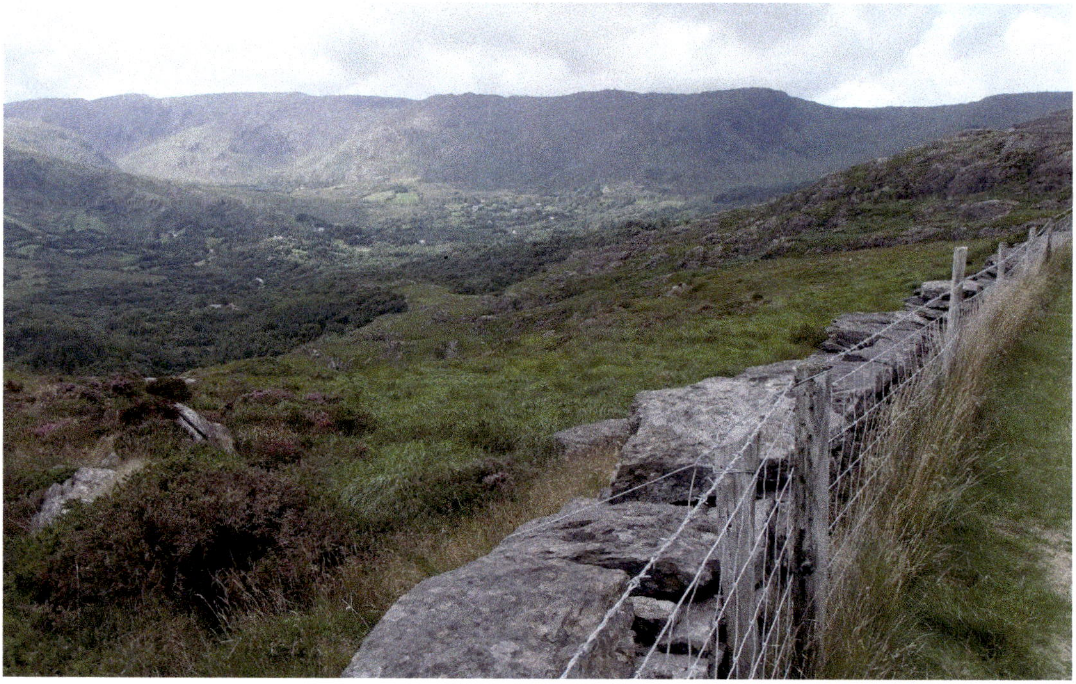

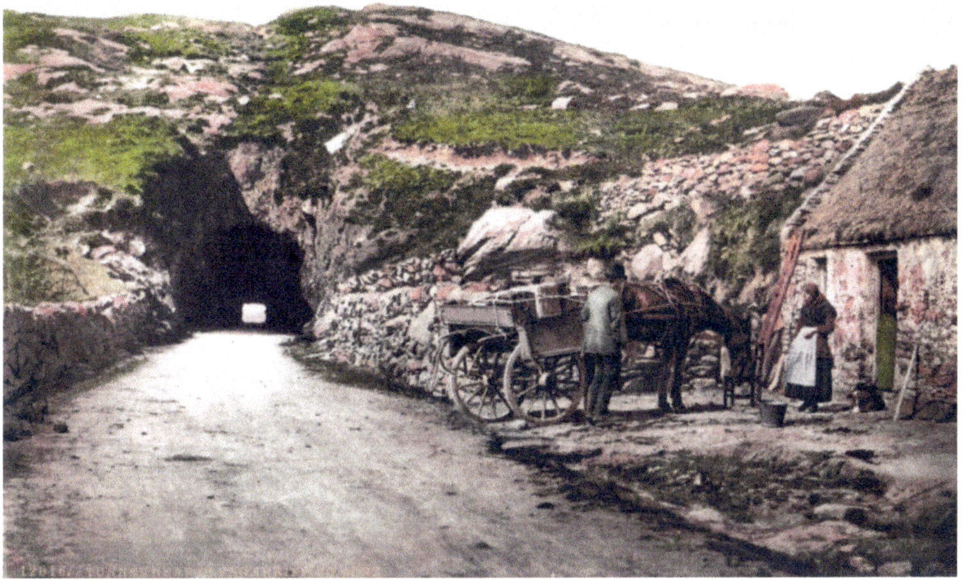

Turner's Tunnels, Glengarriff Tunnel

Turner's Tunnels on the N71 are a series of beautiful, hand-hewn rock tunnels. At a height of 1,200 feet, the main tunnel on the Cork-Kerry border is pictured above and is known as the Caha Pass. On the Kerry side, the main tunnel is followed by three more mini tunnels, a set of twin tunnels and a final short tunnel. These tunnels were constructed as a relief work following the great famine of 1847. It is also located at the border of County Cork and County Kerry. The ruins of the cottage on the right can still be viewed at the site today. It seems Turner was the local landowner at one time.

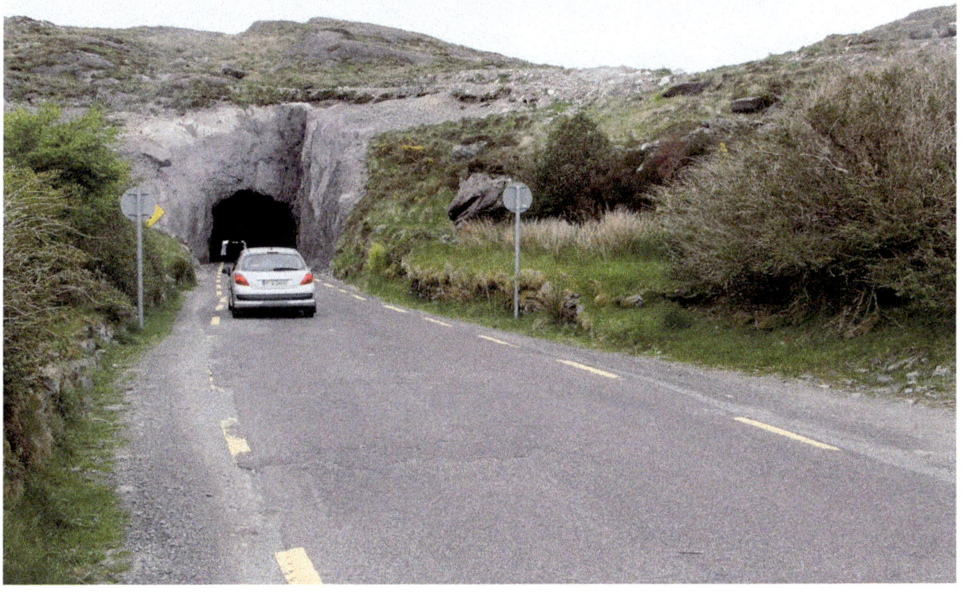

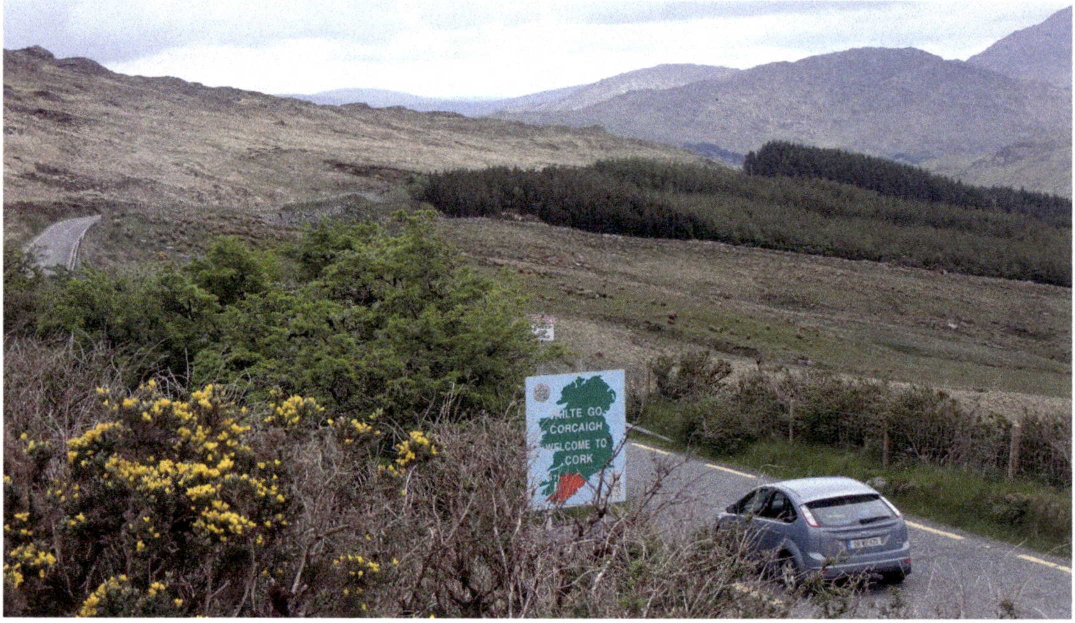

Caha Pass, the Borders of a County

Emerging from Turner's Tunnels, the visitor is welcomed to County Cork. Ahead is the vast expanse of Bantry Bay and the island-dotted harbour of Glengarriff. An account of the Guy's *Topographical Directory of County Cork* in 1897 describes the surface of the county as of considerable variety, from bold, rocky mountainous in the west to the richness and fertility of soils in the north and east. Being the largest county, Cork had 243 parishes and 5,473 townlands, with nearly 13 per cent under barren mountain lands. The house at the tunnel was a typical labourer's cottage 100 years ago with stone walls and a thatched roof.

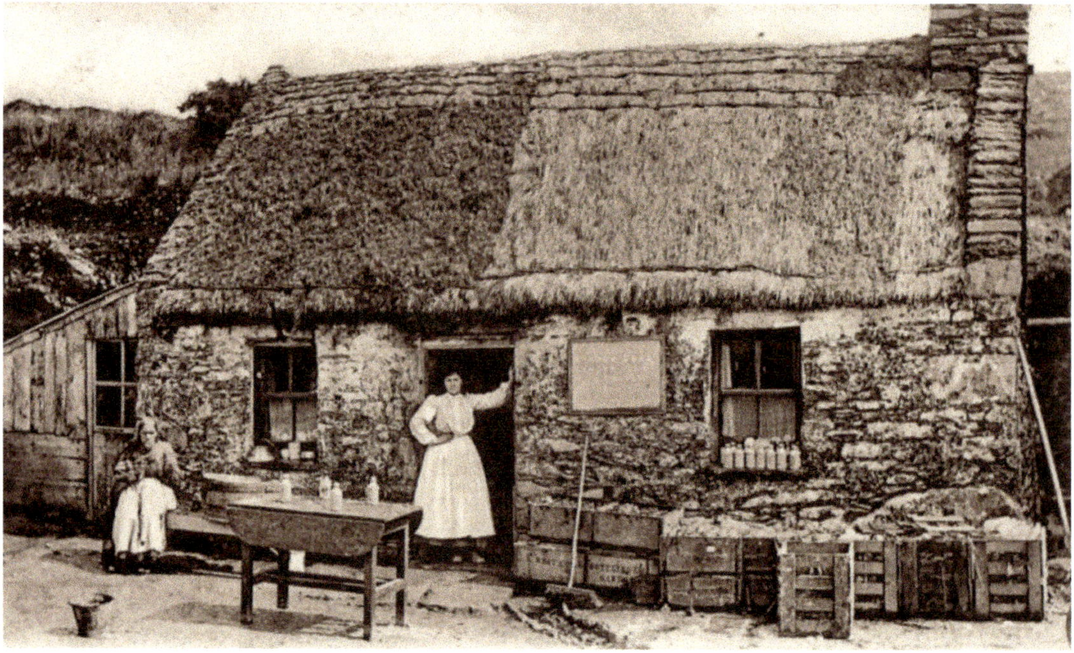

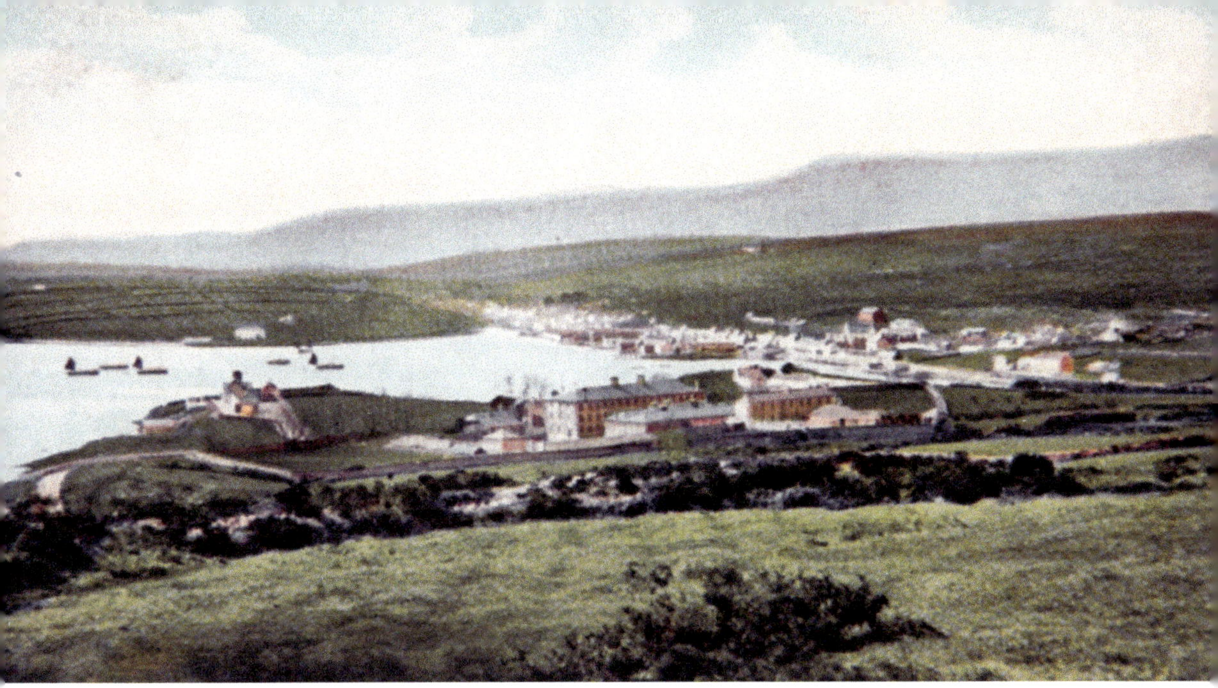

Castletownbere Haven

During his travels in 1750 in County Cork's most westerly peninsula, Beara, Charles Smith wrote that Castletown, alias Castledermot, is a 'small village of little note, opposite to the island of Berehaven'. In 1758, Pococke, who travelled by sea from Bantry to Berehaven Harbour, wrote: 'There is no village at this harbour, only small houses.' The large British military and naval base on Bere Island during the early decades of the 1900s, and especially during the First World War, provided a period of economic prosperity in Castletownbere. In the picture above, navy vessels in the harbour are shown, as well as a workhouse in the centre.

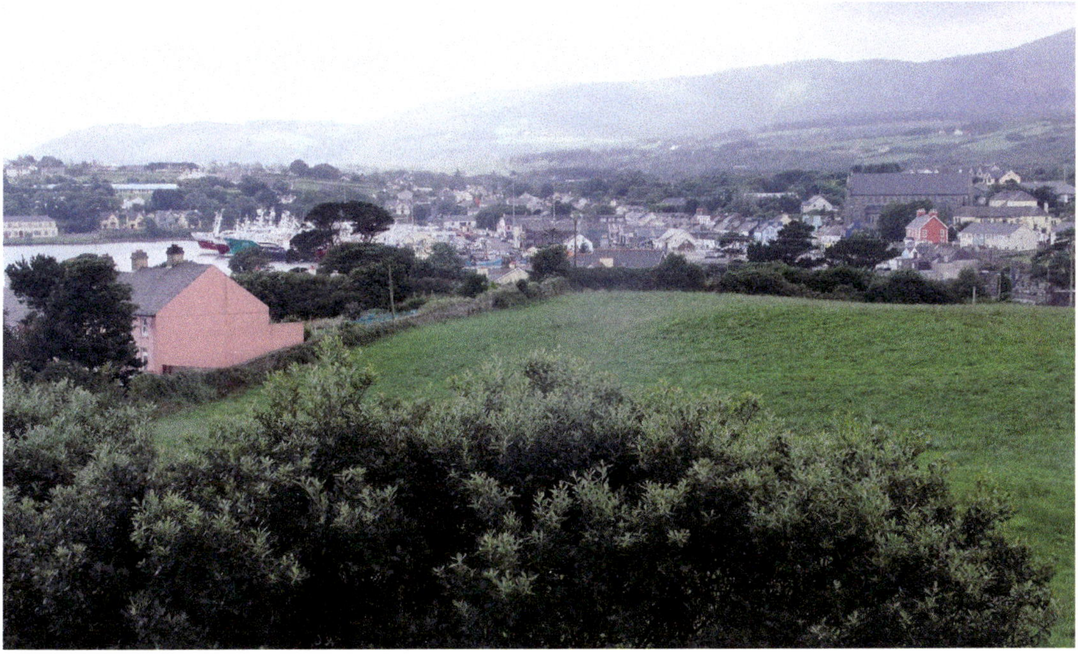

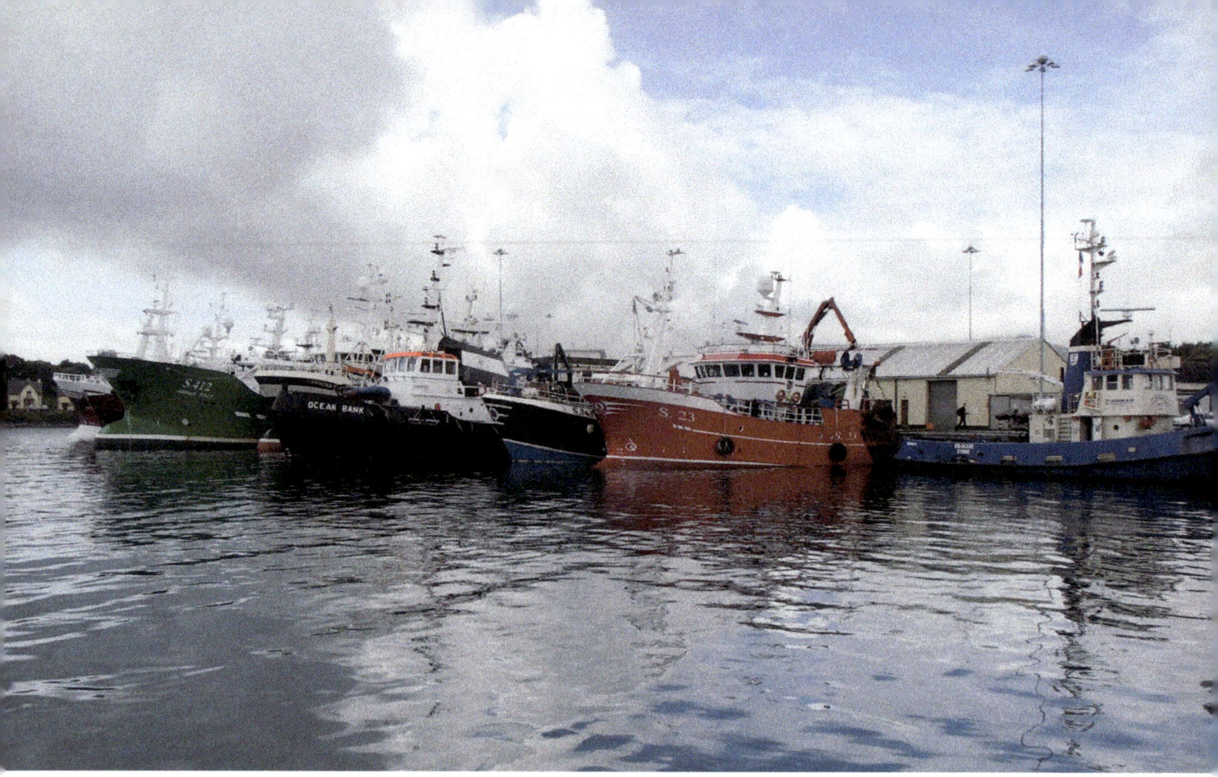

Coastguard Station, Castletownbere

During the second half of the 1800s, the Beara Bay Hotel, including the terrace of houses on its west side, was sold for use as a coastguard station. By 1910, a new coastguard station was built where St Joseph's Hospital is now. In the 1960s, Castletownbere Harbour was developed as the major fishing port for south-west Ireland. Fish processing factories provided much-needed employment along the shore, as viewed above, and these eliminated the view in the old picture below.

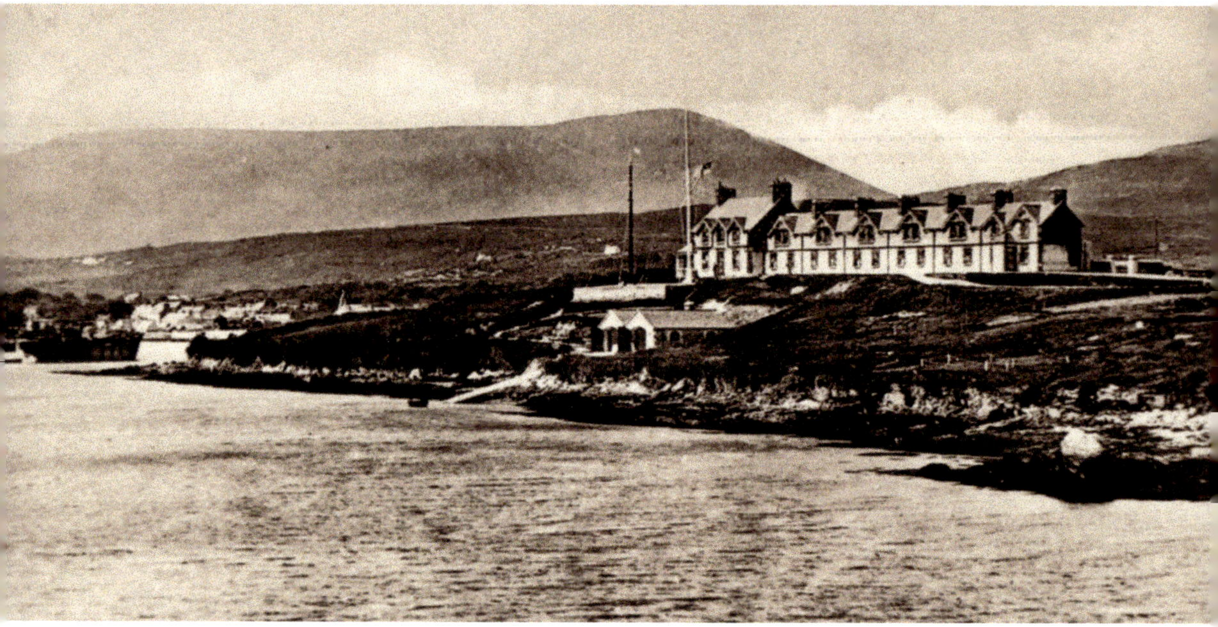

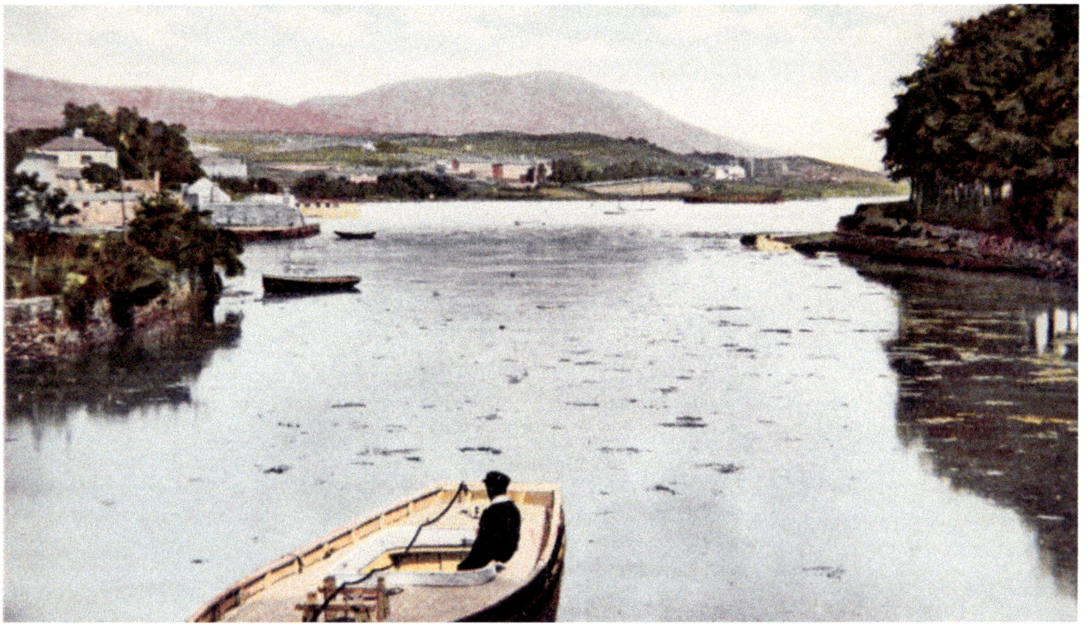

Castletownbere Haven

Castletownbere is known for the diverse range and top quality of its fish, not just in Ireland but throughout Europe. The Slieve Miskish and Caha Mountain ranges of the Beara Peninsula tower over the area, providing a dramatic backdrop. The Beara Peninsula is some 45 km long and 15 km wide at its widest point. It is surrounded by the crystal-clear waters of the Atlantic, and is lapped by the warm waters of the Gulf Stream during the summer months.

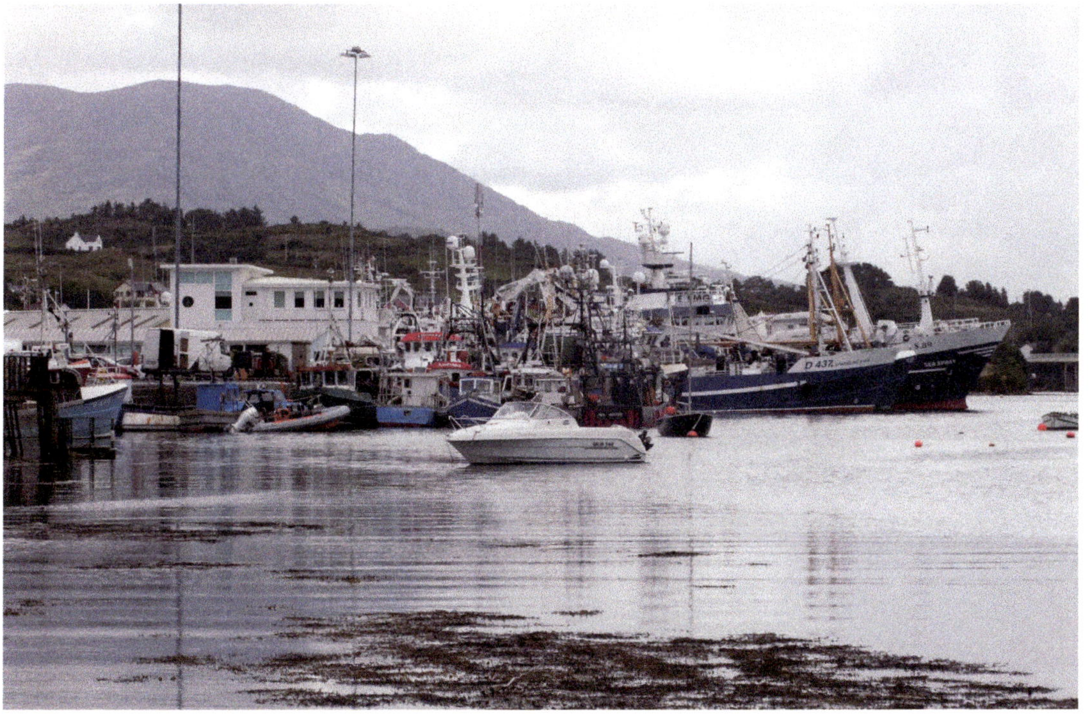

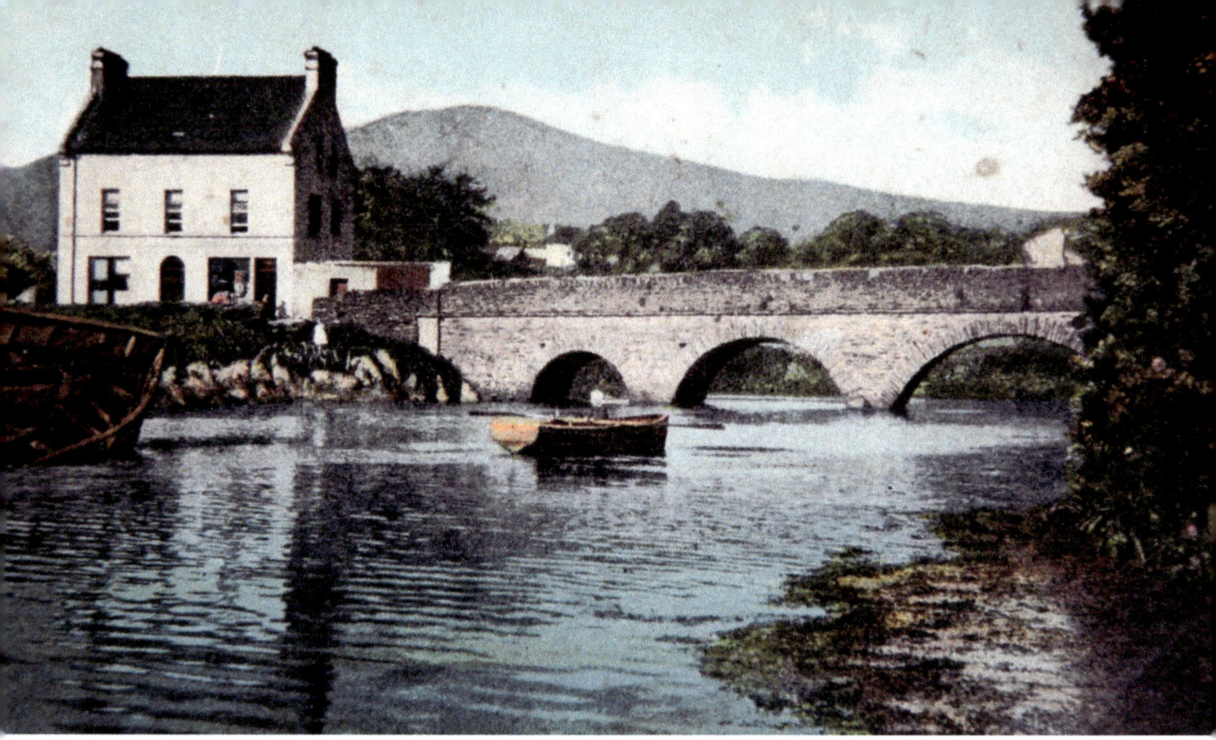

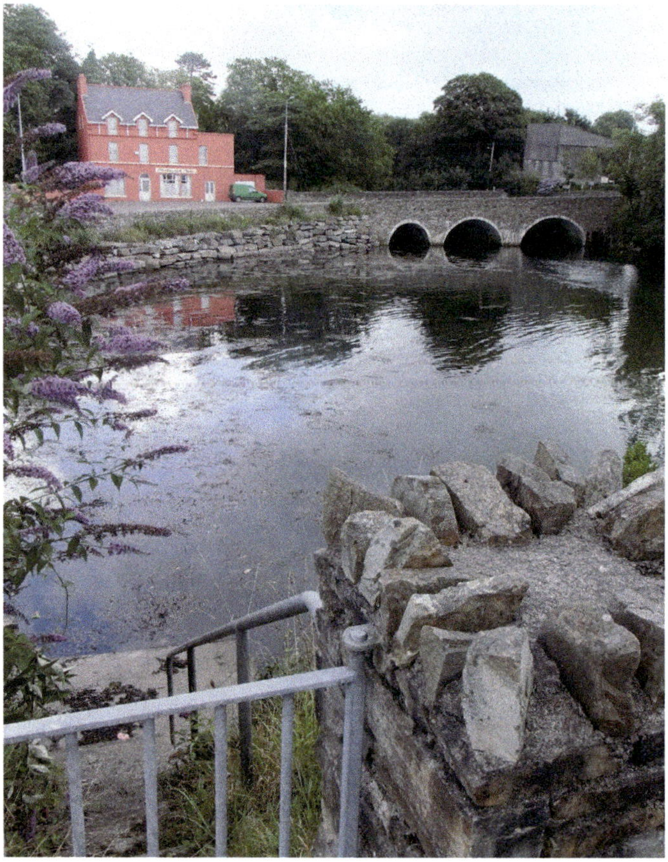

An Epic March, Castletownbere, Bridge

A plaque at the site of this photograph highlights the history of the O'Sullivan family. Donal Cam was the last independent ruler of the O'Sullivan Beara clan in the wake of English attempts to secure rule over the whole of Ireland. Following defeat in the Battle of Kinsale in 1601, Donal Cam made the decision to withdraw from his lands and undertake an epic march to Breifine, County Leitrim. Donal and his family sailed for Spain to settle in 1604. He was killed by a servant in 1618 and is buried in Coruna in northern Spain.

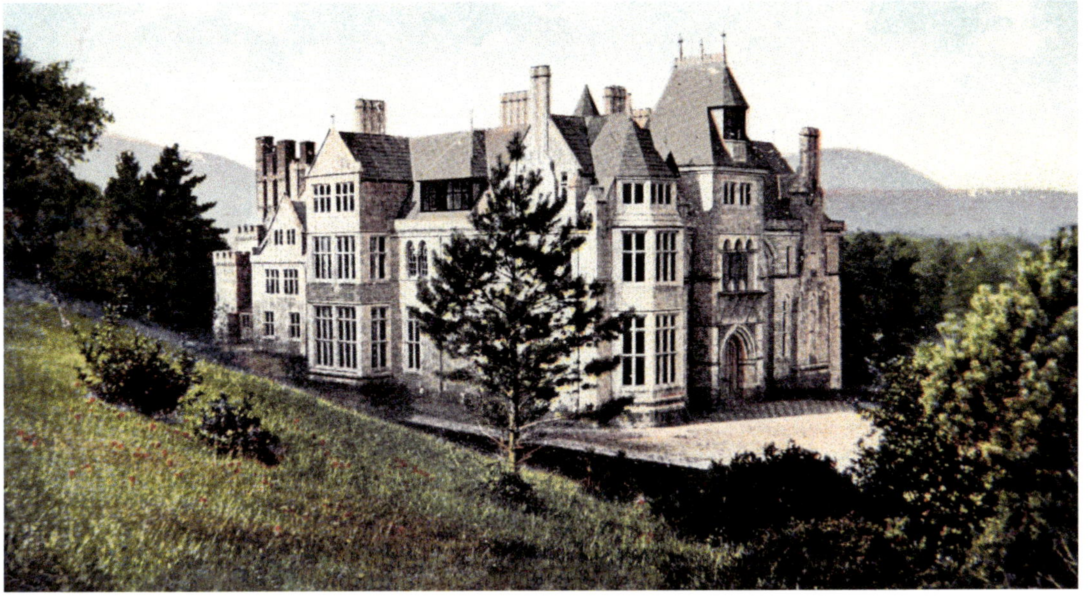

Puxley's Castle

The big house at Dunboy was built by Henry and John Puxley in 1739, the family having been granted the lands previously belonging to the O'Sullivan clan. The family prospered thanks to smuggling and nearby copper mining in Allihies. In 1866 their descendant, Henry Lavallin Puxley, began extensive alterations to the castle. However, Henry's beloved wife died in 1872, and he was so devastated by her death that he left Ireland, never to return. The house was never properly finished and even in recent times, despite renovations during Ireland's economic boom (*below*), the idea for a hotel on the site has never materialised.

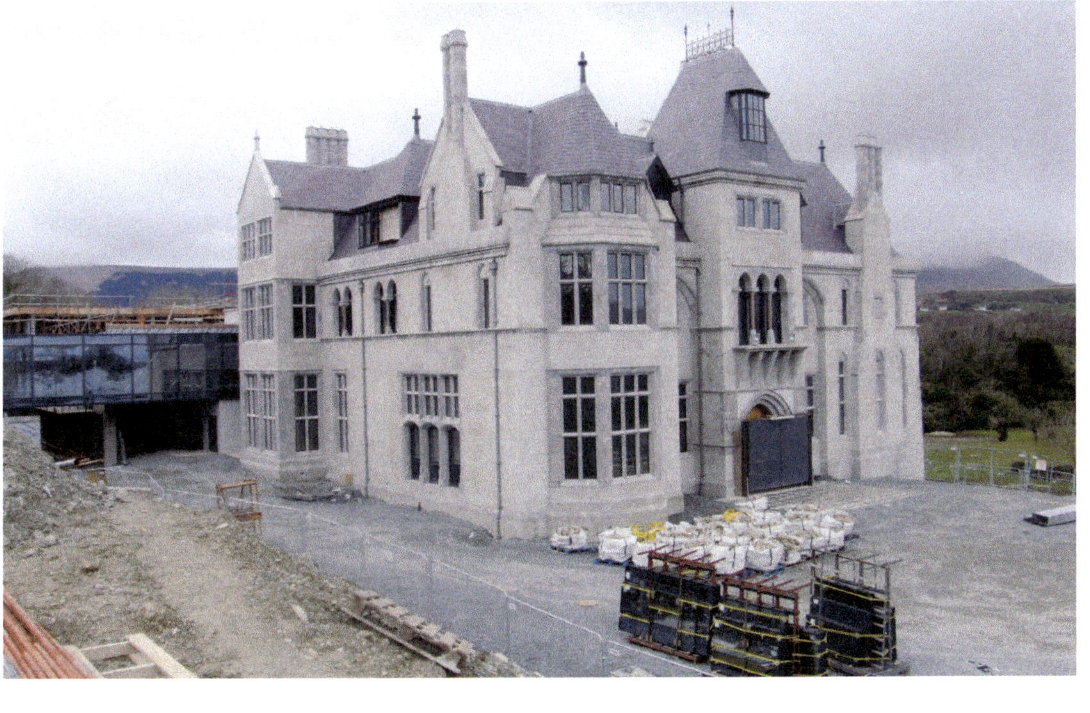

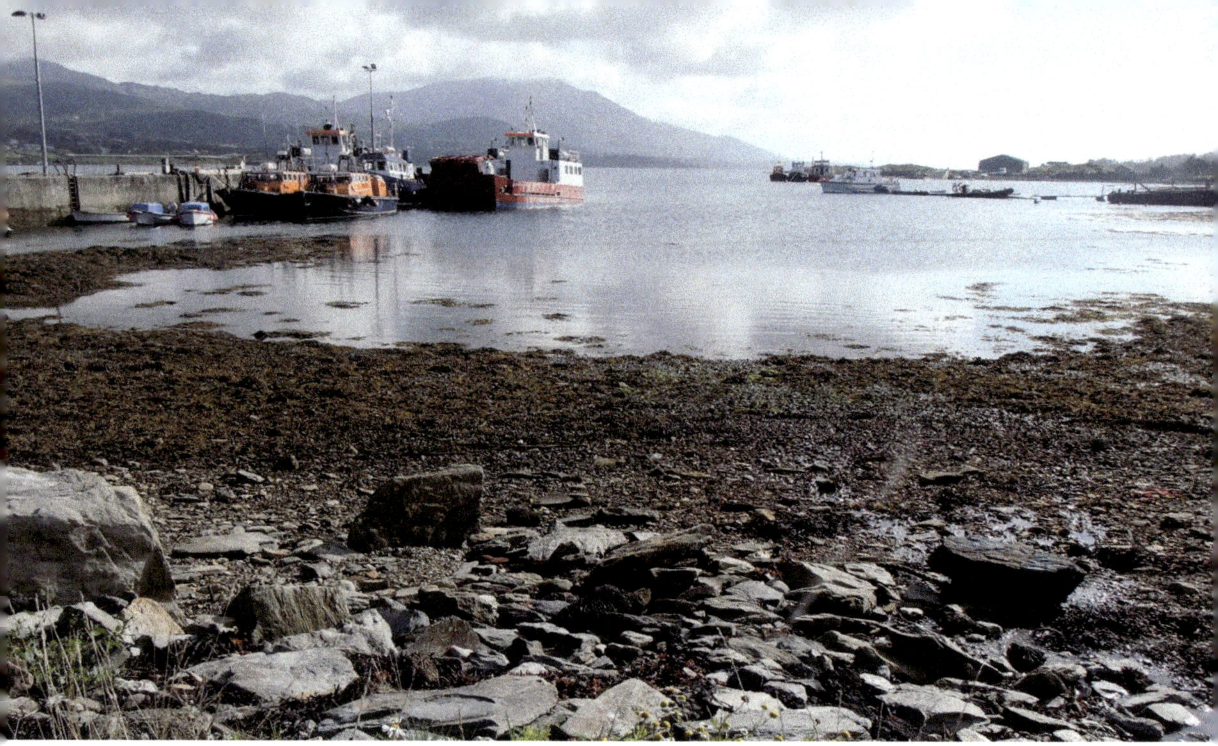

Ferry at Bere Island

Bere Island is roughly 11 km by 5 km in size and has a population of 200. It is just 2 km offshore from the town of Castletownbere. Two ferries service two locations on the island. The island is rich in archaeological sites, dating from the Bronze Age through to medieval times, including ring forts, standing stones and wedge tombs. The British Navy constructed Martello towers, a signal tower, military barracks and a military fortification on it, some of which can be explored up close.

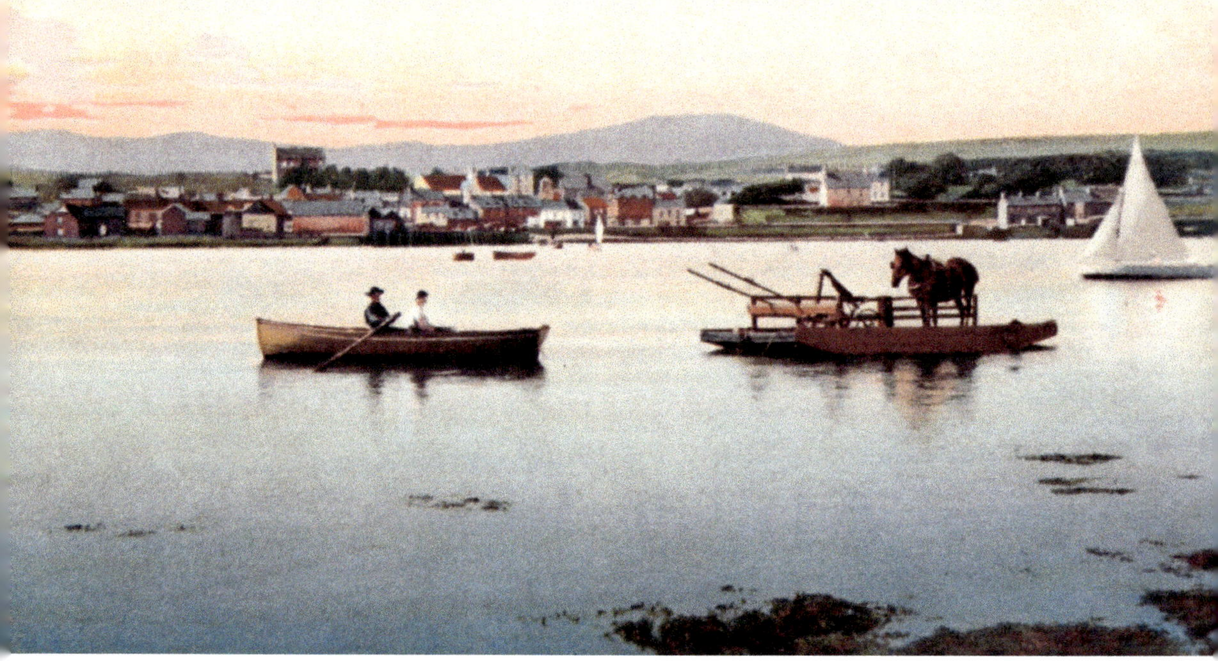

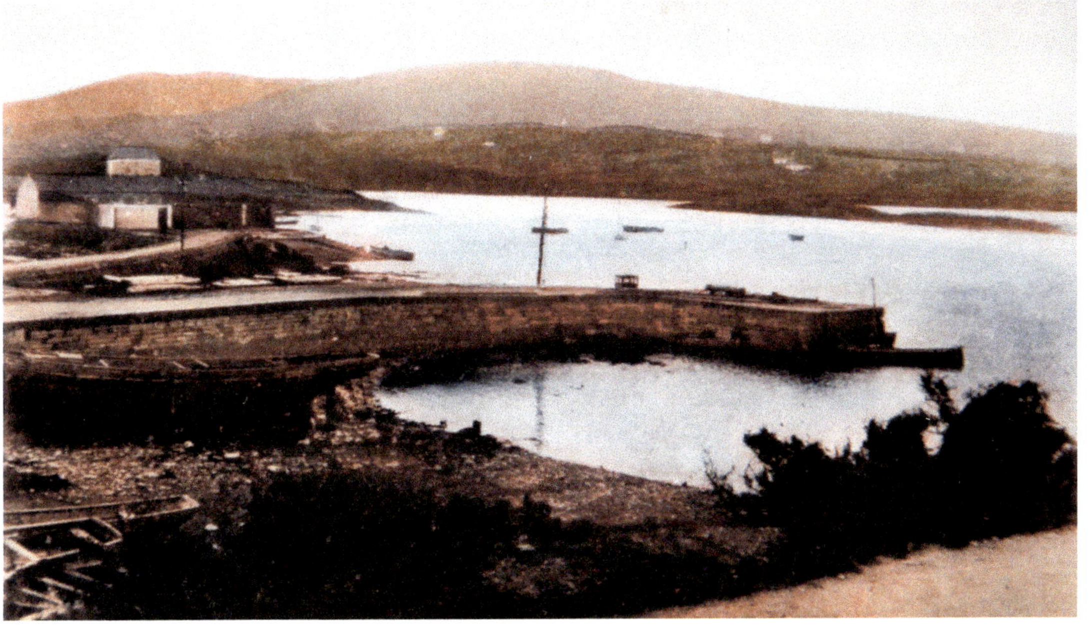

Lawrence Cove, Bere Island

The construction of the stone pier at Lawrence Cove commenced in 1797, just a year after an attempted French invasion of the south coast of Ireland. It was the first construction work to be carried out by the British Navy on the island. In recent years, the pier has served the needs of locals and the Irish army who have a training station at Lonehort Battery. Near the pier is a new, modern marina area – run by the Harrington family – for boats and yachts visiting the island during the summer season (*inset*).

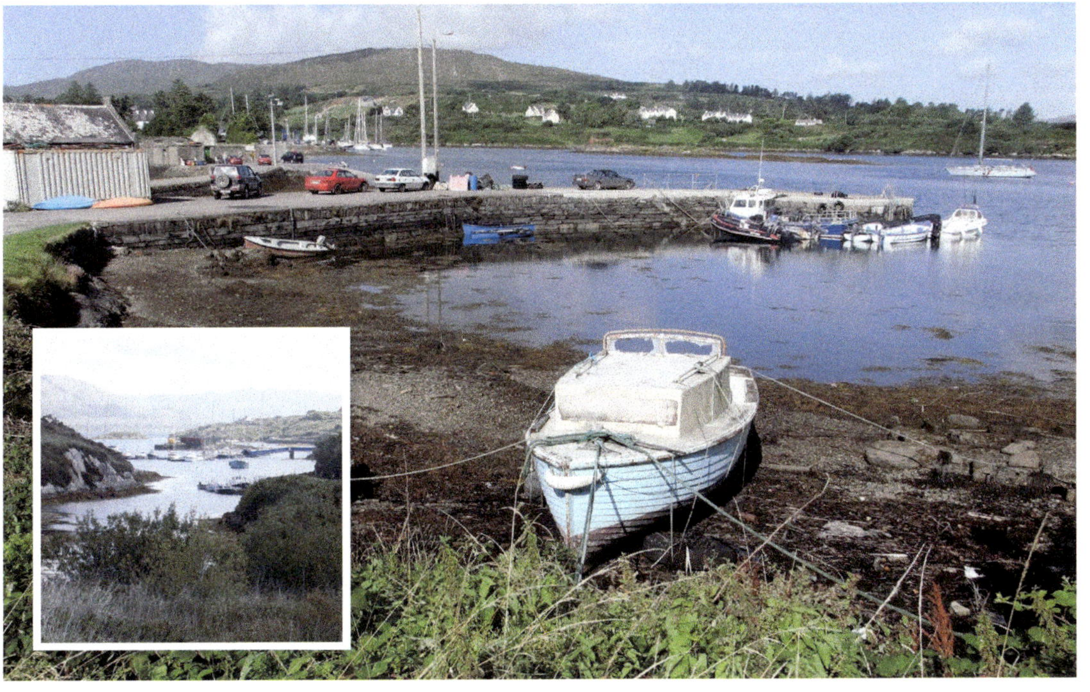

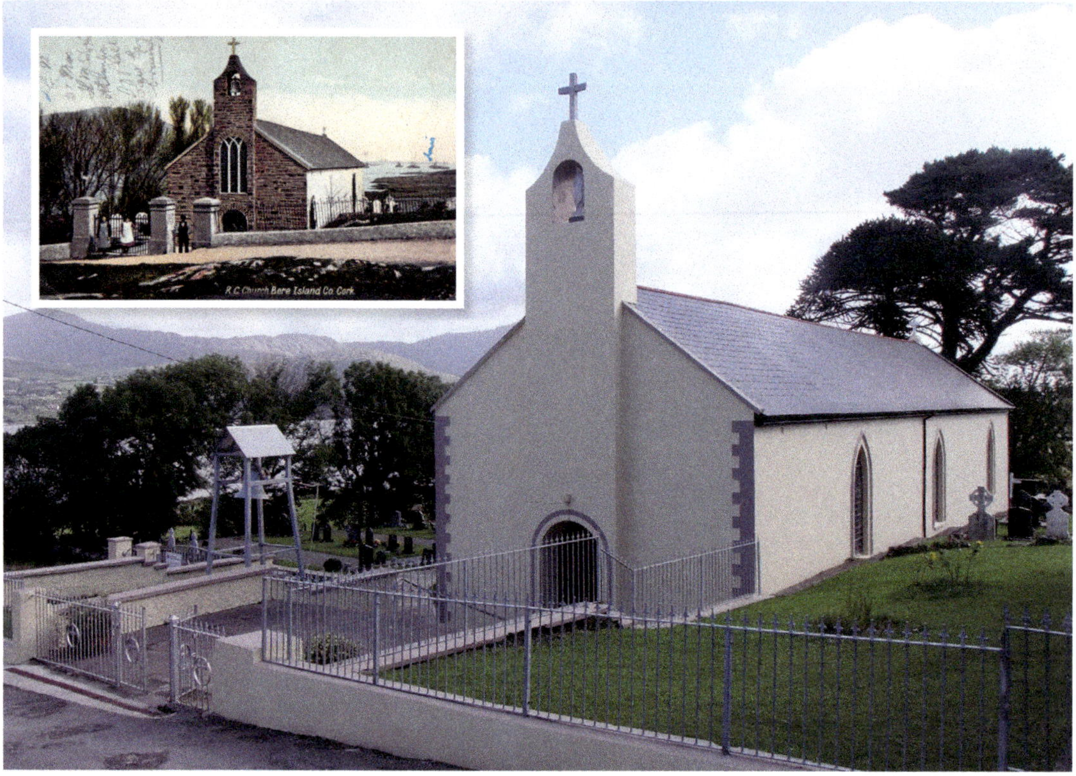

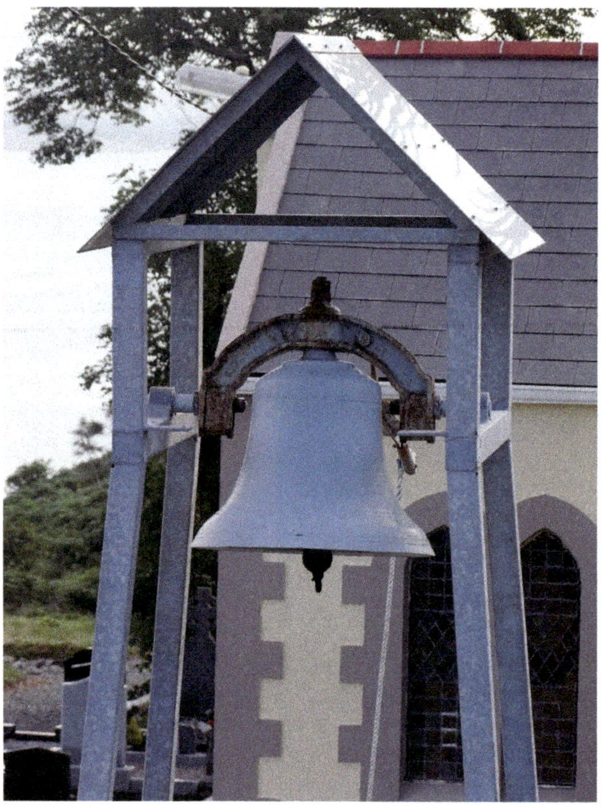

St Michael's Church, Bere Island

Bere Island's church was built in 1843, and enlarged in 1900. The graveyard hosts Catholic, Protestant, Irish and English graves, including some British military graves. The old church bell stands adjacent the church. St Michael is Bere Island's patron saint and devotions, or a 'pattern', were held here annually on the nearest Sunday to his feast day.

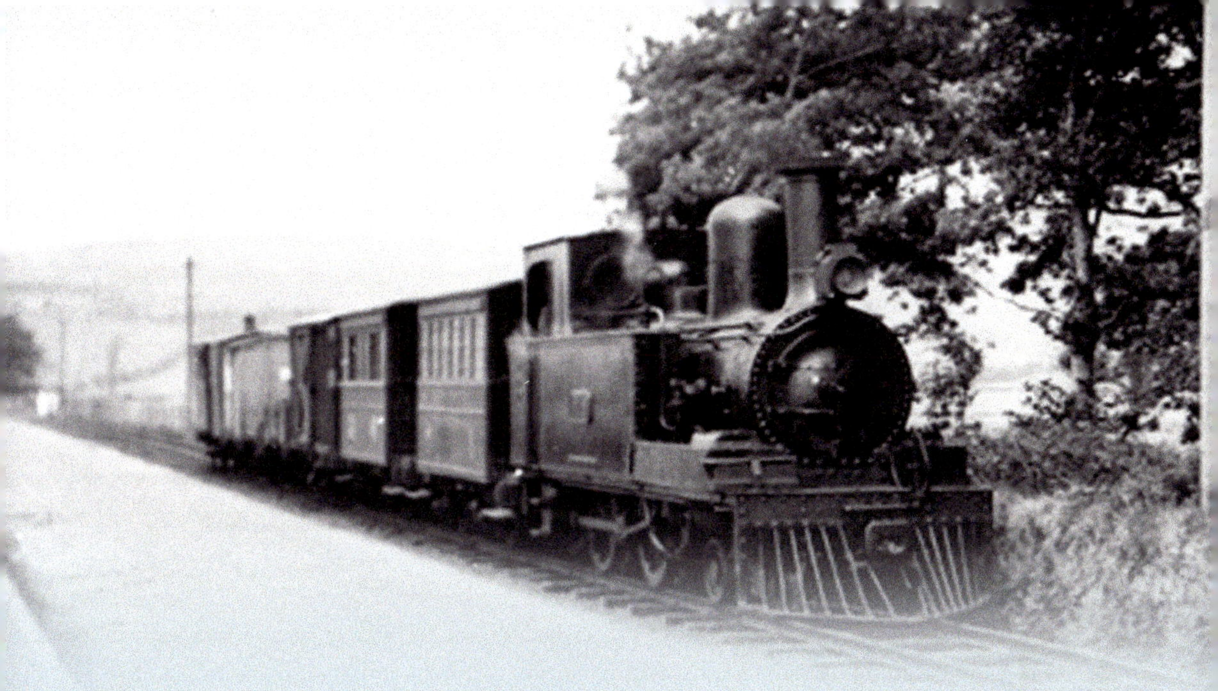

CHAPTER 5

Railway Ventures – A Tracked History

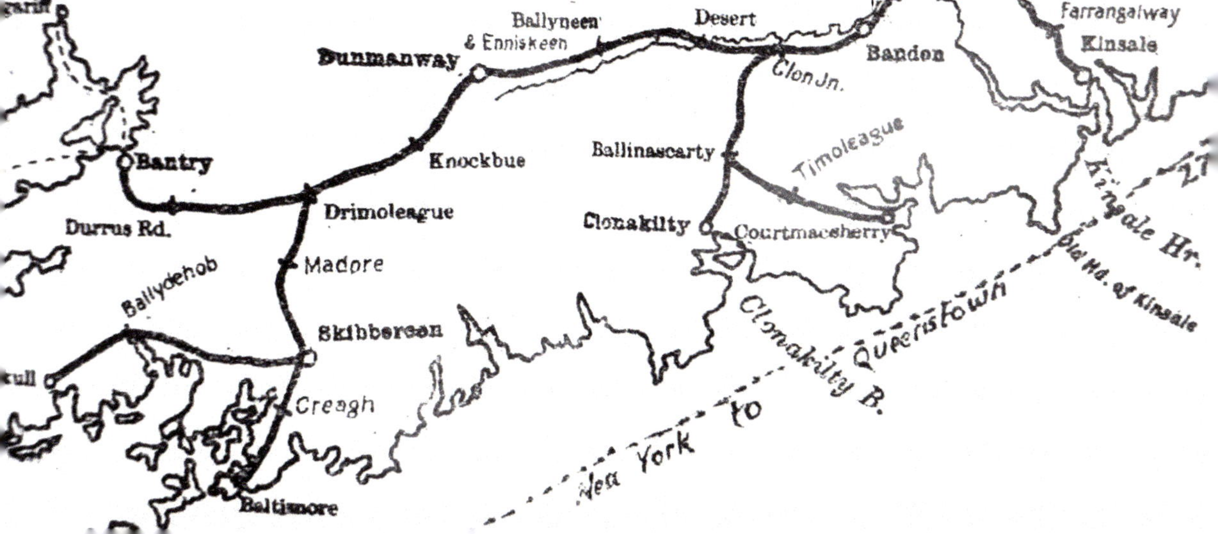

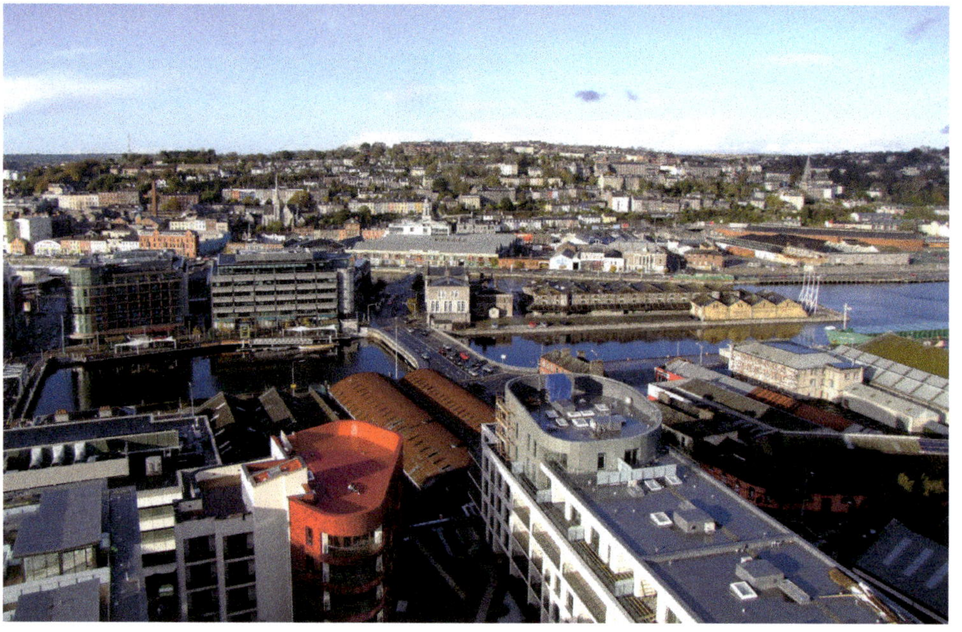

Albert Quay Terminus

Providing access between West Cork and Cork City for the general public, including visitors and farmers, was the Cork, Bandon and South Coast Railway line. The Cork to Bandon line opened to the public on 6 December 1851. The Cork terminus was on Albert Quay, which had three passenger platforms, a carriage storage area, and sidings into the Cork Corporation's stone yard and the corn market. Feeder lines were also added in the early twentieth century to the roller-milling complex on Victoria Quay and to the Ford tractor works on Cork's marina. Today, Ireland's tallest building, the Elysian tower, occupies the railway yards. The picture above is taken from the top of the Elysian.

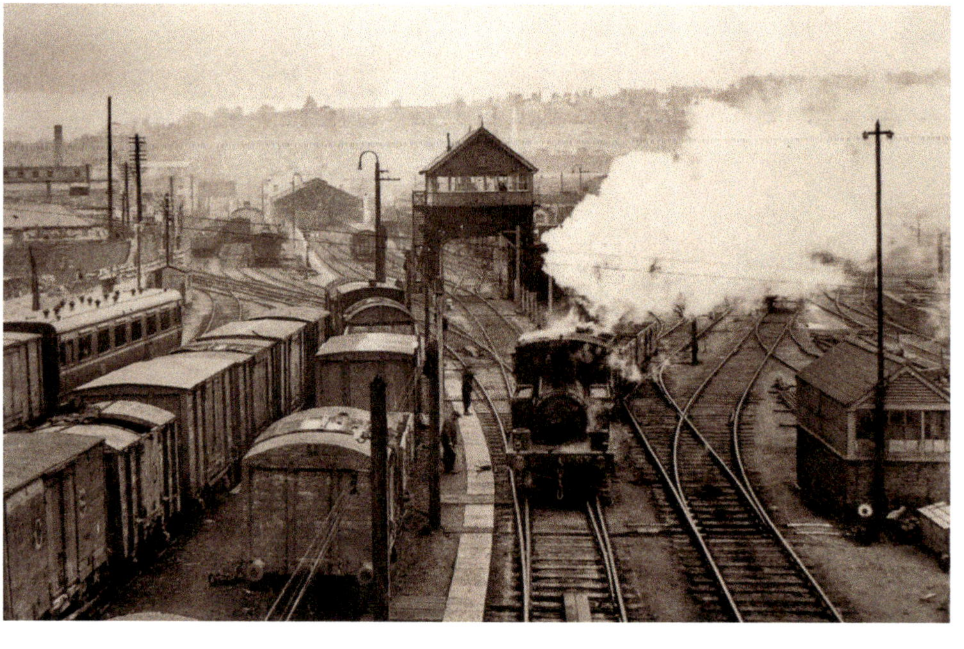

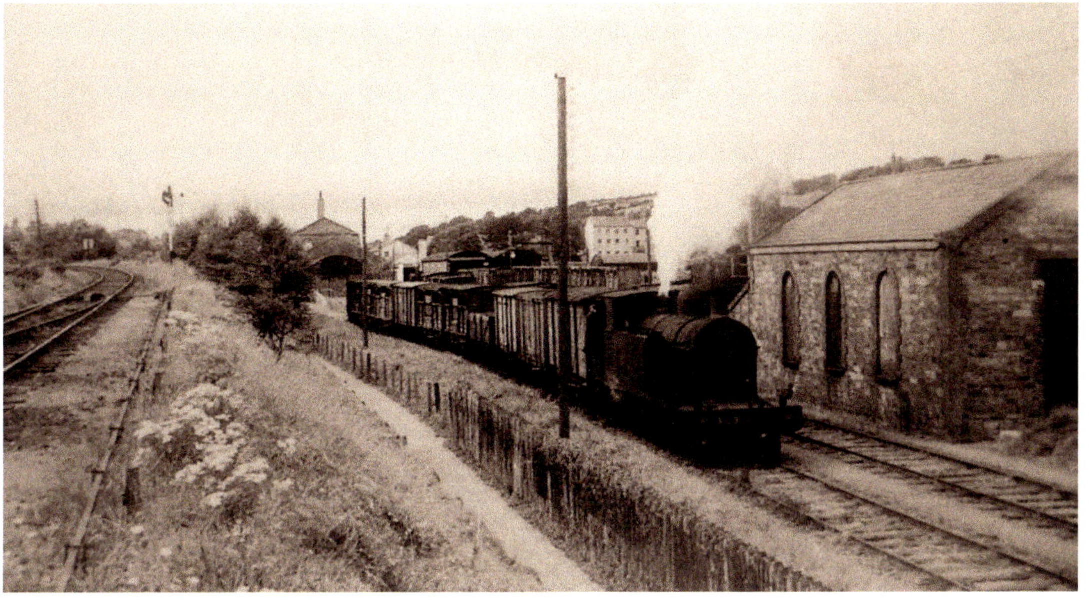

Bandon Terminus

The Cork to Bandon Railway project was an enormous undertaking. The main parts included the longest railway tunnel in Ireland at Goggins Hill, the Chetwynd Viaduct, a short tunnel bridge under old Blackrock Road near the Albert Quay terminus, twenty-one cuttings, nineteen embankments and fifteen road bridges. The Bandon terminus is now the offices of the Bandon Urban District Council.

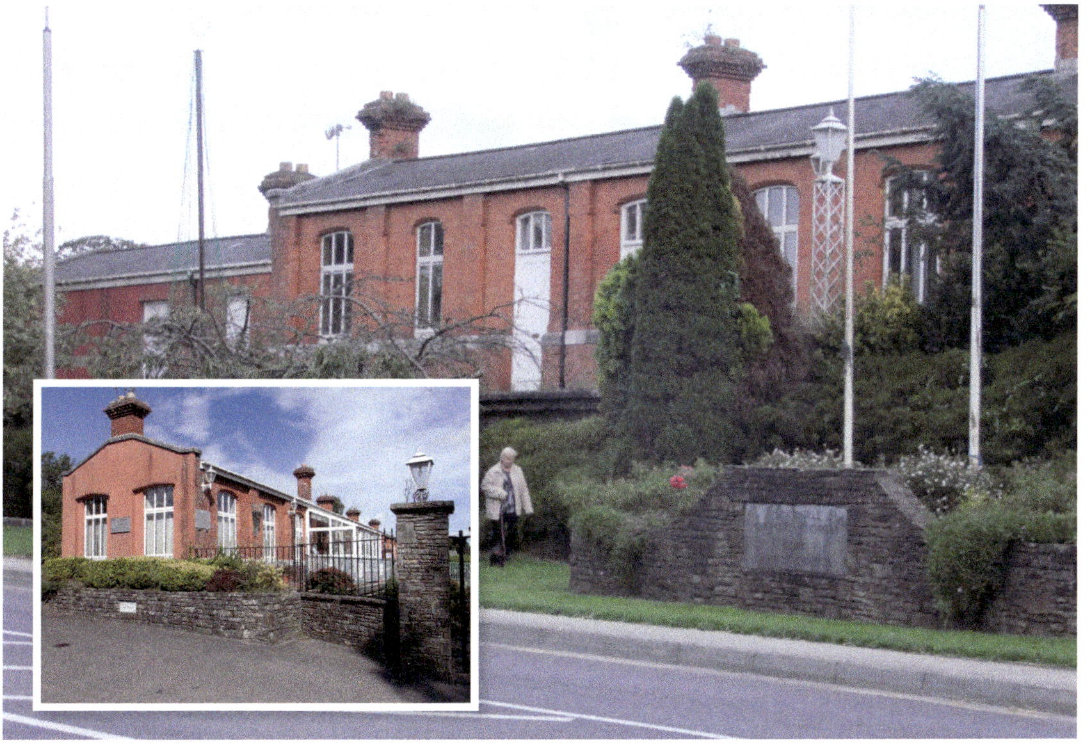

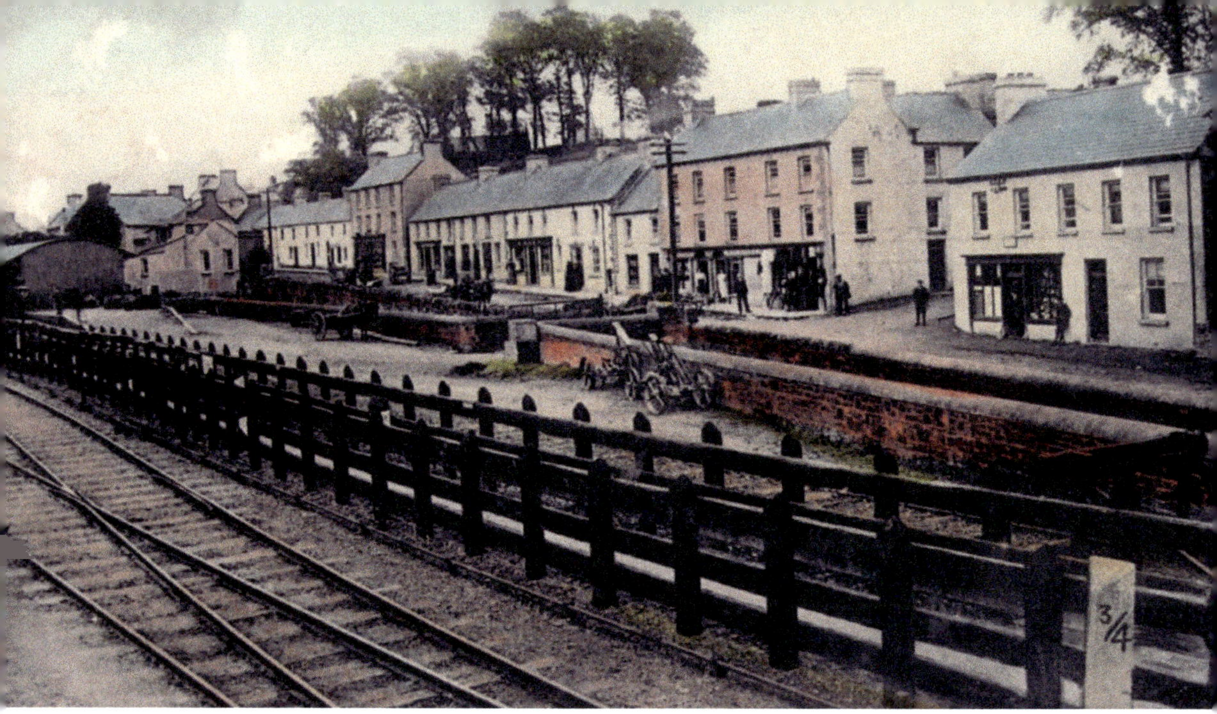

Drimoleague Terminus

Between 1852 and 1894, a further twenty-five engines were acquired by the railway company. Between 1851 and 1893, the mileage of the West Cork line extended from 25 to 94 miles. Many West Cork towns gained their own railway stations: Kinsale (1863), Clonakilty (1866), Dunmanway (1866), Drimoleague (1877), Skibbereen (1877), Bantry (1881), Timoleague & Courtmacsherry (1890), Bantry Bay (1892), and Baltimore (1893). Several of the stations and platforms, such as those in Drimoleague, have survived since the line's closure in 1961 (due to faster modes of travel such as buses and cars).

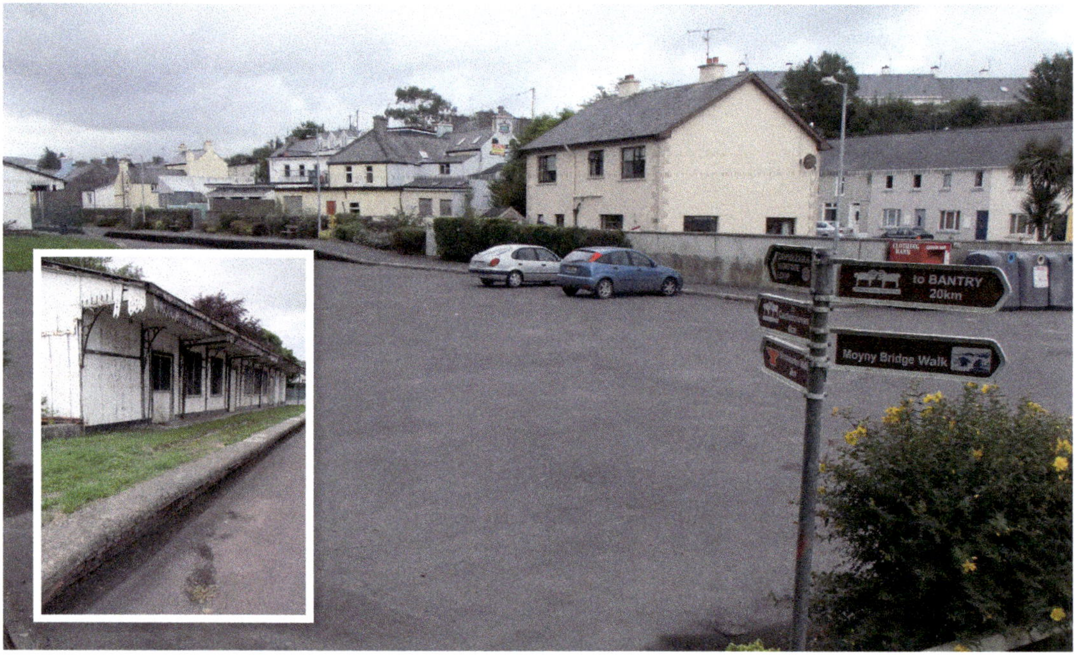

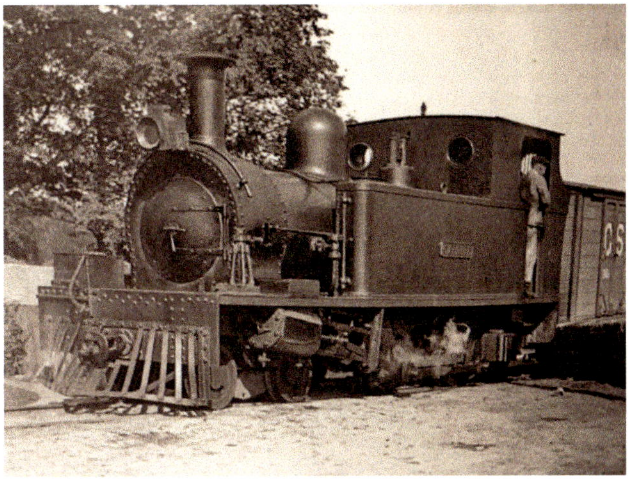

Skibbereen Station

Opened in 1886, the Skibbereen to Schull line had numerous problems, both geological and mechanical. The terrain was a constant problem. The gradients and rough land meant that locomotives could only pull three or four times their own weight. This meant that engines like the 'Gabriel' (*above*), named after a mountain to the north of Schull, which started work in 1906, could only attain a maximum speed of 15 mph. The viaduct (*centre*) can be seen next to the remnants of the Skibbereen station (*below*).

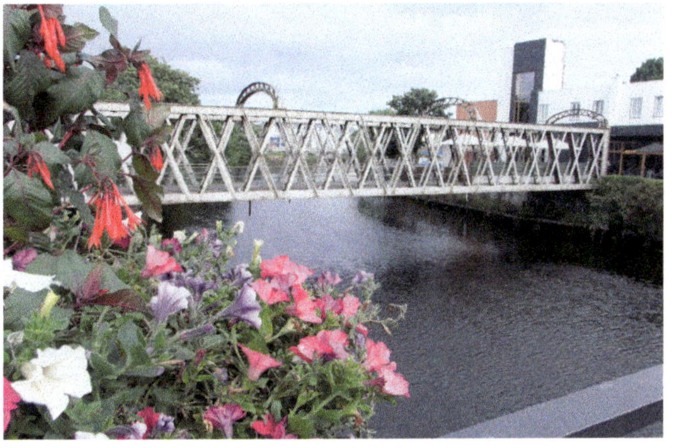

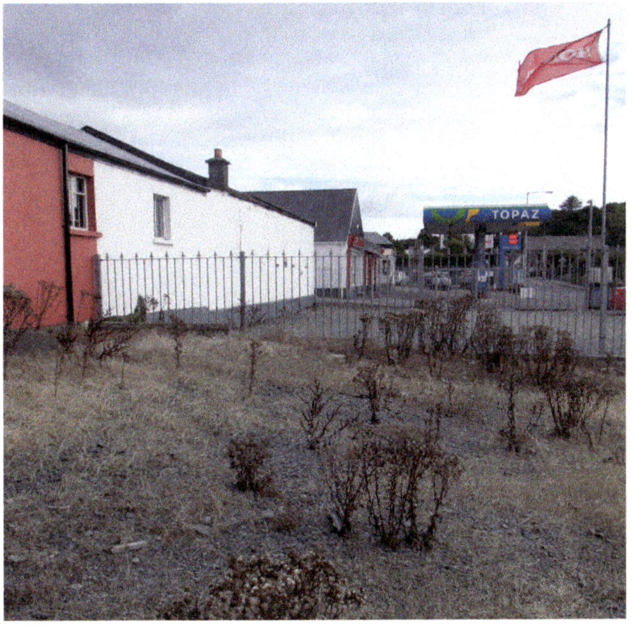

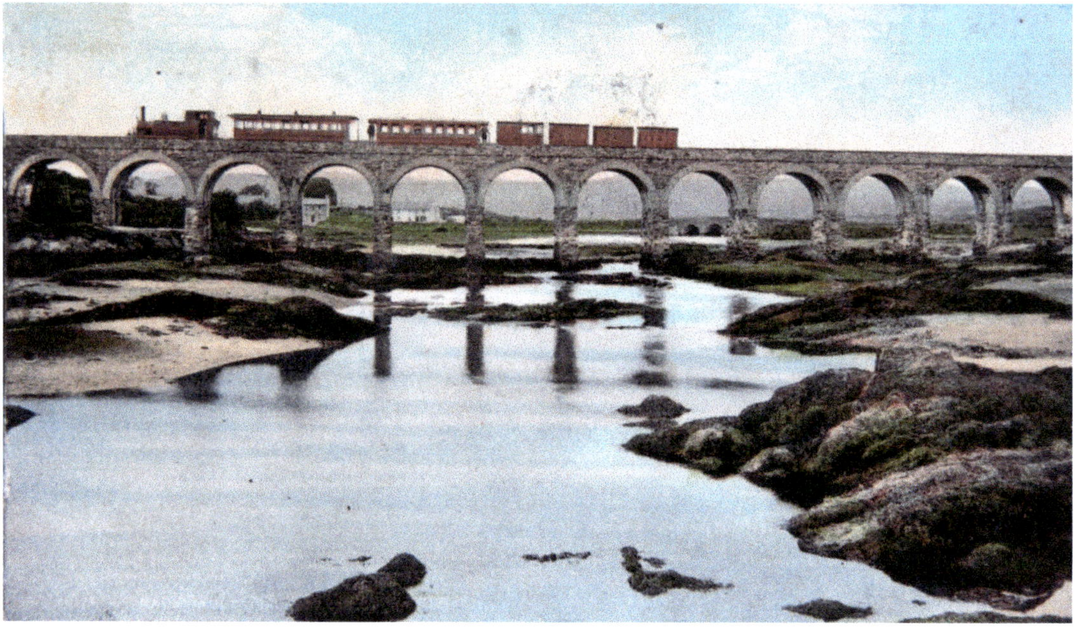

Viaduct, Ballydehob

The Skibbereen and Schull Light Tramway ran beside the main road from Skibbereen to Schull and westward through Ballydehob – a distance of 15 miles. At Roaring Water Bay, the inlet is spanned by an impressive twelve-arch viaduct, which is the only major engineering work on the line. In the picture above, a Schull-bound train has been stopped especially for the photographer. The train comprises 'Gabriel', coaches and vans. 'Gabriel' is known for being christened by the parish priest in 1906 with the help of a bottle of champagne.

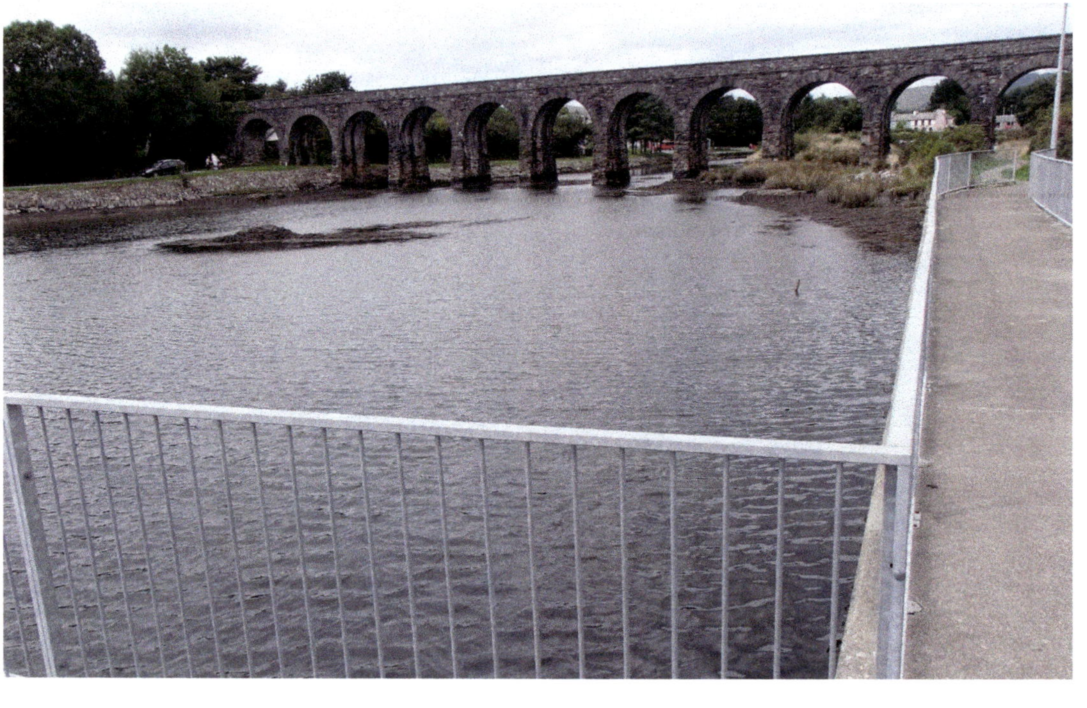

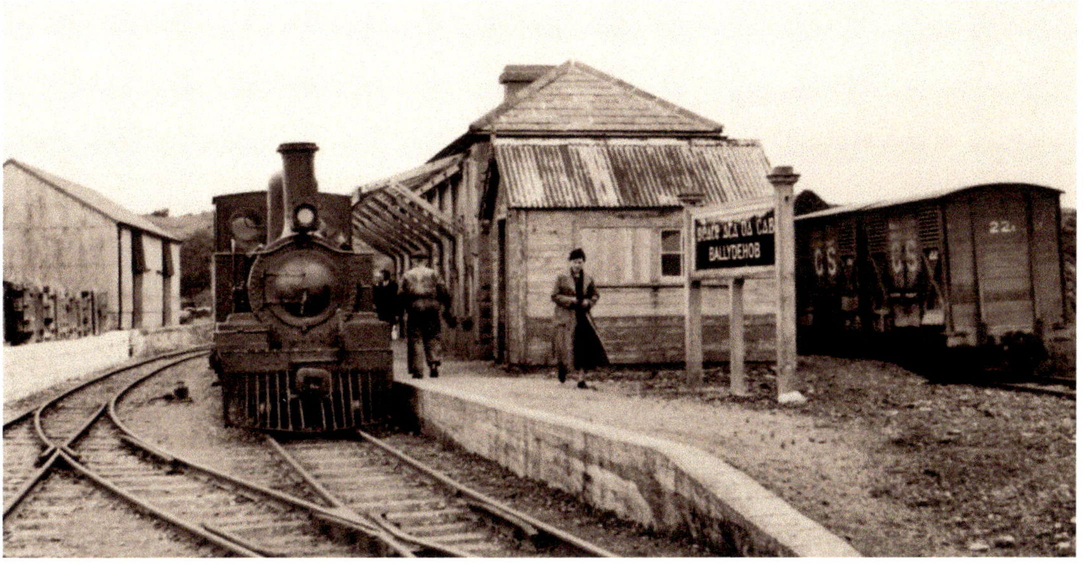

Ballydehob Train

Ballydehob was 9 miles by track from Skibbereen. Due to the contours of the landscape and the need to serve passengers and the farming community, the train was rarely on time and never really stuck to advertised times. The station had the only intermediate passing loop on the line, which can be viewed in the picture above. Apart from the goods sheds, some of which survive, the stationmaster's house is now a private residence. The water tank for locomotives, which stood at the west end of the platform, was fed from a local spring. A view from the viaduct into the former station site can be viewed in the inset.

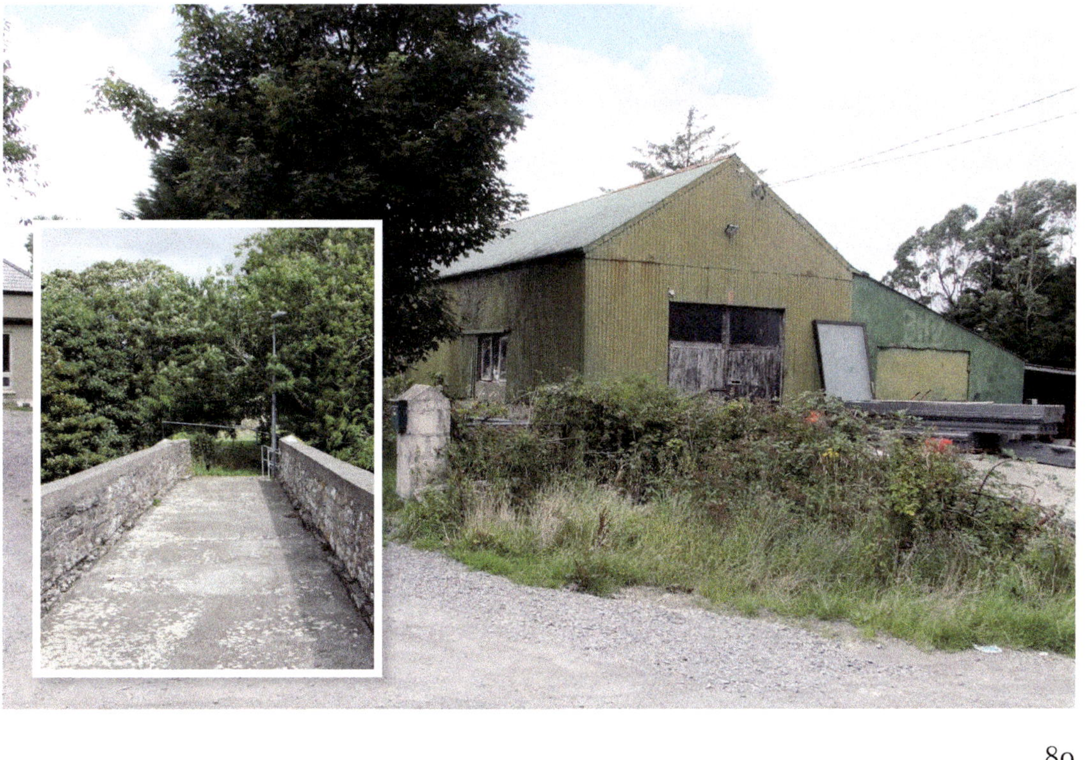

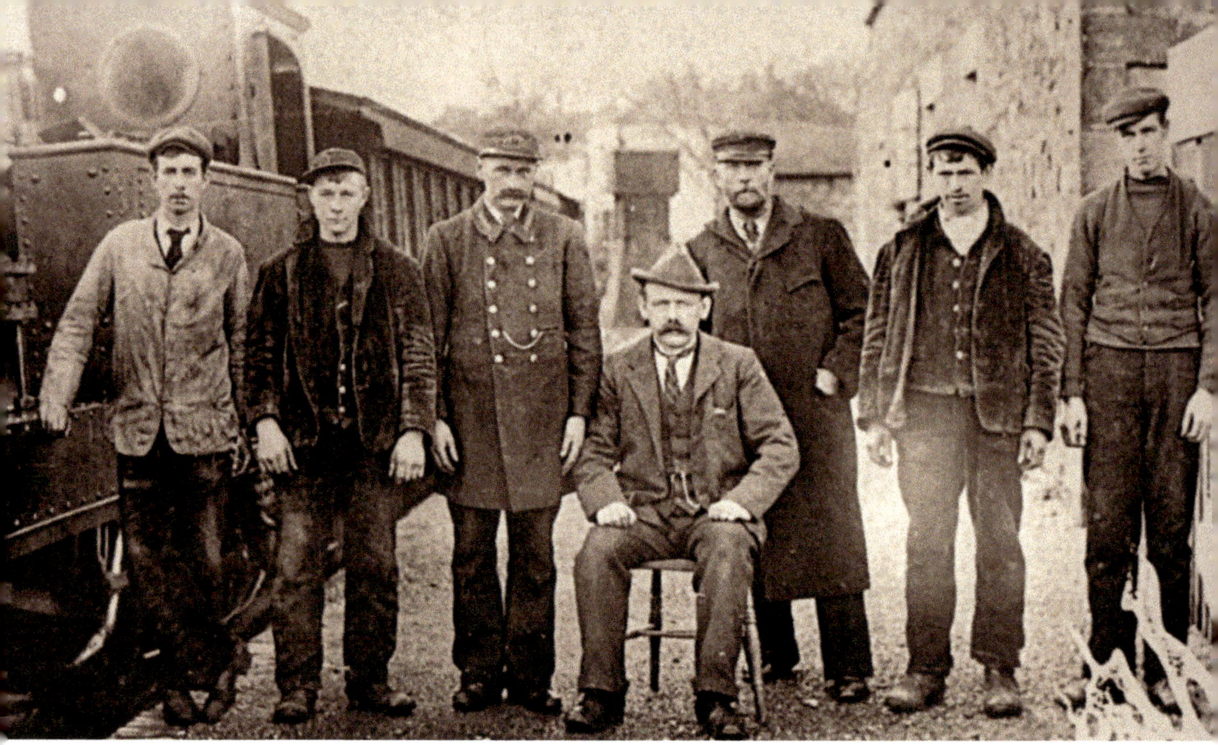

Schull Station

A rare picture of railway employees posing for the camera at Schull railway station, around 1899. Several extensions were made in the years following the 1886 opening of this station: a protective sea wall, a new carriage shed and a pier extension. The station also had a cattle dock, fitting shop, a carriage shed, an engine shed and a coastguard station rocket house. Several of these features can still be viewed, despite the line's closure over fifty years ago.

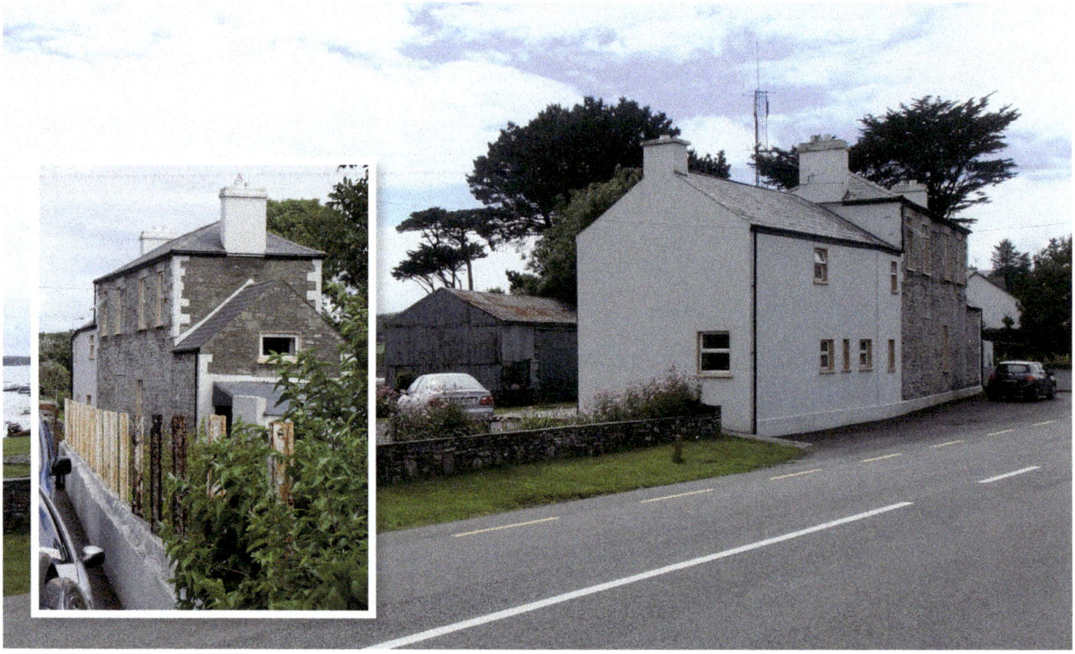

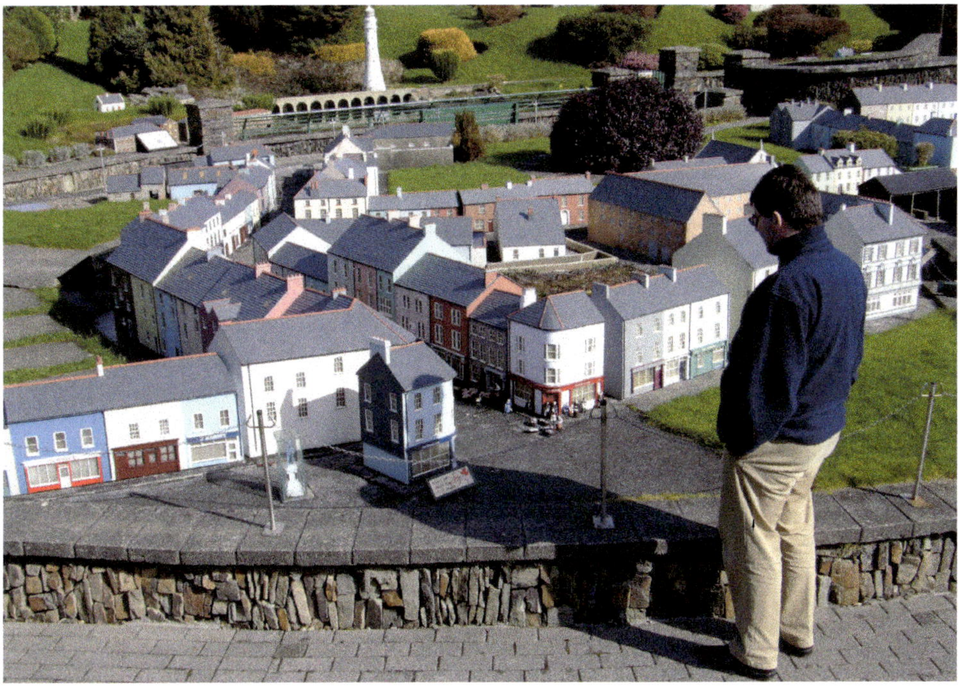

Clonakilty Model Railway

Celebrating the railway heritage of West Cork is the model railway village of Clonakilty. You can step back in time and see what life was like on early twentieth-century trains. A miniature version of the Cork, Bandon and South Coast Railway line, you can enjoy a unique overview of the character and history of each heritage town that the line passed through in West Cork.

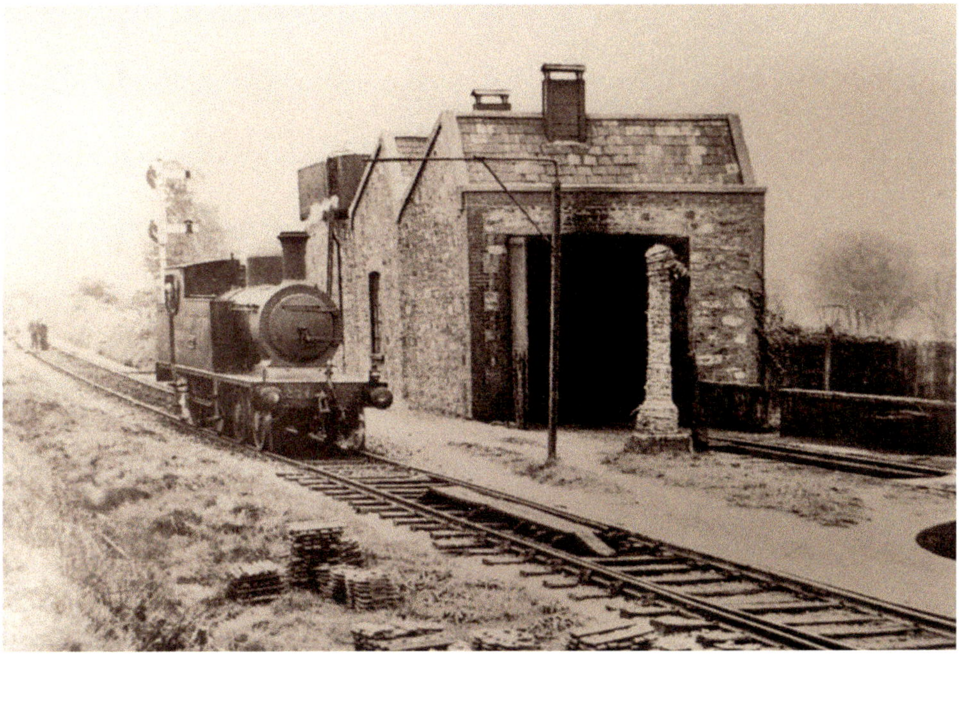

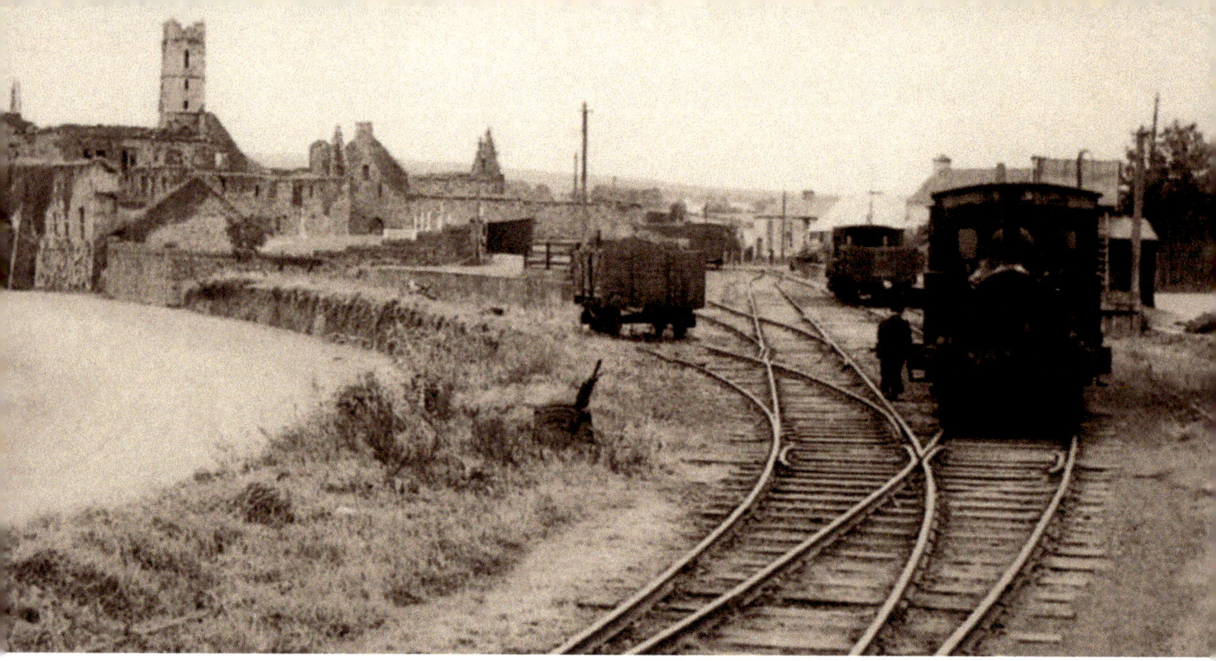

Timoleague Station

Perched at the edge of a long sea inlet, Timoleague is dominated by the ruins of a thirteenth-century abbey, which once overlooked Timoleague railway station (established 1891). The abbey was founded by the Franciscan order in AD 1240, on the site of a sixth-century monastic settlement, founded by Saint Molaga. The name Timoleague comes from the Irish for House of Molaga, *Tigh Molaga*. When John Edmund De Courcy OFM, Bishop of Clogher, resided here in 1495, he built the tower, the dormitory, the infirmary and the library.

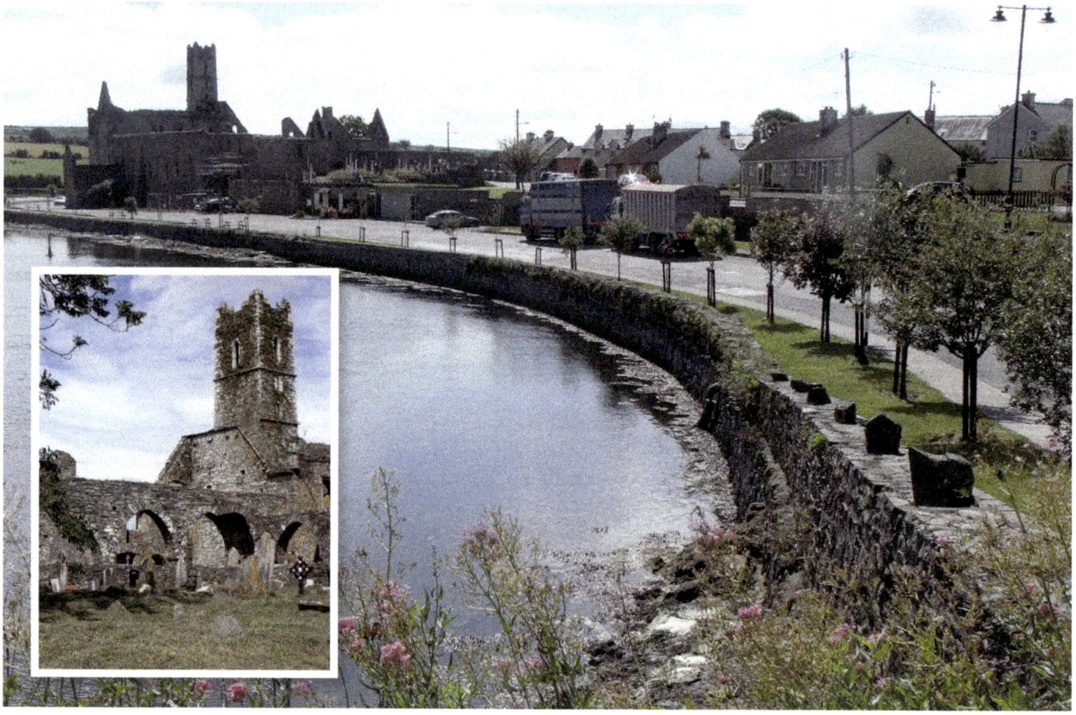

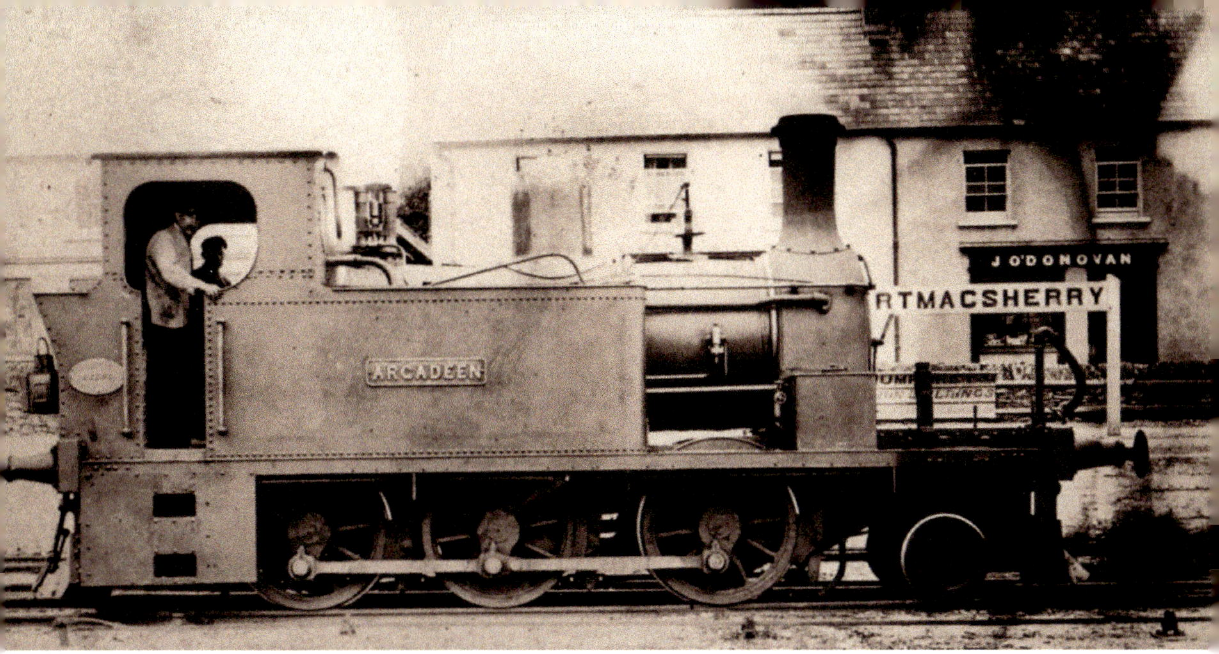

Courtmacsherry Station

The first train arrived in Courtmacsherry on 23 April 1891. Two separate companies connected Courtmacsherry with the Clonakilty line at Ballinascarty junction. The railway opened up a golden age for the area. Three engines worked the line, bringing summer excursions, trains and exporting quantities of winter sugar beet grown by local farmers. The terminus for Courtmacsherry was on its own pier, now the grassy area in the picture below. A scenic pedestrian walkway follows the line from Timoleague to Courtmacsherry pier, and along the inner part of the bay. The line closed in January 1962, at the end of another busy beet season.

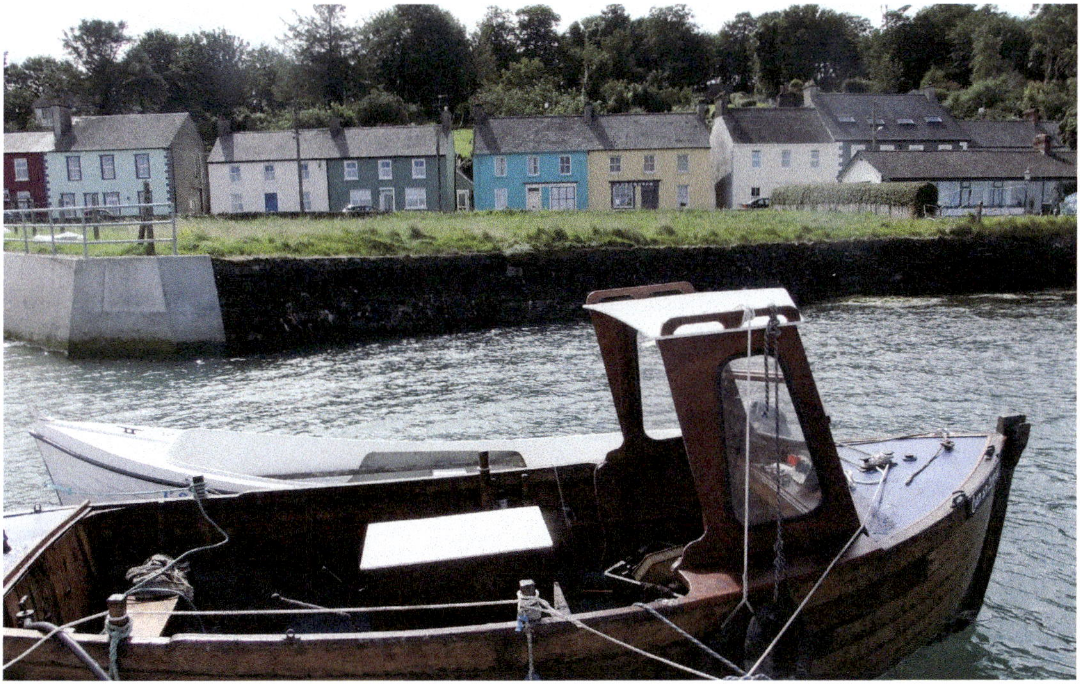

Biographies

Daniel Breen

Daniel Breen was born in Ballincollig, County Cork in 1979. Having graduated with a degree in history and archaeology from University College Cork in 2001, he achieved an MA from Sheffield University in European Historical Archaeology in 2002. While in college, Daniel spent his summer months working on various archaeological sites throughout Ireland. Since graduation, he has worked in Cork Public Museum, where he now holds the position of assistant curator. He co-wrote *Cork City Through Time* with Kieran McCarthy in 2012. He is currently finishing a book with local historian Tom Spalding on the history of the 1902/03 Cork International Exhibition.

Kieran McCarthy

For twenty years, Kieran has actively promoted Cork's heritage, and its various communities and people. He has led and continues to lead successful heritage initiatives through his community talks, city and county school heritage programmes, walking tours, newspaper articles, books and his work through his heritage consultancy business. For the past fourteen years, Kieran has written a local heritage column in the *Cork Independent* on the history, geography and the intersection of modern-day life in communities in Cork City and County. He is the author of twelve books: *Pathways Through Time, Historical Walking Trails of Cork City* (2001), *Cork: A Pictorial Journey* (co-written in 2001), *Discover Cork* (2003), *A Dream Unfolding, Portrait of St Patrick's Hospital* (2004), *Voices of Cork: The Knitting Map Speaks* (2005), *In the Steps of St Finbarre, Voices and Memories of the Lee Valley* (2006), *Generations: Memories of the Lee Hydroelectric Scheme* (co-edited, 2008), *Inheritance, Heritage and Memory in the Lee Valley, Co. Cork* (2010), *Royal Cork Institution, Pioneer of Education* (2010), *Munster Agricultural Society, The Story of the Cork Showgrounds* (2010), *Cork City Through Time* (co-written, 2012), and *Journeys of Faith, Our Lady of Lourdes Church Ballinlough, Celebrating 75 Years* (2013). In June 2009, Kieran was elected as a local government councillor (Independent) to Cork City Council. More on Kieran's work can be seen at www.corkheritage.ie and www.kieranmccarthy.ie.

Cork Public Museum

The postcards shown in this book come from the archives of Cork Public Museum, which was first opened in 1910 and is the longest established local authority museum in Ireland. It is housed in a beautiful Georgian building set in the wonderfully landscaped Fitzgerald Park. During the turbulent pre-Second World War period, the building was utilised for a variety of civic and municipal functions that distracted from its museum role. Finally in 1945, the present incarnation of the Cork Public Museum was officially opened to the public, and it has remained a museum ever since. In 2005, a contemporary and modern extension was added to the existing building, making Cork Public Museum one of the most celebrated public buildings in Cork City. The collections of Cork Public Museum are as rich and diverse as the history of the city itself. The ground floor of the museum has two permanent galleries, each dealing with the historical and archaeological heritage of Cork City and County. A visitor can trace the record from our earliest Mesolithic ancestors to the civic leaders that brought the city into the twentieth century and beyond.

The museum displays some of the most important archaeological pieces known from Cork, including Ireland's oldest pick and shovel from a Bronze Age copper mine, the Iron Age Cork Helmet Horns, and the Garryduff gold bird, a marvel in early medieval craftsmanship. The archaeological section also takes the visitor into what life was like in medieval Cork, where the finds from many recent excavations are exhibited, highlighting the importance of Cork as a trading and economic centre during medieval times. The historic displays focus on many important industrial, social and political aspects of Cork City's development since the eighteenth century. The visitor will see the ebb and flow of Cork's industrial past where butter making, glass manufacture, and silver working were once dominant, but are now non-existent in modern Cork's industrial landscape. The civic exhibition enlivens us to the history of past Cork mayors and the legendary Lord Mayors like Tomás MacCurtain and Terence MacSwiney, who both died in 1920 during the Irish War of Independence. The road to Irish independence is long and detailed, and Cork Public Museum traces the roles played by many Cork people in achieving this aim from the eighteenth to the early twentieth century.

From amateur genealogists to university academics, Cork Public Museum proves invaluable to researchers and students alike. The museum houses a vast amount of artefacts and documents in our reserve collection. Though they may never be publicly exhibited, they need to be protected and preserved so that future generations can have access to this material to aid further research or educate the future about our past. Cork Public Museum has served people from Cork and further afield since 1910, and it is our intent and desire to continue to be custodians of Cork's historical and archaeological legacy for the foreseeable future.

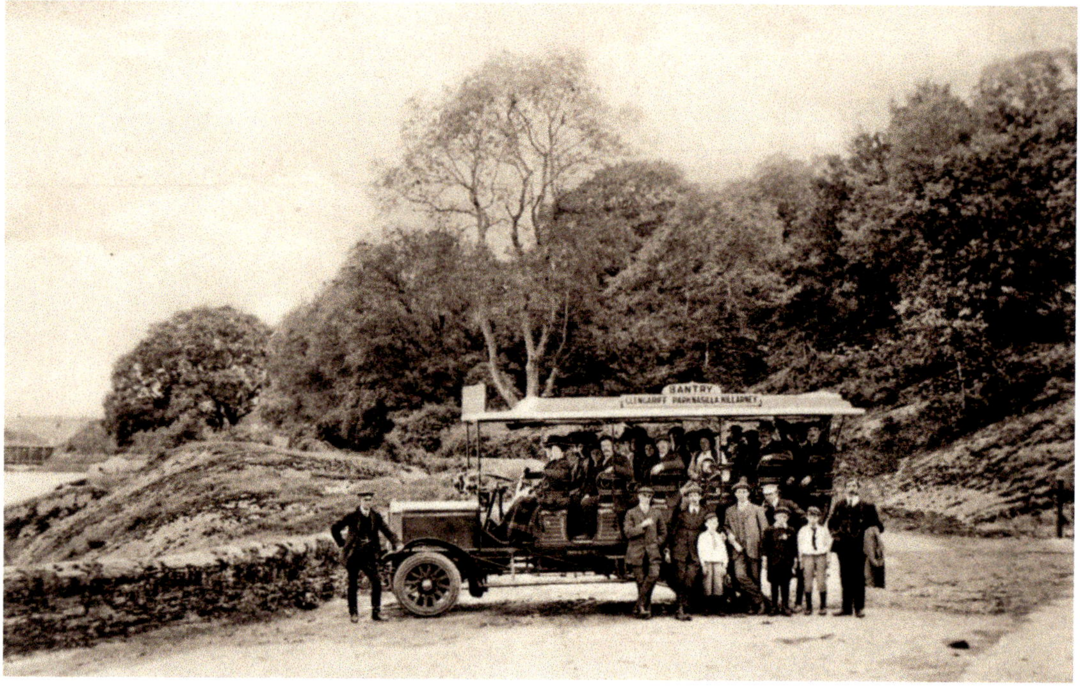

The Tourist Motor Bus at Glengarriff, County Cork, *c.* 1920

The Cork to Glengarriff to Killarney route was popular with tourists 100 years ago. Horse and carriages, trains and early motor cars carried the visitor. Today some of the old routeways have survived, but a lot have been superseded by newer roads, and faster transport routes have emerged since then. The attraction of travelling through West Cork and its coastal, riverine and mountainous terrain still remains. Indeed, many more 'must-see' locations have emerged since then, leaving the region with a myriad of fantastic views, and some visitor experiences with roots going back nearly 200 years to the European Grand Tour era.

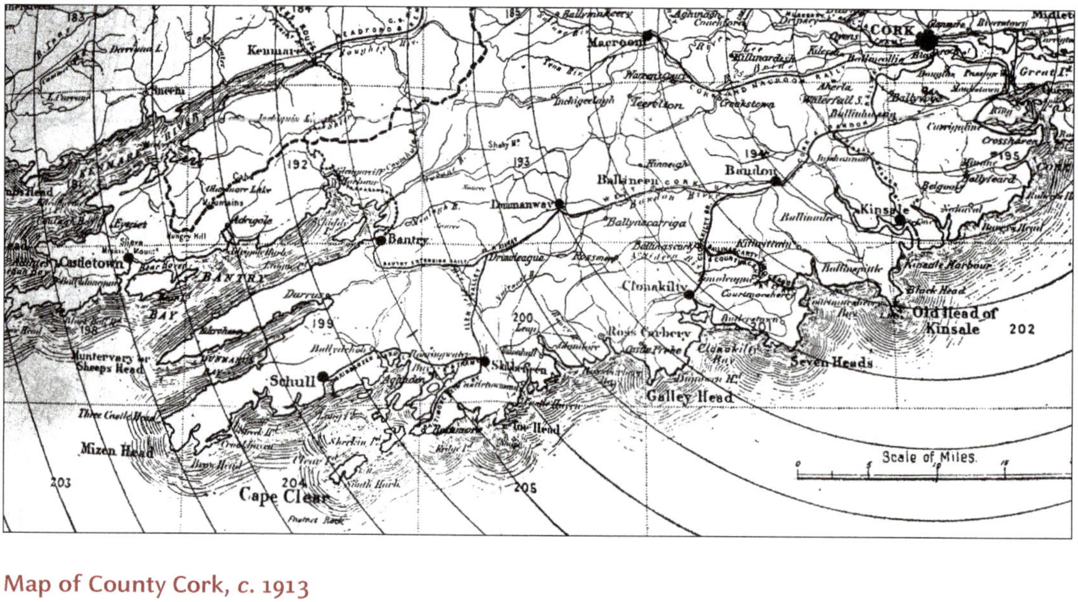

Map of County Cork, *c.* 1913